Magic and the Mind

Magic and the Mind

Mechanisms, Functions, and Development of Magical Thinking and Behavior

Eugene Subbotsky

OXFORD

UNIVERSITY PRESS

2010

OXFORD
UNIVERSITY PRESS

Oxford University Press, Inc., publishes works that further
Oxford University's objective of excellence
in research, scholarship, and education.

Oxford   New York
Auckland   Cape Town   Dar es Salaam   Hong Kong   Karachi
Kuala Lumpur   Madrid   Melbourne   Mexico City   Nairobi
New Delhi   Shanghai   Taipei   Toronto

With offices in
Argentina   Austria   Brazil   Chile   Czech Republic   France   Greece
Guatemala   Hungary   Italy   Japan   Poland   Portugal   Singapore
South Korea   Switzerland   Thailand   Turkey   Ukraine   Vietnam

Library of Congress Cataloging-in-Publication Data

Subbotskii, E. V. (Evgenii Vasil'evich)
Magic and the mind : mechanisms, functions, and development of magical thinking
and behavior / Eugene Subbotsky.
p.   cm.
ISBN 978-0-19-539387-3
1. Magical thinking.   I. Title.
BF1621.S83 2010
153.4′2—dc22
2009031083

1   3   5   7   9   8   6   4   2

Printed in the United States of America
on acid-free paper

Contents

Preface

About 30 years ago, while playing with my young son, I was surprised to see how easy it was for him to solve the most difficult imaginary problems and to find ways out of all the traps that I was trying to set up for him. A giant tiger is attacking him in the forest—no problem, he draws his sword and kills the tiger. A great mountain impedes his way to the treasure—he accelerates and jumps over it. What impressed me most in my son's attitude was not that he was strongly overestimating his abilities and generally ignorant of the limitations of reality; rather, it was his absolute confidence in the idea that nature would be kind to him; that the elements (water, air, gravity) were aware of his presence in the universe, accepting his divine right to be there; and that cultural folk characters such as Santa Claus knew his most secret wishes and were working to make those wishes come true.

Of course, this illusion of childhood is not to last. In fact, outside of play, most children are perfectly aware of their physical and mental limitations. But is this awareness not one of the very reasons that make-believe play is so attractive to a child? Does a child not need, at least sometimes, this wonderful feeling of his or her ultimate power or beauty? As children grow, the limitations of reality gradually co-opt their dreams and play, and they become increasingly aware that in the "real" world even a small achievement requires determination and hard work. Eventually, children learn that nature and the elements are not helping or caring, and that the universe is in the best case indifferent, and sometimes even hostile to their aims. In developmental psychology this process is known as "decentration," but in fact it also represents a growing isolation from the natural world.

This alienation of children from their originally cozy little universe, with some reservations, mimics what has happened to humanity as a whole over time. For millennia, people believed that the universe around them was not only alive but also aware—that the stars and elements were watching them and could respond to their pleas in positive or negative ways. Sophisticated myths and magic were developed to explain the links between a person and the universe. Today, things have changed. Science has exposed the myths and magic as fantasies of the past and replaced the force of sympathy with the force of gravity. Of course, we are in debt to science for its remarkable achievements—modern medicine, elaborate technologies, relatively comfortable lives. Yet the price of such comfort is great: the loss of a meaningful connection between man and nature. Instead of an afterlife, science predicts inevitable and final death for a person, for humankind, and for the universe. Not surprisingly, for many people the perspective of science on their futures is disturbing. Compared with this, even the simplest religious traditions offer a better prospect for the future.

Beyond organized religion and the scientific tradition that has in large part supplanted it, ancient magic, too, lives—even if just in our minds. In dreams and in imagination, in movies and in books, we can see animals talking and humans going through walls. Just one step further and we start to believe that there are people around us who have special powers and who can do magic in the real world. If we take this step, we upgrade our *magical thinking* to the status of a *magical belief*—the belief that magic can happen in the real world. Psychology is quick to reassure: magical thinking and beliefs today are nothing but remnants of the past, mere superstitions, unusual—but quite natural—forms of human behavior. Until fairly recently, most research on magical thinking has been done "under the spell of science"; in other words, science has reduced magical thinking to a vestigial part of the human psyche, or to superstitions that pray on human uncertainties and fears. On the other hand, a traditional respect for science has grown into something of a "religion of science"; we assume that science can explain everything—if not today, then in the future. What is missing from this picture is the notion that science as a discipline aims to explain the laws of nature—laws that are based on physical causality. But the universe is much more than the physical: it includes intangibles such as our mental and emotional lives, human relations and communication, fantasy, dreams, play, and art. The universe also includes religion, politics, commerce, and entertainment. In these domains, can magical thinking be a legitimate way of thinking, just as so-called logical thinking is in science?

Even a brief look back in history shows that viewing magic as a "false science" is misleading; magic is not a less controlled, darker form of science—the two should not be compared as likes. Magic is more akin to art than to science. It is not a coincidence that art and magic/religion appeared simultaneously in the Upper Paleolithic era and preceded science as we know it today by 30,000 years. Both art and magic imply a fusion between mind and nature. They aim at a different goal from that of science; whereas the ultimate goal of science is product, the ultimate goal of art and magic is meaning.

Existential situations that occur in our everyday lives are a good illustration of this point. Years ago, my 2-year-old son and I were strolling quietly in a park area inside the square-shaped enclosure made by a row of flats in Moscow. A shabby-looking contractor's car sat on the pavement next to the building, and some workers nearby were painting a wall. I was looking in the opposite direction at my little son, who was exploring the massive iron fence separating the garden from the driveway. I heard the car engine starting, but paid it no attention until I saw my son's widening eyes. But by then it was too late to react. The contractor's car moved from the pavement into the driveway, but instead of proceeding along the driveway and into the gate, it made a U-turn and bumped into the iron fence a few inches behind my son and me, pushing a massive section of the fence out of its stone base. Only a small fraction of space separated my son and me from painful death. What scared me the most was that this had not happened on a busy street or anywhere one might expect such things to take place and would therefore be alert. The incident was completely unexpected, and that we had not been injured looked to me like the hand of fate.

Although years have passed since that day, I still cannot stop thinking mystically about it. Who, or what, in the world decided about those few inches? Chance? Chance is an impersonal concept developed to account for impersonal and inanimate processes, such as the tossing of a coin. But imagine a situation in which the coin toss determines whether we live or die. Would we still think about the outcome in terms of chance if the outcome allowed us to live? Would a soldier whose mate running next to him was killed by a shell think about staying alive in terms of chance? I do not think so, because in such situations chance becomes an existentially charged event, full of personal meaning. Thinking about life-saving chance in terms of blind coincidence devalues one's life and makes it meaningless. Only if we accept that someone or something with consciousness and intelligence has decided that we are to live can we make sense of our being here in this world—at least, this is how many of us feel, as is evidenced by organized religion. These considerations inspired me to search for magical beliefs in modern people.

I started my exploration by constructing various devices that produced what looked like instances of real magic: objects appeared from thin air or disappeared without a trace, toy animals seemed to be coming to life, magic spells mysteriously changed one object into another one. In reality, these effects were tricks, yet tricks that were notoriously difficult for participants in my research studies to explain. Usually "magic tricks" happen on a stage, near or on a magician's body. Mine occurred in the participants' own hands. In addition, participants were encouraged to investigate the devices, with the purpose of explaining the unusual events. When the investigation failed and participants remained puzzled by what had happened, I started my interrogation. The aim of the interrogation was to suggest that participants had witnessed an event that was indeed magical and that violated known laws of physics.

Very soon I discovered that most preschool children were happy to be persuaded that magic was real. This was not as easy to do with adults, but eventually adults, too, succumbed to magical explanations. Even while denying that they believed in magic, many adults behaved as though they did. Most participants, both children and adults, acknowledged that magical things could happen in their dreams, imaginations, and play, but what these experiments demonstrated was that magical thinking could relatively easily leave its legitimate ground—imagination—and trespass into the realm of physical reality.

But if modern educated adults accept that someone can change physical objects in a magical way, then perhaps they could also accept that their thoughts and imaginations could be affected magically. And indeed, as I will show, adults reported that magical manipulations had little effect on their perceptions of real or imagined physical objects, but had a strong effect on their imagined fantastical objects. Further experiments revealed that participants' personally significant imagined objects, such as their own images of their future lives, were particularly strongly affected by the experimenter's magical manipulations. This brought me to the idea that along with "mind-over-matter" magical events (such as magic spells or wishes directly affecting physical events and processes), a "mind-over-mind" type of magic, or "communication magic," also exists. Communication magic involves magical spells or rituals that aim to affect the minds of others with the purpose of curing, bringing luck, or causing harm. In addition, unlike mind-over-matter magic, which contradicts fundamental physical principles, mind-over-mind magic can occur in the real world, via suggestion and autosuggestion. Although in the modern world suggestion is viewed as a psychological, rather than a magical, process, later in this book I will argue that suggestion (and its results, such as the placebo effect) is a "baby" of magic and is based on the same psychological mechanism as practical magic. A person who believes (explicitly or implicitly) in magic could indeed be affected if magical manipulations were performed on his or her mind with his or her knowledge. For example, Lévy-Bruhl cited the case of a man who believed that he had been cursed to die, and had indeed died because of his belief.

This was a lucky idea for me—it extended my studies of magical thinking into the domain of human communication. First I asked whether the culture of magic in the media could possibly affect children's cognitive development. Indeed, multinational industries such as toy producers and entertainers exploit and support magical beliefs in children, and many television programs for children feature magical characters. Some developmental psychologists argue that early intuitive beliefs in children and adults, including magical beliefs, could be obstacles to science education. On the other hand, it is also possible that involvement in magical thinking, via encouraging children's imaginations, might help children start thinking in more diverse and original ways. Experiments that my students and I conducted have indeed shown that exposing children to a movie that contains strong magical effects significantly increases their performance on creativity tasks.

Further, I assumed that in the early stages of history magical/religious influences on people for the purpose of healing or bringing harm were based on suggestion. With the onset of scientific ideology, overt magical rituals were discarded, yet suggestion remains the most effective way to manipulate mass consciousness in such areas as religion, politics, commerce, and psychotherapy. This brought me to the notion that ordinary suggestion today may be based on the same psychological mechanism as was magical suggestion in the times before science. I conducted a series of experiments that, I believe, showed that this common mechanism does exist. This finding has important implications for understanding the psychological-historical continuity of the techniques used to influence and control people's minds.

In the common view today, political power is based on rationally controlled electoral processes, and not on magical beliefs. Contrary to this view, if magical and ordinary types of suggestion are based on the same psychological mechanism, then suggestive persuasion techniques used in political rhetoric and commercial advertising may be viewed as historically evolving from magical practices. Psychologically, these techniques rely on the individuals' tendency to involuntarily accept messages that they might find unacceptable from a rational standpoint, and in many cases, these persuasion techniques work. For example, influenced by clever advertising, people sometimes buy products that they know they do not need—they just cannot resist. In other words, suggestion is literally the magic of today.

In order to protect themselves from magical manipulation, people develop sophisticated defense mechanisms. Yet throughout their lifespan people remain curious about magical events, and, though subconsciously, many appear to believe in magic. Through experimental research, I have tried to find new evidence that will help us to better understand some old theoretical issues, such as the relationship between magic and science, and magic and religion. Doing research on the development of magical thinking has also helped me to find a common psychological factor that underlies developmental changes in cognitive domains: theory of mind, distinguishing appearance from reality, children's drawings, reality monitoring, and more.

As a result, the development of the human mind can be presented as the growing differentiation and diversification of two main domains of reality: the domain of ordinary reality, in which rational and logical science reigns, and the domain of magical reality, where magic and religion hold sway. In the life of a modern person, magical thinking and magical beliefs, together with religious beliefs, perform many important functions, such as reducing anxiety, boosting creativity, and providing meaning of life. They complement the development of rational and scientific thinking and are a fascinating topic for psychological research.

I began these studies in Moscow in 1982, and continued them in Germany, England, and Mexico. Most of my results have been published in journals such as *Developmental Psychology*, *Developmental Review*, *British Journal of Developmental Psychology*, *British Journal of Psychology,* and *Psychologist*, and some were presented at international conferences. Yet by and large, my studies have remained scattered and fragmented. This book is an attempt to put them together and to place them within the context of other studies on magical thinking. Inevitably, certain material from the book has been adapted from material published in the aforementioned journals. I am grateful to my students who helped me to conduct some of the experiments reviewed in this book. A special thanks to my colleagues Karl Rosengren, Paul Harris, Carl Johnson, Jacqueline Woolley, and Carol Nemeroff for their friendly feedback and support of my work. And of course, my gratitude goes to the editor of this book, Sarah Harrington, for her belief in this project, imaginative and efficient editing, and valuable suggestions.

I dedicate this book to all scientists who can sense the mystery that lay hidden behind the known physical and nonphysical worlds.

Magic and the Mind

1

Magical Reality

At the sunset hour of one nice spring day, one of the main characters of my favorite novel, Mikhail Alexandrovitch Berlioz, editor of a literary magazine and a convinced atheist, was sitting with his companion on a bench in an alley of lime trees in 1920s Moscow. Berlioz was lecturing his companion—a beginning writer—on some literary and historic topics, when suddenly his heart thumped and for the moment vanished.

Just then the sultry air coagulated and wove itself into the shape of a man—a transparent man of the strangest appearance. On his small head was a jockey-cap and he wore a short check bum-freezer made of air. The man was seven feet tall but narrow in the shoulders, incredibly thin and with a face made for derision.

Berlioz's life was so arranged that he was not accustomed to seeing unusual phenomena. Paling even more, he stared and thought in consternation: "It can't be!"

But alas it was, and the tall, transparent gentleman was swaying from left to right in front of him without touching the ground.

Berlioz was so overcome with horror that he shut his eyes. When he opened them he saw that it was all over, the mirage had dissolved, the chequered figure had vanished and the blunt needle had simultaneously removed itself from his heart (Mikhail Bulgakov, 1967, p. 14).

Think about Mikhail Alexandrovitch. Like him, you probably do not believe in magical things, but how would you feel if you were in his shoes? Surprised, scared, confused? The science-based universe is a fragile construction. Like an inflated balloon, it can only exist in its wholeness; if it

3

is punctured by a single hole, it will burst. At present our universe looks fine, yet magical things are all around us. They happen in fiction, movies, cartoons, commercial clips, computer games, art, and theater. We see them in our dreams and assert them in prayer and superstitious behaviors. We teach them to our children through fairy tales and references to folk magical characters (like Santa Claus, the Tooth Fairy, and the Easter Bunny). We hear about them in the narratives of those who think they "saw something" supernatural. With so much magic around, why do so many of us fail to take it seriously?

The phenomenology of magical beliefs is also diverse: it includes belief in witches, ghosts, spirits, premonitions, reincarnation, astrology, palm reading, omens, UFOs, aliens, and immortal souls. Of course the most sophisticated, historically developed, and powerful example of magical reality is religion. Anthropological research has shown that originally the two concepts we think of as religion and magic were once the same (Frazer, 1923; Lévy-Brühl, 1966; Malinowski, 1935; Tambiah, 1990). In early religions, people worshipped ancestral spirits and animal spirits, and those were their gods. As Steven Mithen (2005) writes, "Many of the new behaviors . . . , such as the anthropomorphic images in the cave paintings and the burial of people with grave goods, suggest that these Upper Palaeolithic people were the first to have beliefs in supernatural beings and possibly an afterlife. We are indeed seeing here the first appearance of religious ideologies" (p. 198). Some forms of tribal religions today, and even major religions like Hinduism, retain features such as these. However, as monotheistic religions (such as Judaism or Christianity) emerged, religion gradually separated itself from everyday magic and became an established and legitimized institution of magical thinking and magical beliefs. This institution became highly powerful and demanded a monopoly on magical beliefs. As a result, common magical beliefs were ousted into the subconscious by both religion and science. Science opposes magical thinking and magical beliefs on rational grounds, declaring them to be false reasoning (Feynman, 1974). Religion recognizes the power of magical thinking over people's minds, yet declares magical thinking and beliefs (outside of accepted religious forms of magic) to be immoral and associated with bad powers like the devil, evil spirits, and paganism (Strandberg & Terry, 2004). Not surprisingly, most religious believers would oppose the idea that they actually believe in magic. But the belief in an almighty and omnipotent God who can do miracles and in a petitionary prayer that can affect physical, biological, or psychological events (Barett, 2001) is undeniably belief in the magical. In one study conducted by a student of mine, religious students scored significantly higher than nonreligious students on Eckblad and Chapman's (1983) Magical Ideation scale, and on a 30-item magical beliefs questionnaire specially designed for the study to measure magical beliefs in adults (Sasaki, 2006). Interestingly, the "art versus engineering" variable that was ortho-gonal to the "religious beliefs" variable in this study showed that art students scored significantly higher than engineering students on both scales, sup-porting the idea that artistic ability, religious beliefs, and magical beliefs are connected.

All the aforementioned beliefs share a common feature: they violate phy-sical causality and our intuitive expectations about objects, people, and animals. For example, witches, as usually conceived, can do magic by affecting people and objects through their magic spells; ghosts and spirits violate principles of physical space, time, and object permanence, being able to go through physical obstacles, appear and disappear without a trace, or "live" for centuries. Astrology teaches us that our fates are written in the skies. Religions assert that God is in many places at one time and can do miracles (bring a dead person to life, exorcise evil spirits, change water into wine in an instant). Since notions of physical space, time, causality, and object perma-nence are interdependent, violation of any of these tacitly implies violation of all the others (Subbotsky, 1993).

MAGICAL CAUSATION: MIND OVER MATTER AND MIND OVER MIND

The aforementioned phenomenology of magical beliefs is a part of what I call *magical reality*. In contrast to physical reality, magical reality is based on *magical causation*. At least four types of causal effects can be qualified as truly magical: (*1*) the direct effect of consciousness over matter, such as affecting or creating physical objects through the effort of will (*mind-over-matter magic*); (*2*) the sudden acquisition of spontaneity by a nonanimate physical object (*animation magic*); (*3*) a violation of the fundamental laws of object permanence, physical space, and time, such as one physical object inexplicably turning into another physical object in an instant (*nonperma-nence magic*); and (*4*) when certain objects or events affect other objects or events in a nonphysical way, through similarity or contagion (*sympathetic magic*) (Frazer, 1923; Johnson & Harris, 1994; Nemeroff & Rozin, 2000; Tambiah, 1990; Vyse, 1997).

These kinds of magical causality are interdependent: they are different facets of a single type—counterphysical supernatural causation. For example, animation magic is a variation of nonpermanence magic, because transformation of an inanimate object into an animate one changes phy-sical features of this object by adding to it, for instance, a functioning brain, intestines, and movements. Mind-over-matter magic is a generic kind of magic because it implicitly involves animation magic (God or a sorcerer bringing a dead person to life), nonpermanence magic (a witch turning a girl into a frog), and sympathetic magic (a sorcerer killing a person by stabbing a clay figurine representing that person). This allows a researcher on magical thinking to use a simple heuristic: *instead of studying the whole bulk of magical causal events, or even their representative sample, we may study the generic kind with the assumption that the results will be transferable.* In most studies reviewed in this book, mind-over-matter magic was targeted. I chose this kind of magic because it implicitly involves all other kinds of magical causation. *Thus, by studying mind-over-matter magic, one can study the whole spectrum of magical phenomena, which is reflected in mind-over-matter magic just as a whole garden can be reflected in a single dewdrop.*

A social offshoot of mind-over-matter magic is *mind-over-mind* magic. As defined previously, mind-over-matter magic implies that mental processes (like wishing or casting a magic spell) can affect physical events, like the weather or harvest, in a supernatural way (see Frazer, 1923; Vyse, 1997; Woolley, 2000). However, some researchers extend the scope of magical causality to include its effects on mental, rather than physical, reality (mind-over-mind magic). For example, when a medicine man uses his power for healing, he influences a sick person's mind in a magical way by encouraging the person to observe healing rituals performed on the magician's own body (Frazer, 1923). As I briefly mentioned in the Preface, Lévy-Brühl (1966) cited an example of black witchcraft "by effigy." In this case a person who believed that he had been cursed to die "had fretted so much about it that he died" (p. 343). This type of witchcraft has also been observed in some modern traditional cultures (Cannon, 1957).

Theoretically, there is no reason to reject the idea that magical manipulations can affect individuals' subjective experiences, such as emotional states, thoughts, and perceptions. Indeed, mind-over-matter magic contradicts fundamental physical principles, whereas mind-over-mind magic does not. To a large extent, human communication is free from the constraints of physical causality, and influencing individuals' subjective experiences by magical manipulations (such as spells and rituals) is a special kind of human communication.

Studying communication magic extends the studies on magical thinking and magical beliefs beyond the area of cognitive processes by including a vast and important psychological domain—human personality and social interaction. These studies illuminate the link that exists between an individual's susceptibility to influences based on magical causality and more commonly known reactions to social influence, such as suggestibility, compliance, and obedience.

MAGICAL THINKING, MAGICAL BELIEFS, MAGICAL BEHAVIOR, AND OTHER CONSTRUCTS

An important distinction to make is that between *magical thinking* and *magical beliefs*. In contrast to magical thinking, which confines magical characters and events to the domain of imagination, magical beliefs imply that the magical characters or events exist in the real physical world. For example, in dreams we can see animals turning into humans, or people going through solid walls. Immersed in the imaginary world of Harry Potter while reading the book or watching the movie, we dream of witches and wizards who practice mind-over-matter magic, and of all sorts of other magical events. Magical events that we entertain in our dreams, narratives, arts, play, and fantasies are instances of magical thinking, not of magical beliefs. Whereas magical beliefs are in contradiction with the view that perceived physical reality strictly conforms to the laws of physics, magical thinking is not. One can think or dream about getting a nice house or a car by just thinking about it or saying a magic spell, yet one knows that in the real world this is impossible.

Magical behavior is a kind of behavior that asserts magical thinking and/or magical beliefs. Examples of magical behavior that asserts magical thinking include playing games of pretend with magical characters or events, drawing magical objects, and telling magical stories. Examples of magical behavior that asserts magical beliefs include chanting a magic spell (or, conversely, trying to avoid the spell to be chanted) in the hope that the spell would work, carrying out magical rituals with the aim of affecting natural objects or people, wearing a lucky charm, or praying to God.

It is also necessary to distinguish between *magical thinking* and other theoretical constructs, such as *autistic thinking*. Magical thinking, as stated earlier, is the type of thinking that involves violations of physical and mental causality. In contrast, autistic thinking is a kind of thinking that conflates fantasy with reality without necessarily violating principles of physical causality (Bleuler, 1951). A person with autistic thinking ignores the resistance of reality, builds up an image of himself or herself that fulfills the person's most secret desires, and behaves as if his or her fantasy is real (for instance, that he or she is a famous historical character, such as the Virgin Mary or Napoleon). Unlike a playing child who is pretending to be Batman or Cinderella but does not really believe that he or she *is* Batman or Cinderella, a person with autistic thinking really believes that he or she is a famous historical character. Another feature that separates magical thinking from autistic thinking is the understanding of theory of mind. Studies of autistic children have shown that some of these children have a limited understanding of the idea that other people have representations and beliefs about reality that are different from their own, and that these beliefs can sometimes be wrong (Baron-Cohen, Leslie, & Frith, 1985). In contrast, magical thinking by definition is animistic—it implies that, not only people and gods, but also animals and even inanimate objects have some kind of mind and their own beliefs about the world (Frazer, 1923; Tambiah, 1990). Finally, whereas autistic thinking is primarily directed toward fulfillment of desires, magical thinking deals with both desirable and undesirable outcomes. Just like rational thinking, magical thinking can be used both for achieving desirable goals and for protecting a person against real or imagined dangers.

Another construct from which magical thinking should be distinguished is *fantasy orientation*. Fantasy orientation is a construct that evaluates children's interest in fantasy and is usually measured by interviewing children about their imaginary companions and imaginary play predispositions (Sharon & Woolley, 2004; Taylor & Carlson, 1997). For example, if children report having imaginary friends, favor stories and TV shows with fantastic characters, or prefer to engage in pretend play rather than just playing with objects, these children score high on the fantasy orientation scale. Although fantasy orientation contains certain elements of the imaginary magical world (such as reading stories and watching TV shows with fantastic characters), most items that fantasy orientation involves (such as pretending to be an animal or another person, having imaginary friends, playing games of pretend, and others) are not specifically magical. More important, however, is the difference in causality: whereas magical thinking is defined as a kind of thinking that violates known principles of physical or mental causality, fantasy orientation does not necessarily imply such violations.

THE SCIENCE OF MAGIC AND THE MAGIC OF SCIENCE

One should also distinguish between *magical beliefs* and the *beliefs in the almighty power of science*, which sometimes appear similar to magical beliefs. Indeed, due to the astonishing achievements of science in the contemporary world, there is a commonly held view that science can explain virtually everything—if not now, then in the future. This idea is grounded in the fact that many of the achievements of science (the remote transmission of visual and auditory signals, flying in air and space, seeing small creatures invisible to the unarmed eye) in previous centuries would indeed have been viewed as magical (see Nemeroff & Rozin, 2000; Tambiah, 1990). This belief in the potential omnipotence of science has resulted, for instance, in the interpretation of parapsychological phenomena as physical phenomena whose mechanisms have not yet been discovered by science (Bem & Honorton, 1994).

Yet there is a crucial difference between explanations in terms of "physical yet unknown" forces and in terms of magical forces. In contrast to natural forces (such as gravity or electromagnetic fields), which operate in a predictable way and are devoid of any consciousness, magical forces assume implicit communication between a person and the world (Luhrman, 1989). Gravity attracts physical objects in a mechanical way, whereas a magic spell may imply, for instance, that a meaningful message is sent to the "spirits" that nest in the targeted object or process, with the assumption that these spirits are capable of understanding this message in the same way that humans can understand language—they can become happy or angry because of what these messages mean to them. This also implies that in sending magical messages, people inevitably have to make inferences about what the spiritual agents will think or wish; that is, they have to attribute inanimate things with a certain "theory of mind," a concept that is alien to the objects of science. The assumption that *physical objects at the receptive end of a communicative process have some kind of consciousness* is what distinguishes magical communication from the nonmagical variety.[1] Indeed, cell phones, computers, and text messages can be viewed as devices that receive and process information, yet they cannot "understand" this information in the way that a subject with consciousness can.[2]

Drawing the line between magical and scientific causation is important for psychological research. Theoretically, this distinction is necessary because recent advances in science—computers, cell phones, quantum effects, the idea that a particle can go through two different slits at the same time—have made it appear as though the line between magical and scientific effects is fading. However, in order to be able to make such a judgment or to call a scientific effect "magical," we must know the difference between magical and nonmagical (scientific) effects. This implies that *a logical definition of the difference between magical and scientific causation precedes any empirically based generalization* (for instance, that a cell phone is or is not magical). This also makes a definition of magic safe from any further advances of science. Indeed, one might ask, "What will happen to the definition of magic such as mind over matter and mind over mind when and if field theories and data concerning nonlocal effects in quantum physics tell us that such things are not impossible?" (Some people might argue that we are already at that point.) "Will the definitions shift to exclude these as magic, because they are now science?" My answer is no, because the effects in quantum physics are confined to the micro-world of elementary particles, whereas laws of magic have been defined as alternatives to those of Newtonian physics that are, in turn, based on our "intuitive physics." Instead of surrendering the definition of magic, we will have to acknowledge that quantum effects no longer exclusively belong to the realm of physics; rather, they belong to a special realm that is a bridge between scientific and magical realities.

In recent decades, evidence has been accumulating that the human mind can produce small but replicable direct effects on physical processes. It has been reported that, under certain laboratory conditions, human operators were able to produce a significant shift from the curve of normal distribution of the Random Mechanical Cascade (a device that allows 9,000 polystyrene balls to drop through a matrix of 330 pegs, scattering them into 19 collecting bins) (Dunne, Nelson, & Jahn, 1988). In another experiment, operators showed the capacity to decrease or increase the damping rate of a pendulum—a 2-inch crystal ball suspended by a fused silica rod (Nelson, Bradish, Jahn, & Dunne, 1994). In experiments with the microelectronic random event generator (REG), some operators have been able to shift the means of output distributions of generated events in the direction of their shared intentions (Dunne, 1991).

Being initially skeptical toward psi (this term includes effects like extrasensory perception [ESP]), I recently undertook an experiment in collaboration with Adrian Ryan (Subbotsky & Ryan, 2009). University graduates and undergraduates were randomly assigned to either a high-reward or control group. Participants in the high-reward group, on top of their regular payment of £4 for their time, were promised a reward of £80 for successfully performing on the remote viewing task; participants in the control group only received their regular payment. The aim of introducing the high-reward condition was to examine whether an increased need to succeed would improve the ESP performance, as this would follow from the Psi-mediated Instrumental Response (PMIR) model (Stanford & Rust, 1977). Using the method developed by May (2006), the participants individually attempted to remotely view a photograph that they would see in their near future. They created drawings and/or written notes of their impressions, which the experimenter then compared to five photographs chosen randomly by computer out of the pool of 300 photographs, assigning each a rating between 0 and 100 to indicate the degree of similarity. The database of target photographs described by May and colleagues (1999) was used. After ratings for all five photographs had been stored on the computer's disk, the computer randomly selected one of the five photographs as the target and this was displayed to the participant. Contrary to the expectation, participants in the high-reward group scored at chance level, whereas participants in the control group scored significantly above chance. A possible explanation for the high-reward group failure is that high motivation for success increased anxiety and this impeded the performance (see Eysenck & Sargent, 1993, for the discussion of a possible negative effect of high motivation on ESP). What is important, however, is that when a standard procedure was followed (control group), participants scored reliably above chance and exactly at the same level of significance as in earlier experiments (May, 2009, personal communication).

Although such effects are well documented, they are small and hard to achieve. The effects also appear to be insensitive to basic physical coordinates, including distance and time. Instead, they correlate with various subjective parameters, such as intention, emotional resonance, uncertainty, attitude, meaning, and information processing at an unconscious level. If these mind-over-matter effects are to become established beyond doubt, this will have different implications for scientific and magical thinking. For scientific thinking, conceding such effects involves a reconsideration of the fundamental assumption that observed physical effects are independent from the observer's conscious states. In contrast, for magical thinking and magical beliefs, acknowledging such effects does not have revolutionary consequences; rather, these effects support the view that mind-over-matter magic is not confined to the realm of imagination but can produce effects in physical reality. At present, the results of research on psi suggest that the bridge between scientific and magical realities does indeed exist, though this bridge is hard to maintain by empirical means from within ordinary reality.

In terms of practical importance, establishing the conceptual difference between magic and science authorizes magical and scientific thinking (beliefs) as two separate research areas. If the distinction between magical and scientific causation indeed vanished, then the whole point of studying magical thinking would disappear, as magical thinking would be indistinguishable from scientific thinking. Yet there is no proof to date that "clever devices," such as computers and particles, possess consciousness of the human type,[3] and objects having consciousness is a fundamental assumption behind magical thinking (Frazer, 1923; Lévy-Brühl, 1966; Piaget, 1927). Another factor that determines the importance of the magic/science distinction comes from the area of education. Some developmental psychologists argue that early intuitive beliefs in children and adults could be obstacles to science education (Bloom & Weisberg, 2007). If this is true, then magical thinking may be one of those intuitive beliefs. It has long been established that in their early years children intuitively assume that animals and even inanimate objects have consciousness similar to their own (Laurendeau & Pinard, 1962; Piaget, 1927). As long as this assumption ("animism") contradicts the scientific view on the physical world, it can be a factor of resistance to scientific education. In the end, it is a matter of experimental research to determine if magical thinking is an obstacle to cognitive development or if it enhances such development.

It could be the case that magical beliefs impede cognitive development in certain domains while boosting such development in others at the same time.

MAGIC AND RELIGION: INSTITUTIONALIZED AND NONINSTITUTIONALIZED MAGICAL BELIEFS

Finally, two types of magical beliefs can be distinguished from one another. *Noninstitutionalized magical beliefs* (NIMBs) are magical beliefs that are unrelated to any "official" religious doctrine. Most beliefs in mind-over-matter and mind-over-mind everyday magic (witchcraft, power of cursing, astrology, palm reading, everyday superstitions) belong to NIMBs. In contrast, *institutionalized magical beliefs* are magical beliefs that are accepted by an official religious ideology. For example, in Christianity such beliefs are those in the almighty God, Christ, angels, prayer, and holy miracles. According to the teaching of theism, God can suspend or cancel physical laws of nature, but the same power is not allowed to people (Swinburne, 1979, 1996). As long as divine intervention into natural laws is exceptionally rare, God is viewed as a keeper of natural laws who supports their stable and universal nature. This allows for science to thrive. At the same time, by positioning God at the very end of the causal chain and giving God the role of *causa finalis*, theism has distanced God from an individual's everyday life. Since noninstitutionalized magic may be used by some people to fill in the gap, religion may rightly consider magic as a competitor.

As a result, NIMBs experience powerful resistance from both science and religion. Science rejects magic because magic is in contradiction with science's fundamental principles, such as the principle of laws of nature operating independently from an observer. In contrast, religion recognizes the power of magical beliefs, yet demands monopoly on these beliefs by declaring all unconventional magical beliefs to be linked with evil. In the Bible we read, "You must not preserve a sorceress alive" (Exodus, 22:18). If religion may be threatened by unconventional (noninstitutionalized) magic so much that it demands a sorceress to be killed, this means that the sorceress is important enough to present danger to religion (recognition of the importance of unconventional magic) and that she should be killed (leaving all the magic to the religion—the demand for monopoly). At the same time, institutionalized magical beliefs gain support from church and religion. Altogether, the scope of magical reality can be presented as in Figure 1.1.

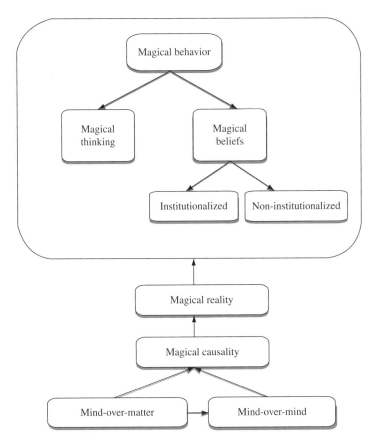

FIGURE 1.1. The structure of magical reality.

THE STATE OF THE PROBLEM

Studies of magical beliefs in children have produced a bunch of fascinating results, yet the interpretation of these results is hindered by methodological problems (see Chapter 2). In adults, studies of magical thinking targeted a wide range of phenomena, from parapsychology and superstitions to placebo effects. Reviews of these studies (Vyse, 1997; Zusne & Jones, 1989) were meant to reflect the state of the science in the field of research on magical thinking, yet the message that they delivered was biased by scientific ideology. Until relatively recently, most research on magical thinking was based on the assumption that magic is a misleading alternative to science. It was also assumed that, for unclear reasons, magical thought had managed to survive the "scientific revolution" even though it historically belongs to the past stages of human mental development.

With regard to children, magical thinking has been predominantly viewed as a by-product of cognitive development that occurs naturally in the early and preschool years of childhood but eventually gives way to scientific reasoning (Piaget). In adults, beliefs in magic have been labeled as superstitions that develop as a means of dealing with frustrations, uncertainties, and the unpredictable nature of certain human activities—for example, the belief that wearing a certain item of clothing can affect the outcome of a sporting competition or gambling. Even religion has been discounted as a delusion—a system of false beliefs that impede our understanding of how the world works (Dawkins, 2006). Some researchers (Langer, 1975; Vyse, 1997) have acknowledged that certain aspects of magical beliefs and superstitions, such as the "illusion of control," may contribute to the development of problem-coping strategies, but their role was viewed as far less significant than that of logic and scientific thought. Viewed in this light, magical reality is nothing but a curious phenomenon of human psychology that is secondary to the overwhelmingly superior scientific reality.

Researchers such as Nemeroff and Rozin (2000) place a greater emphasis than others in the field on the role that magical thinking plays in the functioning of the human mind, such as the role of heuristics. These researchers theorized that magical beliefs could operate consciously or unconsciously, while noting that cultural context may help to determine the level of awareness at which they operate. Nevertheless, they concentrated their research on sympathetic magical thinking in adults, which in Western cultures operates predominantly subconsciously. *The psychological mechanisms of children's and adults' beliefs in mind-over-matter and mind-over-mind magic, at both conscious and subconscious levels, remain largely unexplored.*

To summarize, the studies reviewed in this book aimed to provide an unbiased view of the role that magical reality plays both in the cognitive development of children and in the functioning of the adult mind. On one hand, rather than being a host for wrong beliefs and superstitions, magical reality provides a person with coping strategies for problems that are beyond the reach of scientific thinking. Because magical reality deals with meaning, emotions, and communication, it can peacefully coexist with, and productively complement, scientific reality. On the other hand, magical reality opens the door to manipulation of human minds on a grand scale, with the purpose of influence and control. This makes people vulnerable to indirect persuasion techniques that can be exploitative and potentially dangerous.

HYPOTHESES AND PREDICTIONS

The studies reported in this book are the studies of magical thinking, NIMBs, and magical behavior. The main hypothesis behind these studies was that *initially, NIMBs appear in children as a legitimate, conscious form of beliefs that coexist with the belief in physical causality; later, under pressure from science and religion, NIMBs go into the domain of the subconscious.* If this main hypothesis is true, then the following specific hypotheses follow from it.

Young and preschool children should endorse NIMBs to the same extent that they endorse the belief in physical causality, both in their verbal explanations of unusual effects and in their behavioral reactions. Justification: children's NIMBs have not yet experienced the pressure of scientific and religious education, the two forces that confront NIMBs and exile them into the subconscious. This specific hypothesis is discussed in Chapter 2.

At a certain period of school age, magical explanations disappear from children's verbal accounts about causes of physical effects, yet they can be easily reactivated if unexplained causal effects that assert magic are shown to them. Justification: in the beginning of scientific and religious education, the retreat of NIMBs into the subconscious is not yet complete, and these beliefs fluctuate between the domains of conscious and subconscious (Chapter 3).

Being a significant part of preschool and elementary school children's everyday experience, early magical thinking positively affects children's performance on cognitive tasks. Justification: children's early magical thinking and magical beliefs receive support from children's social environment, in the form of maintaining children's belief in folk magical characters (Santa, the Tooth Fairy) as well as the industry of toys and entertainment, books, and movies for children. This systematic (and expensive) support can only be justified if children's caretakers (parents, teachers, psychologists) intuitively realize that magical thinking entails benefits for children's cognitive development (Chapter 4).

When asked to explain unusual causal effects that assert mind-over-matter magic, adults will deny magical explanations of such effects, even if these effects are repeatedly shown to them. Justification: in their explicit judgments, most adults want to be in accord with science and religion (Chapter 5).

When psychological defense against magical influence is relaxed (for example, when denying the possibility of magic involves a high cost or when magic affects fantastic and not real objects), rational adults will retreat to magical behavior. Justification: in adults, beliefs in NIMBs do not disappear but are subconscious. As follows from psychoanalysis, when defenses are overcome, subconscious thoughts and beliefs ascend to the surface of consciousness (Chapter 5).

In contrast to Western educated adults, uneducated participants from developing cultures will endorse magical beliefs both in their verbal explanations and in their nonverbal behavior. Justification: in many developing cultures, NIMBs are not suppressed by science and religion and remain in the domain of consciousness (Chapter 6).

When faced with magical effects in situations where these effects do not challenge their rational beliefs, such as in situations of exploration, Western adults will show curiosity toward such effects and be likely to explore these effects. Justification: the energy of the repressed NIMBs requires an outlet into the domain of consciousness, and exploratory behavior (along with dreams and imagination) provides such an outlet (Chapter 7).

In the domains that are viewed as inaccessible for physical causality (such as the domain of fantasy), adults would be prepared to accept magical causation. Justification: the belief that magic can work in such domains as fantasy does not challenge the dominant belief in scientific rationality, and this makes magical causality acceptable (Chapter 8).

Mind-over-mind magic, which in the earlier historic epochs was employed in order to manipulate mass consciousness and consolidate a community, remains in modern societies. However, under the pressure of science and religion, mind-over-mind magic is stripped of its sacred context and renamed as suggestion and indirect persuasion. Justification: as a social offshoot of NIMBs, mind-over-mind magic is in confrontation with religion and science. In order to avoid this confrontation, mind-over-mind magic must shed its association with magic and adopt secular forms of suggestion and indirect persuasion (Chapter 9).

When confronted with magical intervention in their lives, either in the form of observing magical phenomena (cognitive intervention) or in the form of a sorcerer trying to exert influence with the help of magic (emotional intervention), adults will resist such intervention: they will either ignore magical phenomena (cognitive defense) or deny that magical influence had any effect on their lives (emotional defense). Justification: modern religion associates NIMBs with bad forces (the devil, evil spirits, paganism). This creates in adults the fear of magic and triggers psychological defenses against magical intervention (Chapter 10).

Social institutions, such as political power, commercial groups, and religious sects, exploit NIMBs, aiming to control, manipulate, and make financial or psychological profit. Justification: anthropological and historical studies have shown that in the early stages of history these institutions used magic for manipulation and control over minds. With the onset of science, NIMBs retreated into the subconscious, yet their energy can be reached via psychological techniques, such as suggestion and indirect persuasion, and exploited for extracting political, economic or psychological benefits (Chapters 9 and 10).

In modern Western cultures, a person has to maintain a special activity in order to keep magical reality from entering his or her everyday life. Justification: magical reality is suppressed by science and religion, yet it is constantly present in a person's subconscious thoughts and desires; therefore, the person has to make an effort not to allow his or her magical thoughts and beliefs to surface (Chapter 11).

Unlike NIMBs, magical thinking based on NIMBs thrives unimpeded in the domain of consciousness throughout the lifespan. Justification: magical thinking is carried out through play, dreams, art, and imagination, which, in the Western cultural tradition, do not have the ontological status of true reality and do not threaten the power of science and religion (Chapter 12).

This book is like a Russian nesting doll: it involves a bunch of specific hypotheses, each of which is subordinate to, or nested within, the central (main) hypothesis. For example, in Chapter 7 the specific hypothesis is that adults will have a stronger interest in exploring an impossible magical effect than an identical counterintuitive physical effect. But testing this specific hypothesis *at the same time tests the main hypothesis*, because the predicted effect is caused by the subconscious power of NIMBs. As each chapter involves a lot of special features and details, it will be necessary, from time to time, to remind the reader that what he or she is reading has a double aim—to examine the specific chapter hypothesis and the book's main hypothesis at the same time.

2

Children and Magic

It has long been assumed that in their verbal reasoning about physical objects and events, preschool and elementary school children progressively acquire a natural view of the world. Thus, in their replication of Piaget's early data (Piaget, 1927), Laurendeau and Pinard (1962) reported that in children between 5 and 11 years of age, physical explanations of natural phenomena gradually replaced "precausal" explanations (animistic, artificialistic, and magical). This shift from precausal to causal thinking has been observed by other researches as well (Carey, 1985; Carey & Spelke, 1994; Huang, 1930; Rosengren, Kalish, Hickling, & Gelman, 1994; Samarapungavan, 1992; Schultz, Fisher, Pratt, & Rulf, 1986; Smith, Carey, & Wiser, 1985).

Along with this, psychologists have long noticed that preschool children in Western cultures remain open to the possibility that magic is real. Jean Piaget (1971) provided multiple examples of preschool children's magical behavior, such as one boy who believed that by saying their names, he could cause gorgeous birds and butterflies in his father's illustrated manual "to come to life and fly out of the book, leaving holes behind them" (p. 135). Harris, Brown, Marriot, Whittal, and Harmer (1991) asked children aged 4 and 6 years to pretend that there was a creature (a rabbit or a monster) in an empty box. When left alone, some children behaved as if the pretend creature were really in the box.

In one of my own earlier studies, in Experiment 1, children aged 4, 5, and 6 years were presented with a magic box that could turn pictures of attractive objects into real objects if a magic spell was cast (mind-over-matter magic) (Subbotsky, 1985). When asked if such things can happen in real life, almost all children denied this. But when the experimenter went out of the room "to make a phone call," up to 90% of the children tried to magically convert pictures into objects and were bitterly disappointed when this did not happen (see results shown in Figure 2.1).

In Experiment 2 of this study, children of the same age were told the story of a girl who had received a magic table as a birthday present. The table could turn toy figures of animals into real live ones. Again, asked if this could happen in real life, only a few 4-year-olds said yes. Yet, when the children had an opportunity to see a real table that looked exactly like the one in the story and saw that a small plastic lion started moving on the table (through the use of magnets), only a few of the children behaved in a rational manner (looked for the mechanism, searched for the wires). The rest of the children either ran away, fearing that the lion was coming to life, or applied a magic wand they had been given to stop the lion from moving (see results shown in Figure 2.2).

Another experiment targeted children's belief in nonpermanence magic. In their judgments, most preschoolers denied the possibility of moving through walls or going back in time. However, when shown a magic trick that made these events seem to have happened, the majority of 4- and 5-year-olds and some 6-year-olds tried to pass their hand through a glass wall (in order to

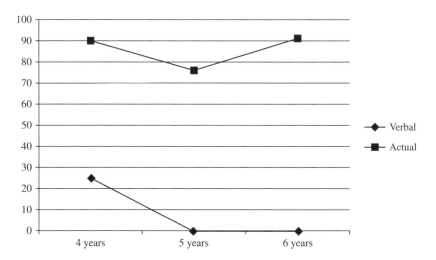

Figure 2.1. Percent of children who showed their belief in magic in their verbal judgments (Verbal) and actual behavior (Actual) in Experiment 1.

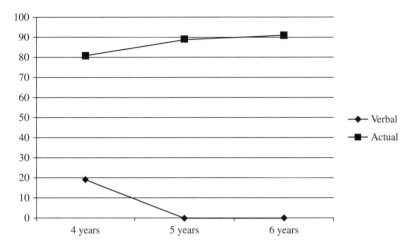

Figure 2.2. Percent of children who showed their belief in magic in their verbal judgments (Verbal) and actual behavior (Actual) in Experiment 2.

obtain an attractive object) and refused to drink "magic" water (fearing to become infants again), thereby revealing their belief in the potentially unusual properties of space and time in everyday reality (Subbotsky, 1994).

CHILDREN'S MAGICAL BEHAVIOR: A BELIEF OR A MISUNDERSTANDING?

But what do these experiments really show? In the modern world, even young children are systematically exposed to the achievements of technology, such as television and remote-control cars. "How could they know that technology for time travel, transforming drawings into objects, and age regression is not quite there yet?" (Bloom, 2004, p. 218). Indeed, when preschool children call a certain causal event "magical," do they really mean magic, or is this simply a word used for complex and unknown but possible physical effects? By saying that event A (a magic spell) caused event B (a change of a physical object in an apparently empty box) by magic, do children mean a really magical effect (that a spiritual force within the inanimate object consciously complied with the magician's request) or do they refer to a possible physical effect (that an unknown physical force within a technical device remotely reacted to the experimenter's words or actions)?

In order to answer this question, 6- and 9-year-olds were shown two unusual effects that looked similar but were supposedly caused by two different causal mechanisms: magical (the experimenter cut a piece of paper in half with a pair of scissors while wishing at the same time that a brand new postage stamp be cut in half in an empty box) and physical (the experimenter switched the controlling device and a remote-control car was set into motion) (Subbotsky, 1997a). In both cases, participants were asked if the effect they saw was magic or not magic, and asked to explain the answers. In addition, in Trial 2 of this experiment, the question about cutting the stamp in half by cutting a piece of paper and making a wish was repeated after the demonstration of the remote-control car. This was done in order to alert children that an explanation alternative to magic is possible. If the children realized that the experimenter could in fact act upon a physical object (a car) at a distance without touching it and still insisted that the original effect (cutting a postage stamp in half without touching it) was magic (whereas moving a car was not), then this would increase the probability that what the children meant by "magic" was not just a trick involving an unknown physical force.

The results indicated that only a few 6-year-olds thought that moving a remote-control car was magic, whereas the great majority called cutting the postage stamp in the box "magical" and did not change their opinion after they had been told about the possibility of the science-based explanation. This reduced the plausibility of viewing children's references to magic as an over-extension of the term "magic" to include normal events with an unknown physical force involved. Rather, what children meant when they said that the division of a postage stamp by means of cutting a square of paper and making a wish was magic, was a version of mind-over-matter magic.

But perhaps children referred to magic because the adult (who was likely to be viewed by the child as a person with superior powers) carried out the actions? In order to examine this possibility, in another experiment in the same study, the "paper-stamp" manipulation was performed by one of the children's peers trained to act as an experimenter's assistant. The results showed that the children were equally prepared to call the unusual effect magical when this effect was performed by an adult or by one of their peers.

WHEN MAGIC MEETS SCIENCE: CAN CHILDREN BELIEVE BOTH?

So, elementary school children can indeed distinguish between counterintuitive physical effects (one physical device acting on another physical device at a distance) and magical effects (a magic manipulation or spell acting on a physical object at a distance). But would they prefer a physical explanation to a magical one if both explanations referred to the same effect? As long as schooling is supposed to provide children with scientific alternatives to their spontaneous explanations, which are often magical (Piaget, 1927), one would expect the answer to be positive.

To examine this, 6- and 9-year-olds were shown an unusual effect (a brand new postage stamp was destroyed in an apparently empty box) in a magical (a magic spell was cast on the box before the event happened) or scientific (an unknown physical device was switched on and off again before the event) context. Contrary to expectation, in their judgments, children of both groups endorsed magical and scientific explanations to an equal extent (Figure 2.3). In their actions, 9-year-olds showed a significant drop in their credulity toward physical, but not toward magical, explanations; most of them refused to allow the experimenter to repeat his magic spell while the children's own valuable objects were in the closed box.

Taken together, the aforementioned experiments raise a problem of stability, or entrenchment, of children's magical beliefs. When children are interviewed about hypothetical magical events, even most 4-year-olds deny that magic can happen in real life. Yet, when presented with the visual effects that look like instances of real magic, most 6- and 9-year-olds are prepared to endorse magical explanations to the same extent as physical explanations, in both their verbal judgments and behavior. Why do children as old as that both deny the reality of magic and believe in it at the same time? Could this be due to a special balance between the costs and benefits of engaging in magical behavior in different circumstances, as some psychologists believe (Woolley, 1997; Woolley & Phelps, 1994)? For instance, in an interview situation about hypothetical instances of magic, children are likely to show rational and logical thinking because an interviewer expects this from them, whereas thinking in a magical way brings no benefit to them. The balance of costs and benefits was reversed in the situation when the same children felt in

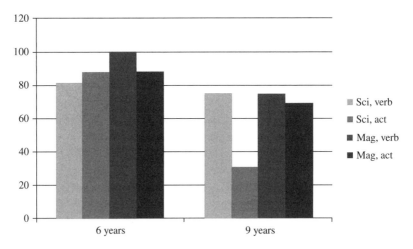

FIGURE 2.3. Percent of children who endorsed magical ("Mag") and scientific ("Sci") explanations in their judgments ("verb") and actual behavior ("act").

danger of not getting (or losing) their valuable object if they disregarded the possibility of the magical explanation.

Without denying the validity of the "cost–benefit balance" argument, one could inquire whether the high cost of denying magical explanations in psychological experiments is the only cause of children's magical beliefs. After all, even in the lives of children, to say nothing of adults, magical effects do not happen quite so often. If children's causal beliefs were shaped by their everyday experience only, then early magical beliefs should be gone by the age of 5 years—yet evidence exists that these beliefs continue much beyond this age. The question arises, What makes early magical beliefs so resistant to everyday experience?

Verbal Magical Beliefs and Children's Everyday Experience

Magical experiences do happen in young children's lives. Occasionally, children discover objects that are allegedly left or taken by magical characters, such as Santa Claus or the Tooth Fairy. Since these experiences are not so frequent and run against the mundane order of everyday life, even children cannot help viewing them as anomalous. This fact puts the issue of children's magical beliefs in the general context of people's capacity to handle anomalous causal events. The fact that anomalous data (data that contradict established views) are often ignored or reinterpreted to make them fit established views has long been acknowledged in philosophy of science (Humphreys, 1968; Kuhn, 1970; Lacatos, 1970). It has also been shown in developmental research that students often retain their naïve physical (Champagne, Gunstone, & Klopfer, 1985; Chi, 1992; Kuhn, 1989; Levin, Siegler, Druyan, & Gardosh, 1990; McCloskey, 1983) and psychological (Nemeroff & Rozin, 2000; Subbotsky, 1997b, 2000b) theories, even after they have received appropriate scientific instruction.

MAGIC AS AN ANOMALOUS EXPERIENCE

In their comprehensive account of people's reactions to anomalous data, Chinn and Brewer (1993) argued that preserving an original theory includes six main forms of responding to anomalous data: (*1*) ignoring the data, (*2*) rejecting the data, (*3*) excluding the data, (*4*) holding the data in abeyance, (*5*) reinterpreting the data, and (*6*) making minor peripheral changes to the original theory. The authors presented ample evidence from both the history of science and psychological research showing that scientists and students use similar strategies to discount anomalous data before they succumb to those data and change their original theories. Among the factors that influence the way in which people respond to anomalous data, Chinn and Brewer mentioned characteristics of prior knowledge, such as the entrenchment of the original theory, and characteristics of the anomalous data, such as the credibility of the data.

Although the majority of examples discussed by the aforementioned researchers fall into various specific domains (biology, physics, and geography), the authors suggest that there exists a special set of beliefs—ontological beliefs—that is particularly deeply entrenched and hard to change (Chinn & Brewer, 2000). Ontological beliefs include beliefs about the most basic properties of the world, such as the belief about the structure of matter. Children's beliefs about mind-over-matter magic belong to this class of beliefs.

Indeed, the belief that the law of physical causality unconditionally governs the natural world belongs to the scope of ontological beliefs, and this belief is incompatible with the belief in mind-over-matter magic. As argued in the previous chapter, in their judgments, preschool children increasingly rely on nonmagical causal explanations of physical effects (Carey, 1985; Laurendeau & Pinard, 1962; Piaget, 1927; Rosengren, Kalish, Hickling, & Gelman, 1994; Samarapungavan, 1992; Shultz, Fisher, Pratt, & Rulf, 1986; Smith, Carey, & Wiser, 1985). Regarding manual, sensorimotor objects, this shift from magical to physical thinking occurs even at an earlier age. According to Piaget (1937), at around 2 years of age, children start handling manual objects in accord with the objects' physical and spatial properties. As a result, early beliefs in magical causality eventually die out, at least as far as children's verbal judgments about physical objects that are within the scope of the their everyday practical experience is concerned. At the same time, some questions about this fundamental shift in causal reasoning remain unanswered, specifically: (*1*) At exactly what age do children start viewing magical events as anomalous? (*2*) To what extent are early verbal magical beliefs entrenched in preschoolers and children of various school ages? (*3*) Can these beliefs be undermined by an explanation that an apparently magical event is, in fact, an ordinary event or a trick?

By the same token, the belief in the universal power of physical causality,[1] which replaces early magical beliefs, can vary in its degree of entrenchment as well. One might expect preschool children, when shown an anomalous event that looks like magic, to be quick in dropping their newly acquired scientific causal beliefs and acknowledging that magic is real, whereas schoolchildren would resist the anomalous experience by ignoring, rejecting, or reinterpreting the anomalous data. In other words, the studies presented in this chapter aimed to examine the extent to which children's verbal causal beliefs could be affected by the presentation of anomalous (magical) causal events.

In the studies related to the problem, three main issues were addressed. The first issue dealt with the problem of how frequently children of varying ages refer to magic in their spontaneous explanations of phenomena unknown to them. It has been reported that even 4- and 5-year-old children can discriminate between possible and impossible transformations without spontaneously invoking the concept of magic (Huang, 1930; Rosengren et al., 1994). In other reports, however, children aged 4, 6, and 8 years quite often used the term "magic" when confronted with phenomena for which they did not have correct physical explanations (Chandler & Lalonde, 1994; Phelps & Woolley, 1994).

These conflicting reports raise the question of what children of varying ages actually mean by "magic." In some studies on children's magical thinking, it remains unclear whether children who used the concept of magic meant real magic that involved supernatural powers or just tricks and parlor magic (Chandler & Lalonde, 1994; Rosengren & Hickling, 1994; Rosengren et al., 1994). In other studies, children's responses indicated their growing awareness of magic as events different from tricks and involving violations of fundamental physical laws (for instance, in Phelps and Woolley's 1994 study, one 8-year-old commented that magicians cannot make a house appear in an instant, while a fairy can make it appear "just like that"). Altogether, there is some evidence that at the age of 5 or 6 years, children acquire an understanding that genuine magic is different from stage magic and is impossible in the real world.

This research only examined children's verbal reactions to magic. The second issue targeted children's behavioral responses to events that involve magical transformations, different from their verbal responses. Some researchers suggest that children's tendency to engage in magical practices during an experiment is a function of the "cost" of these practices for participants (Woolley & Phelps, 1994). In their verbal judgments, school-children usually show skepticism toward magic. Yet, if skepticism toward magic involved a potentially high cost, children (Harris, Brown, Mariott, Whittall, & Harmer, 1991; Johnson & Harris, 1994; Subbotsky, 1985, 1994) and even adults (Rozin, Markwith, & Ross, 1990; Rozin, Millman, & Nemeroff, 1986; Subbotsky, 1997a; Subbotsky & Quinteros, 2002) behaved as if they believed in magic.

The third issue is most closely related to the problem raised in the present study: at what age do children start viewing events that violate physical laws as anomalous and dismiss or reinterpret these events to preserve their scientific view of the world? In a study by DeLoache, Miller, and Rosengren (1997), 2½-year-old children typically failed to repeat scientific explanations of magical phenomena when describing the experiment to a nonaccompanying parent; instead, they said that a real magical transformation had been observed. In another study, 4- and 5-year-old children were confronted with commonplace and impossible transformations after they were asked to judge the possibility of these transformations (Rosengren & Hickling, 1994). Although in the beginning most children denied the reality of impossible transformations, after seeing the "impossible" events, many 4-year-olds changed their minds and acknowledged these events to be "really magical," whereas 5-year-olds insisted that they were tricks. This suggests that at the age of 5, children already hold the belief in the universal power of physical causality.

Altogether, the reviewed studies illuminate a number of important questions in the development of causal thinking, yet they also share some methodological limitations. In some of these studies, participants did not really observe any magical transformations, and in others, the phenomena that were supposed to look magical were, in fact, classic tricks with which children could have been familiar from their past experience (watching movies or TV programs or going to the circus). This created ambiguity in interpreting children's answers; most children would view these phenomena as tricks, even if they labeled them as magic. If this were the case, observing these phenomena could not present a serious challenge to the older children's belief in the universal power of physical causality. To overcome these methodological limitations, two conditions should be met: (*1*) children should be able to clearly discriminate between instances of true magic² and magic tricks, and (*2*) an inexplicable causal effect should be presented that does not come from a traditional set of tricks available in magic shops and would, therefore, look more convincingly like an instance of true magic.

To summarize, the shift from early verbal magical beliefs to the belief in the universal power of physical causality warrants more systematic examination. Specifically, the following question remains open: is the acquisition of the knowledge that magical events are incompatible with physical laws a sufficient condition for children to drop their belief in magic?

THE BELIEF IN QUESTION: TESTING THE ENTRENCHMENT OF MAGICAL BELIEFS

Theoretically, there can be two types of judgment about magic: a conceptual judgment and an ontological judgment. On the conceptual level, a person whose magical beliefs are examined has to be able to distinguish truly magical effects from (*1*) ordinary (nonmagical) events and (*2*) tricks that look like magical effects. In other words, the person has to have a concept of magical events as events that violate known physical laws. As argued in Chapter 1, such violations include at least four types of events: mind-over-matter magic, animation magic, nonpermanence magic, and sympathetic magic. If a person can clearly distinguish true magical events (such as a piece of paper changing its shape as a result of a magic spell) from ordinary events (a piece of paper changed by applying a physical force to it) and from a similar-looking trick (a piece of paper changing by inconspicuously being replaced by another one), then the person can be qualified as having a true concept of the mind-over-matter magic. Yet, to qualify a person as a believer or nonbeliever in magic, along with the person's conceptual understanding of magic, his or her ontological judgment needs to be examined. If a person who has a proper concept of true magic also thinks that true magic is possible in the real world, then this person can be viewed as a believer in magic, at least as far as the person's verbal responses are concerned.

Accordingly, one goal of this study was to examine at what age children acquire the knowledge of true magical events as something that violates known physical principles (testing the conceptual understanding of true magic). Another goal was to find out at what age children start viewing true magical events as anomalous and nonexistent in the real world (testing the ontological dismissal of true magic from the real world). The third goal was to investigate under what conditions children are prepared to abandon their belief that true magic does not exist in the real world—if they are faced with anomalous causal events that look like instances of true magic (testing the entrenchment of children's belief in the universal power of physical causality). What if children who deny that a certain hypothetical event that violates known physical laws is magical are shown this event "for real"? Would the children be able to retain their rational views and dismiss the effect as a trick? Or would they be quick to change their minds and say that the effect was true magic? If, in this situation, they embraced a magical explanation, it would mean that children are ready to change their disbelief in magic even when the cost–benefit balance remains constant. In other words, at a certain age both children's magical beliefs and their beliefs in physical causality are unstable and easily traded one for the other depending on the availability of evidence supporting or falsifying these beliefs.

To examine this, a $15 \times 11 \times 11$-cm wooden box was used for the demonstration of "magical" phenomena (Subbotsky, 2004). A special construction of the lid and a hidden trap door produced an event that looked like a violation of object permanence: a new postage stamp placed in the box could change into another postage stamp, for example, into a half-burned one. The box could be manipulated (turned upside down or shaken) without revealing the secret of the mechanism through which the postage stamps (the new one and the burned one) were apparently exchanged. The burned postage stamp was hidden between the trap door and the box's wall.

In the *interview trial* of this experiment, the children were questioned on their understanding of the difference between proper magic and magic tricks. This precaution was necessary because in English the word "magic" can stand for both true magic and stage magic (see Kuhn, Amlani, & Rensink, 2008). Children were shown two pictures of a wizard who performed the unusual events. The pictures differed only in the color of one of the following features: a cap, buttons, shoes, or a beard.

The children were then told that one of the two men was a real wizard and could do true magic, while the other only pretended that he could do true magic but, in reality, could only show tricks that looked like magic. The children were then presented with four pairs of test items. In each pair, one item presented an instance of true magic that involved a violation of known physical principles (the mind-over-matter type of magic) and the other, a magic trick that produced the same result as did the mind-over-matter magic. In order to pass the test on understanding the difference between magic and magic tricks, children had to correctly identify most of the eight items as magical or nonmagical and identify the real wizard for each pair of items (the children had to be correct on 10 out of 12 distinctions between true magical effects and magic tricks). As Figure 3.1 shows, for most 5-year-olds, understanding the difference between true magic and tricks proved a difficult task.

Children who understood the concept of true magic were then asked an ontological question of whether they believed that true magic could happen in real life. Percentages of the children's answers are shown in Figure 3.2. The results indicated that 58% of 5-year-olds, 81% of 6-year-olds, and 70% of 9-year-olds deny that true magic can happen in the real world.

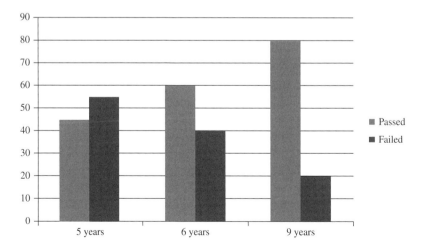

FIGURE 3.1. Percent of children who passed and failed the test on understanding the difference between true magical effects and tricks that looked like magic.

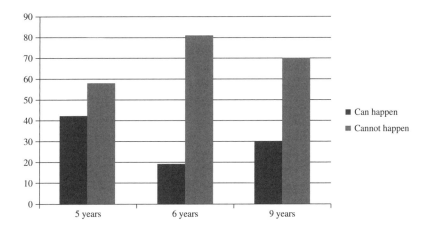

FIGURE 3.2. Percent of children who understood the difference between true magic and tricks and answered that true magic can or cannot happen in real life.

The *demonstration trial* followed. In this trial, I presented the children who denied that true magic could be a reality with a causal effect that looked like an instance of true magic: I asked children to put a new postage stamp in an apparently empty box, and then cast a magic spell on the box in which I ordered the postage stamp to be burned. When the children opened the box, they found a half-burned stamp. The children were asked whether the effect they had seen was an instance of true magic or a magic trick. All 5-year-olds and most 6-year-olds abandoned their skepticism and accepted magical explanations, even though the cost–benefit balance was the same before and after the demonstration. In 9-year-olds, however, only half of the children dropped their original skeptical view, while the other half maintained that this was a trick (see Figure 3.3).

Children who originally believed in magic or accepted magical explanations in the demonstration trial were then shown the trap door in the box and given an explanation of how it worked. They were asked again to explain the cause of the magical effect they had seen. In 5-year-olds, magical beliefs were so strong that even after the trick was explained, 91% persisted in their magical explanations (see Figure 3.4). In contrast, older children quickly recovered their skepticism toward magic after the trick was explained.

Altogether, the data showed that in 5-year-olds, verbal beliefs in physical causality have no advantage over beliefs in magical causality. Furthermore, in children of this age, verbal magical beliefs are deeply entrenched, and vice versa: in those 5-year-olds who showed disbelief in magic (and, as a consequence, the belief in the universal power of physical causality), this disbelief (belief) proved not to be entrenched. This explains the earlier

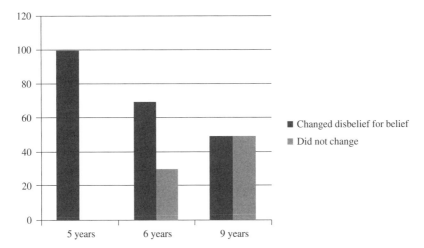

FIGURE 3.3. Percent of nonbelievers in magic who changed or did not change their disbelief in magic for belief.

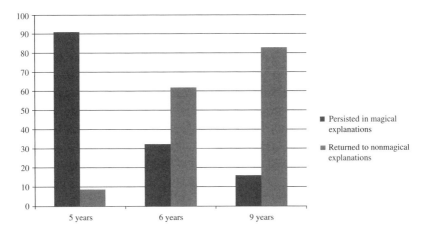

FIGURE 3.4. Percent of children who persisted in their magical explanations and those who returned to nonmagical explanations after the trick had been explained.

reported data, according to which, in one kind of circumstance, children of this age (and younger) show a good grasp of physical causation in their reasoning (Bullock & Gelman, 1979; Kun, 1978; Shultz et al., 1986), and in another kind of circumstance, they are prepared to explain causal events in terms of magic (Bullock, 1985; Rosengren et al., 1994). To summarize, in 5-year-olds' causal judgments, beliefs in physical and magical causal explanations coexist with a certain prevalence of magical beliefs. This prevalence of magical explanations over physical explanations disappears in 6-year-olds.

At this age, an overwhelming majority of children deny the possibility of magic in the real world and view magical outcomes as anomalous causal events. In those 6-year-olds who showed verbal magical beliefs, these beliefs were no longer entrenched. Along with this relaxation of their magical view of the world, most 6-year-olds develop the belief in the universal power of physical causality. However, in 6-year-olds, as in younger children, the belief in the universal power of physical causality is not entrenched, and most children are quick to retreat back to magical explanations if confronted with anomalous causal phenomena.

In other words, in 6-year-olds' verbal judgments, magical and physical beliefs coexist in more or less equal terms—a certain balance is achieved between children's preparedness to go either for magical or for physical explanations. In 9-year-olds, this balance is no longer observed; 50% of children showed an entrenched belief in the universal power of physical causality. At the same time, in those 9-year-old children who still hold magical beliefs, these beliefs are no longer entrenched. In sum, whereas in 5-year-old children magical explanations prevailed over physical ones, in 9-year-olds the relation was reversed. Not only did the majority of 9-year-olds deny the reality of magic in their ontological judgments, but also a large number of children refused to accept magical causal explanations when confronted with the anomalous events. Eighty-five percent of 9-year-old children who accepted or produced magical explanations abandoned these explanations as soon as the trick was explained to them.

The experiment confirmed the notion that in preschool and primary school children, verbal disbelief in magic is only superficial. Despite the prevalence of physical causal events in children's everyday experience, at this age children are happy to be reassured about magic's existence. Caught between two conflicting traditions in a modern society—the tradition of science (cultivated at school) and the tradition of magic (cultivated in "folk culture" and in children's culture)—children are ready to accept both. According to the existing evidence, most parents acknowledge that they go along with their preschool children's magical beliefs but show less support for such beliefs as children get older (Rosengren & Hickling, 1994). Some studies indicated that at the end of the preschool period (at about 6 years of age), children's verbal belief in the efficacy of wishing fades (Woolley, 2000). The study presented in this chapter, with some correction on age, supported this view. It showed that between 6 and 9 years of age, children's verbal belief in the mind-over-matter magic rapidly decreases— a change that can be a result of a group of factors, such as the termination of parental support of early magical beliefs, systematic school education, and religious education. *This change can be viewed as the beginning of separation between noninstitutionalized magical beliefs (NIMBs) and institutionalized magical beliefs. Whereas institutionalized magical beliefs are promoted by religious education, NIMBs begin their descent into the depths of the subconscious.*

In Chapters 5 and 6, we will meet NIMBs again—this time in adults. But before that, I will discuss an important issue: does children's magical thinking matter?

Magical Thinking and Children's Cognitive Development

Multinational industries (such as toy production and entertainment) exploit and support magical beliefs in children. By the age of 6, most children have seen the various Harry Potter films, "Superman," and "Spiderman," and have had books about wizards and fairies read to them. In most Western families, children are exposed to magical folk characters such as Santa Claus, the Easter Bunny, and the Tooth Fairy (Clark, 1995; Harris, Brown, Marriot, Whittal, & Harmer, 1991; Prentice, Manosevitz, & Hubs, 1978; Rosengren & Hickling, 1994; Woolley, 1997). Many TV programs for children show magical characters, and the number of readers of the DC Comics comic book series, which employ characters with magical powers, is surely in the millions. Yet, despite the pervasive nature of the phenomenon of magical thinking, surprisingly little is known about its effects on children's cognitive and social development. Is children's magical thinking an epiphenomenon of cognitive development that simply accompanies the development of logical thinking, or does it affect the development of logical thinking and other cognitive processes?

DOES MAGIC PLAY A ROLE?

As I have argued previously, historically, magical thinking has been portrayed as an immature stage in the development of intelligence that is inevitably replaced by logical (socialized) thinking (Piaget, 1962). In more recent studies, it has been shown that older children, and even adults, engage in magical thinking (Harris et al., 1991; Nemeroff & Rozin, 2000; Subbotsky, 1985). The coexistence of magical thinking with logical thinking throughout the lifespan does not, however, answer the question of whether magical thinking also affects logical thinking or other cognitive abilities. Apart from being a curious aspect of human behavior (Vyse, 1997) that is worthy of study and even admiration, is magical thinking also a useful ability from which other aspects of human cognitive functioning can benefit? In other words, is involvement in magical thinking confined to entertainment, or has it also to do with more practical aspects of children's lives, such as learning and social communication?

   The existing evidence suggests a positive answer to this question, but only indirectly. For example, research has indicated that in 4-year-olds, but not in 3-year-olds, having imaginary companions predicts understanding of theory of mind, as measured by tests on appearance-reality, false belief, perspective taking, and representational change, with the children's measure of verbal intelligence being controlled (Taylor & Carlson, 1997). As stated in Chapter 1, an imaginary companion is a measure of fantasy orientation and not of magical thinking, yet, indirectly, the association between playing with an imaginary companion and improving one's theory-of-mind abilities may suggest a similar association between engaging in magical thinking and improving understanding of others' minds. Indeed, many magical stories (such as Little Red Riding Hood) are based on understanding false belief (the understanding that the girl in Little Red Riding Hood failed to read the mind of the wolf from his questions and thus put her grandmother and herself in danger). Singer and Singer (1990) also found that fantasy proneness is correlated with more advanced theory-of-mind abilities. Dias and Harris (1988) showed that a pretence stance can help children to solve counterfactual syllogisms, and similar results were confirmed with autistic children (Scott, Baron-Cohen, & Leslie, 1999). Fantasy also influences children's ability to reason about analogies (Richert, 2003). Four-year-olds' understanding of the role of mental representation in pretence improved when put in fantasy contexts (Sobel, 2006). Principe and Smith (2008) reported that 5- and 6-year-olds who strongly believed in a fantastic entity—the Tooth Fairy— gave different reports of their most recent primary tooth loss from those who believed in the Tooth Fairy to a lesser extent. Not only were the believers' reports more complex and voluminous than were those of non-believers, but they also "recollected" more supernatural occurrences, including actually having heard or seen the Tooth Fairy. This study showed that belief in a magical entity could have negative cognitive effects (for instance, they may lead to false memories of actually seeing or hearing the entity), suggesting that having magical beliefs is related to real-world thinking in both positive (by making children's memory reports richer in content) and negative (by making the children report false events) ways.

Altogether, the reviewed research provides some evidence that fantasy and imagination affect children's performance on certain cognitive tasks, such as understanding theory of mind, understanding pretence, syllogistic and analogical reasoning, and false reports of past events. However, as stated in Chapter 1, magical thinking is different from fantasy orientation. There is no direct evidence to date that not only imagination and fantasy but also magical thinking can affect children's performance on cognitive tasks. The studies also showed that children's beliefs in a magical character affected their memories. Can engagement in magical thinking, just like having magical beliefs, also produce effects on real-world thinking? The answer to this question is unclear; at least, I failed to find evidence of this in the literature.

In order to partially remedy the aforementioned gaps in research, the study reported in this chapter examined the hypothesis that *magical thinking positively affects children's cognitive development, by enhancing their creative thinking.*

A positive role of creative thinking for intellectual performance in both adults and children has long been emphasized in psychology (Feldhusen & Treffinger, 1975; Guilford, 1950; Sternberg, 1985; Torrance, 1962). Studies have shown that creative students excel in various intellectual and social activities outside the classroom, leading researchers to suggest that schools should provide extracurricular activities to foster the development of creativity (Perleth & Sierwald, 1993). Furthermore, some research suggests that children's creative ability can enhance performance on real-life problems (Richards, 1993), and that creativity is positively correlated with children's ability to use cognitive coping strategies (Christiano & Russ, 1996). Singer and Singer (1990) also found imaginative play to be linked to children's academic adjustment and their flexibility of thought. Russ (1998) discusses the aforementioned research and puts forward the idea of "play intervention" to increase children's creativity in cognitive, emotional, and social adaptive functioning.

Today, *creativity* is typically defined as the capacity to generate "novel behavior that meets a standard of quality or utility" (Eisenberger, Haskins, & Gambleton, 1999, p. 308), although sometimes it is viewed as the capacity to generate novelty in action and thinking independently of whether the new actions have or do not have any utilitarian value (Smith, 2005). In the context of defining creativity, two types of thinking are usually distinguished. *Convergent thinking* is involved in solving tasks that have only one correct solution, whereas *divergent thinking* is necessary to solve problems that allow for multiple correct answers. Divergent thinking is often seen as a component of creativity (Mouchiroud & Lubart, 2001; Russ & Kaugars, 2001; Russ, Robins, & Christiano, 1999). Despite the variety of definitions of magical thinking, the invariant feature it involves is counterintuitiveness—the ability to construct a world that is an alternative to the real world. This ability is akin to divergent thinking—the ability to find solutions to problems that provide alternatives to typical solutions. In other words, creativity was found to comprise divergent thinking (Runco, Nemiro, & Walberg, 1998; Russ & Kaugars, 2001), which is also seen as key in magical thinking. In clinical research, similarities between magical ("paleological") thinking and creativity have also been suggested to exist (Arieti, 1976). These common features make it possible to ask a question about the potential link between magical thinking and creativity. Research to date has highlighted the importance of creativity for children's intellectual and social abilities, yet it has been limited in terms of pinpointing the psychological factors that can boost children's creativity. The aim of the study presented in this chapter was to examine whether encouraging children to think in a magical way by exposing them to the imaginary world in which known physical principles are violated can enhance children's creative performance on cognitive tasks.

MAGICAL THINKING AND CREATIVITY: THE STUDY

A common method of assessing creativity is through divergent thinking measures. Torrance's Thinking Creatively in Action and Movement (TCAM) test was designed to measure 4- to 8-year-olds' capacity to show fluency, originality, and imagination in their thinking through action and movement (Torrance, 1981). Preschool children's scores on the TCAM test have been shown to be significantly correlated with tests of divergent problem solving (a modified Piaget set of measures, and mathematics readiness test), but not with traditional Piaget measures having one correct answer (convergent problem solving) (Reisman, Pellegrini, Floyd, Paguio, & Torrance, 1980). Despite criticism, divergent thinking was found to predict creative achievements in later years (Plucker, 1999). Another way of assessing creativity is through encouraging children to create nonexistent (impossible) objects (Craig & Baron-Cohen, 1999; Karmiloff-Smith, 1989; Leevers & Harris, 1998; Matuga, 2004; Scott & Baron-Cohen, 1996). Since this task requires providing alternatives to familiar real objects, it can be seen as a test of divergent thinking.

Developmental research has shown that exposure to cinema and TV affects children's subsequent behavior. For example, exposure to aggressive models on TV increased children's subsequent aggressive behavior (Comstock & Scharrer, 2006; Huston & Wright, 1998; Huston-Stein, Fox, Greer,

Watkins & Whitaker, 1981), whereas watching altruistic models encouraged children to behave in a prosocial way (Huston & Wright, 1998; Singer & Singer, 2001). Adult participants who watched humorous video clips improved their performance on a divergent creative task (Filipowicz, 2006). Drawing from these data, we hypothesized that showing children a film with magical content could facilitate, albeit temporarily, the children's performance on creative cognitive tasks.[1]

The aim of Experiment 1 (Subbotsky & Hysted, 2008) was therefore to examine whether presenting children with a film display that promotes magical and fantastical thinking is likely to lead to them showing greater creativity in subsequent tests, in comparison to those who have been shown a film that does not include any magical content.

Participants aged 4 and 6 years and recruited from the Greater London area were divided into experimental and control groups and shown a magical or nonmagical intervention film, respectively. The films were composed of scenes from a Harry Potter movie, deemed as having either "magical" or "nonmagical" content. The magical scenes included animals talking and witches and wizards using wands, performing magic spells, and flying on broomsticks. The nonmagical film was made up of scenes with the same characters but in this case having conversations with no mention of any nonstandard behavior or beliefs. Ten judges who were blind to the purpose of the film independently rated both on the following scales: emotional response (neutral, 1, to very positive, 5), magical content (very nonmagical, 1, to very magical, 5), pace (very slow, 1, to very fast, 5), and richness in action (very poor, 1, to very rich, 5). The experimental film scored significantly higher than the control film on magical content. On the other three scales, the differences between the two films were not significant.

Prior to the intervention, the children of both the experimental and control groups were tested on one activity taken from the TCAM test. Six-year-olds were also given the task of drawing two nonexistent objects. The rest of the activities on the TCAM test were given after the intervention, and four more drawings of nonexistent objects were requested.

Results indicated that before the intervention, children in the experimental and control groups scored approximately equally on most measures. After the intervention, children in the experimental group scored significantly higher than children in the control group on the majority of subsequent creativity tests. This was true in both age groups (see Figure 4.1).

In order to see changes over time, average scores in drawings of nonexistent objects were compared before and after the intervention: on both the "originality" and "nonreality" measures, in the experimental group the drawings received significantly higher scores after the intervention than before it, and in the control group the scores stayed about the same (see Figure 4.2).

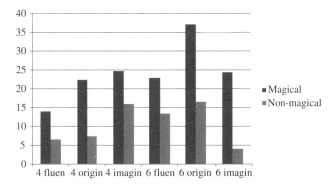

FIGURE 4.1. Means of summarized TCAM scores (fluency ["fluen"], originality ["origin"], and imagination ["imagin"]) as a function of condition (magical versus nonmagical) and age (4 years versus 6 years) in Experiment 1.

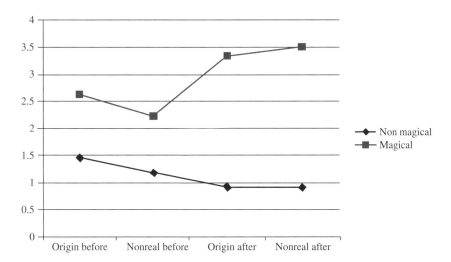

FIGURE 4.2. Average scores for 6-year-olds' drawings' originality ("Origin") and nonreality ("Nonreal") as a function of condition (magical versus nonmagical) and time (before versus after intervention) in Experiment 1.

While this experiment's results can be taken to indicate the possibility of a magical display increasing subsequent creativity, there can be alternative explanations. First, it is possible that children from the experimental group had been exposed, prior to the experiment, to films with magical content more often than had children from the control group, and that this affected the results of the present study. To some extent, this explanation is grounded in the pretest results: although all but one of the differences between the mean raw scores on the pretests were insignificant, all means in the control group were slightly smaller than those in the experimental group. However, even if children in the experimental group had some initial advantage over children in the control group, the fact remains that the intervention markedly increased this advantage, and this fact requires an explanation. The most likely explanation is that exposing the children in the experimental group to the film with highly magical content enhanced their creative behavior to a significantly greater extent than did exposing the children in the control group to the film without the magical content.

Another alternative explanation may be that the higher postintervention performance of the experimental group is due to differences between the experimental and control films, other than having or not having magical content. For example, studies have indicated that positive emotions increase the number of creative responses (Filipowitch, 2006). Although such studies were only performed with adults and the results are contradictory (sometimes the effect of positive mood on creativity was negative), there is still the possibility that a positive effect of the magical display on children's creative behavior was achieved because of the greater emotional lift that the magical display elicited in participants compared with the nonmagical display. However, the expert assessment of both films showed that the films did not differ on emotional response, pace, and richness in action. This makes the second alternative explanation of Experiment 1's results unlikely. Rather, it was the magical effects of the film that led to the increase in creativity.

Finally, it could be argued that increased creativity following exposure to magical events was due to imitation of the content of those events rather than a change in the process by which children generate creative solutions. For example, in the TCAM Activity 1 task, children were encouraged to find ways of getting from one place to another. Might it not be possible that children from the experimental group, who had seen clips of Harry Potter flying on a broomstick and teleporting himself from one location to another, simply imitated these actions as two of their solutions, rather than creatively generating the new ways of moving from one place to another? If this were the case, then the effect of exposure to magical events would be that of encouraging imitation, rather than creativity. Fortunately, all four activities on the TCAM test were scored across the list of prepared responses. These responses included a wide range of possible ways of doing things (such as moving from one place to another or using a cup), but they did not include magical ways. Consequently, the "imitation interpretation" in regard to the TCAM measures can be overruled. In regard to the drawing measures, particularly the non-existence one, this interpretation is more plausible—many of the original pictures of nonexistent objects included objects with animistic properties (a house that is alive and eats cheese). However, in the drawing test, the instruction to both groups encouraged children to produce objects that were unusual and possessed properties that ordinary objects do not possess. This kind of instruction is likely to encourage children to accept the "make-believe" attitude (Dias & Harris, 1988) and produce magical responses independently of the content of the film shown. The inspection of children's drawings has shown that none of these drawings even remotely imitated anything shown in the magical version of the Harry Potter film. This, too, makes the "imitation interpretation" of the effect of the magical film on children's creativity unlikely.

Nevertheless, Experiment 1 involved relatively small samples of participants, and 4-year-olds proved unable to perform on the "picture of a nonexistent item" test. Besides, before the intervention, children in the experimental group showed slightly better performance than children in the control group. Therefore, it was necessary to replicate Experiment 1's results with new samples and an older age range of participants.

Experiment 2 (Subbotsky, Hystead, & Jones, 2009), conducted with children 6 and 8 years of age attending primary schools in Shropshire, England, confirmed the results of Experiment 1. As predicted, exposing children to a film with magical content increased their performance on the TCAM creativity test to a significantly larger extent than did exposing children to a film with the same characters but no magical content (Figure 4.3).

A similar facilitating effect of the magical content on children's creativity was seen on the drawings test. In 6-year-olds, the experimental and control groups scored equally on both the originality and nonreality measures before the intervention; after the intervention, the experimental group scored significantly higher than the control group on both measures. In 8-year-olds,

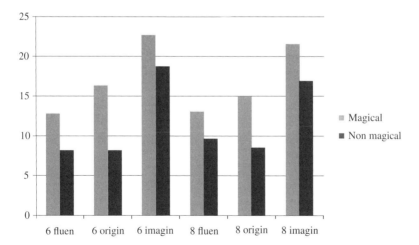

Figure 4.3. Means of summarized TCAM scores (fluency ["fluen"], originality ["origin"], and imagination ["imagin"]) as a function of condition (magical versus nonmagical) and age (6 years versus 8 years) in Experiment 2.

before the intervention the control group scored significantly higher than the experimental group on both measures of drawing creativity; after the intervention, the experimental group caught up with the control group, thus eliminating the differences in creativity of drawings.

Assessment of the direct effect of the intervention via comparison between average scores before and after the intervention revealed significant interaction effects between condition and time in 8-year-olds. On both originality and nonreality measures, in the experimental group drawings received higher scores after the intervention than before it, and in the control group the scores stayed about the same on originality and increased, but to a significantly lesser extent than in the experimental group, on nonreality (Figure 4.4). In 6-year-olds, the interaction plots showed the tendency in the same direction, but the interaction effects between condition and time did not reach a significant level.

Altogether, the findings of the reported study provide support for the hypothesis that showing children a magical display promotes divergent thinking and subsequently increases creativity. This places magical thinking in the broader context of children's cognitive development, linking it with the development of creative thinking and imagination. Rather than a mere epiphenomenon of cognitive development that can be occasionally used for entertainment, magical thinking can be viewed as an enhancer of the development of creative divergent thinking and imagination in children. The link between magical thinking and children's cognitive functioning can explain

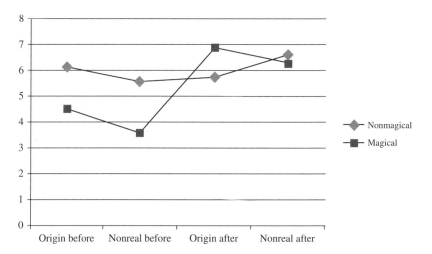

FIGURE 4.4. Average scores for 8-year-olds' drawings' originality ("Origin") and nonreality ("Nonreal") as a function of condition (magical versus nonmagical) and time (before versus after intervention) in Experiment 2.

the persistence of magical thinking throughout childhood, and the support that magical thinking in preschool children gains from children's parents and the existing children's subculture – the two phenomena that otherwise would look unexplained.

Indeed, why does magical thinking, which contradicts scientific thinking and is a "misleading" way to understand natural events, can be found in children as old as 9 years? (see Chapter 3). After all, even most 4-year-olds can understand that magical effects do not happen in the real world (Chapters 2 and 3). And why does magical thinking is supported by our culture, via magical books, movies, and computer games?

In his book on the work of the imagination, Paul Harris (2000, p. 162) writes:

> Under normal circumstances, most allegedly magical phenomena will be impossible to observe and reproduce, and that may mean that children become skeptical about their existence. However, that skepticism need not prevent children from exploring such phenomena in their imaginative excursions. Indeed, they are supported in doing so by many cultural forms, including fairy tales, rituals and religion.

One way to explain this cultural support is to assume that for children magical reality creates the "world of rejected alternatives," which is contrasted with the real world and thus helps children to understand the real world as a unified whole based on the natural laws. Indeed, a substantial amount of evidence shows that children view magical effects as impossible in the real world, and if such events happen (or are declared to be happening), the children view such events as counterintuitive and alternative to ordinary events. Children 4 years and older deny that impossible events (such as eating lightning for dinner) can happen in the real world (Shtulman & Carey, 2007). Three-year-olds and younger 4-year-olds answered that violation of physical laws (a boy turning into a fish) required magic more frequently than violation of social laws (a boy taking a bath with his shoes on) (Brown & Woolley, 2004). Interestingly, this study showed that 4-year-olds also understand that violations of mental laws (a boy turning on a TV with his mind) are impossible and require magic in order to come true. Importantly, preschool children view the magical world not just as a world that lacks causality, but rather as an alternative world based on principles of its own. For example, 3- to 6-year-olds viewed magical causal events (a wish producing direct effects in the physical world) as constrained by the principles of priority (a cause precedes the effect) and exclusivity (an effect cannot result from two independent causes acting simultaneously) (Woolley, Browne, & Boerger, 2006). Preschoolers can also distinguish between different non-real worlds: thus, they understand that Batman and SpongeBob belong to two different fantasy worlds, and that Batman would think that SpongeBob is make-believe (Skolnick & Bloom, 2006). Furthermore, preschool children understand that characters of realistic fiction stories, as well as those of magical and fantastical ones, are not real, yet they claimed that the events in realistic stories could happen in real life more frequently than could the events in the fantastical stories (Woolley & Cox, 2007).

Another way of explaining the support that our culture gives to children's magical thinking is to assume that children's magical thinking directly facilitates their divergent logical thinking and other cognitive processes[2]. It is this explanation that the study presented in this chapter suggests. Just like the play of pretend (Piaget, 1937; Vygotsky, 1999), magical thinking enables children to engage in fantastic imaginary worlds, and thus helps children to start viewing the world and acting upon it from multiple perspectives.

Along with amending our views on some aspects of children's cognitive development, the findings of this experiment could also have implications within a classroom setting. The research reported in this chapter attempted to systematically study whether there are learning benefits of exposing children to magic. The results indicated that exposing children to magic might serve to expand their imagination and get them to think more creatively. Therefore, teachers could use magic in the classroom to enhance interest and increase engagement in the material being taught, and thus facilitate learning. While playing games of pretend with magical characters could facilitate certain aspects of cognitive functioning in preschoolers, in school education, using short magic-themed videos or books might be a more age-appropriate technique for increasing students' creativity than a pretend play intervention, especially as school age children are less ready to engage in pretend play in the school setting. It might also be advantageous to integrate such clips directly into the school day rather than developing separate extracurricular activities.

5

Beyond Childhood

On the basis of the experiments described in the previous chapters, one could assume that adults would be even more skeptical of magic than are 9-year-old children. In order to examine this, 30 university undergraduates were subjected to three trials in which a postage stamp appeared or disappeared in an apparently empty box after the experimenter cast a magic spell on the box, and one trial in which the box stayed empty after the magic spell was not cast (Subbotsky, 2004). Altogether, each participant witnessed four subsequent events in which a change (or no change) in the empty box was observed as a possible result of casting (or not casting) the magic spell. The aim of these manipulations was to examine whether the multiple replications of the apparently magical effect would increase participants' credulity toward a magical explanation of these effects. For each trial, a participant was asked to assess (*1*) the probability that a change occurred in the box after the magic spell was or was not cast and (*2*) the probability that any change that was observed after the box was opened had been caused by the presence or absence of the magic spell. In the pretest interview, all participants correctly distinguished between true magical events and tricks that resembled these events. All participants thought that true magic was impossible in the real world.

The results indicated that although participants' prediction that a change would occur in the box significantly increased in the second trial, their tendency to attribute this change to the magic spell did not. There were, however, marked individual differences observed. Four participants did increase their estimates of probability of magic up to 90%, and 11 participants gave the probability of magic a fair chance (10% or more). All these participants majored in nonscientific subjects or psychology, and all participants who majored in science (five altogether) gave magic a probability of zero.

Altogether, however, adult participants denied magical explanations even though they were repeatedly—four times—faced with anomalous data that challenged their skepticism. This supported the prediction based on the main hypothesis of this book: due to the open confrontation between noninstitutionalized magic beliefs (NIMBs) and the dominant beliefs in the universal power of physical causality, adults would deny having any belief in magic (see Chapter 1). The resistance was so strong that even replication of the magical events was not sufficient to bring the suppressed NIMBs to the domain of consciousness. The question arises of whether adults would be more welcoming toward magical explanations if their resistance were overcome or weakened.

MAGIC WITHOUT MAGIC: ADULTS' REACTIONS TO COUNTERINTUITIVE PHYSICAL EVENTS

One of the important characteristics of the anomalous data that encourages people to change their preinstructional theories is the availability of a plausible alternative theory (Chinn & Brewer, 1993). The alternative theory to explain the magical effect could be, for instance, to view it as an effect of the work of some unknown physical device. If this device, like the magic spell, has no physical link to the box, then the assumption that the device changed something in the box would be viewed as counterintuitive, because in the physical world, all causation occurs through physical contact. The effect of the device also cannot be explained as being caused by electromagnetism, since a piece of paper cannot be destroyed or transformed by a magnetic field. Yet, the assumption that the device is the cause of the effect in the box is not in contradiction with the natural-physical viewpoint. Even if one cannot explain the effect of the device with known physical forces, one can view it as a result of the failure of one's perception, memory, or thinking. In other words, *unlike magical events, the counterintuitive physical event does not challenge the participants' belief in the universal reign of physical causality*.

Further, one could assume that if participants are shown a group of different physical events presented as a cause of the anomalous effect, instead of just one, these events would seem even more compelling to the participants than a single physical event (an action of the device). Indeed, in this case a participant would have a choice of accompanying events, or their combination, with which to explain the anomalous causal effect. On this ground, one can expect that *participants will believe that a counterintuitive physical event happened in front of their eyes to a significantly larger extent than they will believe that a magical event did.*

In order to examine this expectation, in another experiment of the same study, participants (university graduates and undergraduates) were shown an unusual causal effect: a new postage stamp was cut in half in an apparently empty box after the experimenter performed a succession of three actions. The actions included switching an unknown physical device on and off again, cutting a square of paper in half with a pair of scissors, and rolling a Play-Doh ball into a sausage. None of the actions was referred to as or assumed to be magical, yet like the magic spell, these actions did not have any direct physical contact with the box. Participants were asked to explain the effect and say if any of the aforementioned actions had anything to do with the effect.

After the accompanying actions were performed, but before the box was opened, participants were asked whether they believed that the object in the box had changed. None of the participants believed that it had. This indicated that initially, participants did not believe that the accompanying actions had any causal relation to the stamp in the box. Yet, after having seen that the stamp had actually changed, half of participants acknowledged that the accompanying actions might have caused the damage. Seven of these participants chose the device as a possible cause of the effect, and one chose the cutting of a piece of paper. None of the participants, however, could explain exactly how switching on the device or cutting a piece of paper in half could have affected the stamp in the box. Compared to the previous experiment, in which the same effect was presented as the work of a magic spell, this was a significant increase in belief.

In the second part of the experiment (nonverbal processing), the same participants were asked to put their driver's licenses in the box. They were then told that if the experimenter did not reproduce his actions, their licenses would be safe. However, if the actions were performed, the safety of their licenses could not be guaranteed. Participants were then asked if they wanted the experimenter to reproduce the accompanying actions or abstain from the reproduction of these (or some of these) actions. Participants' performance at the level of nonverbal processing was in the same direction. Ten participants (out of the total number of 16) asked the experimenter not to reproduce all or some of the accompanying actions. Five participants chose to ban the action with the device, two chose to ban the cutting, one asked that the paper not be cut and the shape of the Play-Doh ball not be changed ("There might be something in it"), and two banned the reproduction of all actions.

Speaking in rational terms, the action of pronouncing a magic spell is not different from the action of switching on a device or cutting a piece of paper in half, as far as the causal effect of these actions on the object in the box is concerned. Like the magic spell, the latter actions did not have any observed physical link to the postage stamp in the box. The participants' verbal responses prior to observing the object's destruction indicated that none of the participants believed that any of the accompanying actions could have causally affected the object in the box. Yet, a significantly larger number of participants abandoned their skeptical views in the "no magic" theoretical framework (this experiment) than in the "magic" theoretical framework (previous experiment). This supported the idea that in adult participants, repressed magical beliefs (NIMBs) can be promoted to the level of consciousness if these beliefs are framed in a nonmagical context. *Stripped of their magical context and presented as counterintuitive physical events, magical events are allowed to enter the domain of consciousness.*

THE SPECTRUM OF MAGICAL PHENOMENA: EVIDENCE FROM ANTHROPOLOGY, PSYCHOLOGY, AND PSYCHOPATHOLOGY

These experiments confirmed the expectation that in adults, belief in the universal power of physical causality is deeply entrenched. This belief can withstand multiple demonstrations of a causal effect that looks like an instance of true magic.

These data are in contrast with the body of anthropological research, which has shown magical beliefs to be widespread among adults. Luhrman (1989) estimates that in present-day England several thousand people, usually well-educated middle-class individuals, practice magic. Naturalistic observations have shown that out of 51 pedestrians passing a ladder positioned over a pavement, 37 preferred to step into the road to avoid walking under it (Jahoda, 1969). And in their survey of magical beliefs, Zusne and Jones (1982) found that 64% of U.S. college students endorsed at least some magical beliefs—a finding that undermines the assumption that magical beliefs are associated with poor science education. In a recent study on superstitious behavior, a traditional view that links superstitious thinking to maladaptive beliefs and behavior (such as neuroticism and low life satisfaction) was challenged (Wiseman & Watt, 2004). The authors suggested that this view was based on studying negative superstitions (such as that walking under a ladder or breaking a mirror brings bad luck) while ignoring positive superstitions (such as that carrying a lucky charm or that crossing fingers can bring good luck). While negative superstitions may indeed be associated with maladjustment, positive superstitions can be psychologically adaptive. The study supported the prediction: it showed that in regard to positive superstitions, the difference between people high and low on measures of neuroticism and life satisfaction was significantly smaller than in regard to negative superstitions.

Another source of evidence for the presence of magical thinking in adults is psychological research. Paul Rozin and colleagues argued that in disgust and other domains, people's behavior conforms to the main laws of sympathetic magic: contagion ("once in contact, always in contact") and similarity ("the image equals the object"). For example, Rozin, Millman, and Nemeroff (1986) found that university students were reluctant to taste their preferred juice if a sterilized dead cockroach was briefly dipped in it; they were also less willing to try a piece of chocolate if it was shaped in the form of dog feces than if it had the shape of a muffin. When given a choice, the students preferred to taste sugar water from a glass that they themselves had labeled as "sucrose" and not from a glass they had labeled as "cyanide." Amazingly, the preference for a neutrally labeled glass of sugar water was shown even if the alternative glass was labeled negatively ("not cyanide, not poison") (Rozin, Markwith, & Ross, 1990). A similar sympathetic transfer of an undesired quality from a person to an object was shown in the domain of the fear of contagion: students rated a sweater briefly worn by a person with AIDS as significantly less desirable to wear than one worn by a healthy man (Rozin, Markwith, & Nemeroff, 1992).

Normally, the mechanism of sympathetic magic is a useful protective psychological mechanism: although AIDS cannot be transmitted through a sweater, some skin infection could. However, if these mechanisms get out of hand, they can lead to obsessive-compulsive thinking (an illusion that external events that are, in fact, totally irrelevant to a person have a personal meaning and are intended to harm or benefit the person). A study with 5- to 17-year-old children and adolescents showed that in healthy children, there is a significant association between verbal magical beliefs and obsessive-compulsive thoughts and behaviors (Bolton, Dearsley, Madronal-Luque, & Baron-Cohen, 2002). This study did not support the hypothesis that there would be a decline on verbal magical beliefs between young childhood and late adolescence. In another study, 3- to 8-year-old children's beliefs in the power of wishes were shown to be positively associated with the children's ritualistic, compulsive-like behaviors (Evans, Milanak, Medeiros, & Ross, 2002). If pushed still further, obsessive-compulsive thinking can develop into obsessive-compulsive disorder (OCD).

Here, magical thinking enters the area of clinical research. Shafran, Thordarson, and Rachman (1996) suggested that thought–action fusion (TAF) is related to OCD. They distinguished two types of TAF: the likelihood type (the belief that thinking about an unacceptable or disturbing event makes it more likely to happen) and the moral type (the belief that having an unacceptable thought is the moral equivalent of carrying out the unacceptable or disturbing action). The study did indeed reveal that TAF–Likelihood-for-Others (thinking bad thoughts about others may hurt them) was moderately related to the compulsive checking subscale in the obsessive group of participants. Interestingly, the obsessive group endorsed TAF–Likelihood-for-Self (thinking bad thoughts about oneself may make these thoughts come true) to the same extent as TAF–Likelihood-for-Others, whereas comparison groups (students and adult community samples) believed more strongly in TAF–Likelihood-for-Self than in TAF–Likelihood-for-Others. The authors commented that while TAF–Likelihood-for-Self can be rationally comprehended in terms of "self-fulfilling prophecies" (for instance, if I believe that being good to people will make good things happen to me, then this might indeed have real-world consequences), TAF–Likelihood-for-Others cannot. Control participants acknowledged the difference, whereas the obsessional subjects did not. This research supports the idea that people with OCD are prone to believe in mind-over-matter magic. In their study with undergraduates, Einstein and Menzies (2004) also found a link between TAF measures and some measures of OCD; however, this link was mediated by the relationship between TAF scales and Eckblad and Chapman's (1983) Magical Ideation scale. Altogether, this study found magical thinking to be the construct most directly related to obsessive-compulsive symptoms, particularly with the checking subscale. Further, research has shown that schizophrenic patients tend to engage in magically based compulsive thinking to a considerably larger extent than both the general population (Tissot & Burnard, 1980) and nonschizophrenic psychiatric patients (George & Neufeld, 1987). In sum, these studies present magical thinking and behavior as a spectrum of phenomena scattered on a scale from helpful adaptive reactions (disgust, fear of contagion, and positive superstitions) to the reactions of a troubled mind, as in OCD and schizophrenia (see Figure 5.1).[1]

Studies on clinical aspects of magical thinking and behavior could potentially provide insight into the nature of hallucinatory disorders and other

FIGURE 5.1. The spectrum of the phenomena of magical reality.

problems that are based on magical mechanisms, such as religious fanaticism, ethnic conflicts, or suicidal terrorism. For example, the fact that rational people consciously do irrational things that bring about mass loss of human life, including their own, can only be understood in terms of magical beliefs—namely, a feeling of participation in some powerful force (God, destiny) that makes the destructive actions seem rational in the perpetrators' eyes.

BRINGING MAGICAL BELIEFS TO THE SURFACE: THE ROLE OF COST

As with studies involving children, experiments with adults seem to bring researchers to contradictory results. In their conscious judgments, most adults deny the reality of magic, yet in their subconscious reactions, such as disgust and the fear of contagion, they follow the laws of magical thinking. This suggests that in adults, magical beliefs are repressed and may be reactivated given appropriate experimental conditions, with the cost of disregarding magical explanations being one of these conditions. Indeed, would adult participants accept magical explanations if rejecting them levied a relatively high cost?

To examine this, university graduates and undergraduates were shown a "magical effect"—a square plastic card became cut in two places (or badly scratched) in an empty box after either an unknown physical device was switched on and off again or a magic spell was cast on the box (Subbotsky, 2001). Figure 5.2 shows the percentage of participants who endorsed scientific

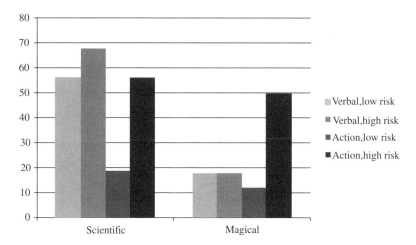

FIGURE 5.2. Percent of adults who agreed that the phenomenon had been caused by the experimenter's manipulation (Verbal) and asked the experimenter not to reproduce the manipulation (Action) as a function of risk: low (damaged driver's licence) versus high (damaged hand).

or magical explanations of the effect under the low-risk (with their driver's licenses at risk of destruction) or high-risk (with participants' own hands as objects at risk of being badly scratched) conditions.

As expected, in their verbal judgments, a large number of participants (around 60%) agreed that the device had been the cause of the unusual effect; far fewer believed that the magic spell was the cause (18%). In their nonverbal actions, however, only a few participants asked the experimenter to abstain from repeating his manipulations under the low-risk condition, and a significantly larger number of participants did this under the high-risk condition—for both "the device" and "the magic spell" manipulations. Not only did many participants prohibit the magical spell in the high-risk condition, but also their explanations of why they had done so revealed that they actually believed that the magic spell could have damaged their hands. In other words, when the cost of not believing in the effect of the magic spell was high (nonverbal behavior under the high-risk condition), adult participants gave considerable credit to the possibility of magic affecting their hands, and their justifications indicated that indeed, most feared that the spell could magically affect their hands. These data extend the results of the experiments discussed in the previous section. They show that when denial of magical beliefs is costly, adult participants are prepared to give up their belief in the almighty power of physical causality and view magical explanations to be as likely as physical ones.

Along with providing support for the "coexistence" model of the development of ontological causal beliefs (Boyer, 1994; Shweder, 1977; Subbotsky, 1993; Zusne, 1985; Zusne & Jones, 1982), the results of the experiments discussed in this chapter also highlight a methodological problem with studying magical beliefs (and other nonphysical causal events) in Western cultures. Insofar as many events that, in earlier centuries, were believed to be magical (transmitting auditory and visual messages remotely, flying in the air and space, and so on) have now become a scientific reality, interpretation of anomalous causal events as unknown physical effects is a possibility. Even psychological phenomena that lack a scientific explanation (such as extrasensory perception and telepathy) are sometimes presented as an effect of some unknown physical "fields" (Bem & Honorton, 1994). Likewise, there is a tendency to reduce nonphysical causal events (such as those that happen in the domains of dreams, feelings, symbolic communication, and perceptual illusions) to physical events in the brain (Aguirre & D'Esposito, 1997; Dennett, 1991; Jackendoff, 1987).

By interpreting magical causal events as unexplained physical events, people retain their belief in the universal power of physical causality and accept their NIMBs at the same time. This suggests that a more comprehensive approach is needed for assessing participants' NIMBs, particularly if this assessment relies solely on participants' verbal responses that can be particularly vulnerable to scientific overinterpretations. This issue highlights the importance of going beyond verbal processing in studying individuals' ontological causal beliefs. A sensible conclusion about participants' NIMBs can only be made on the basis of a general pattern of participants' judgments, nonverbal responses, and explanations of these responses.

One more issue to discuss is whether participants' tendency to accept magical explanations under the high-risk condition can be explained by the rational "weighting" of possible consequences of not believing—a mechanism known as "Pascal's wager."[2] The key issue here is the degree to which the belief in magic is recognized as "firmly held" and "not firmly held." In the study discussed in this chapter, the point was to contrast complete disbelief in magic with having at least some (subconscious) belief. Even when participants were ready to disregard the threat of losing their driver's licenses and approved the magic spell manipulation, in the high-risk condition, 50% of the participants refused to do so and justified this in a way that suggested a belief in magical causation. In my view, this is certainly evidence for some belief that the spell might work.

Essentially, the discrepancy between the "belief in magic" and "Pascal's wager" explanations of magical (superstitious) behavior boils down to the problem of whether beliefs are necessarily subconscious or whether they can also be consciously processed. As Skinner's (1948) famous experiment with pigeons has shown, even nonhuman animals can be conditioned to display behavior that closely resembles superstitious behavior. This kind of behavior can easily be interpreted as an evolutionarily equivalent of Pascal's wager: when the true nature of the problem is unclear, an animal can find a strategy (such as walking in circles) that may produce the desired result, and thereafter have a strong bias to repeat it (Killeen, 1977). This "playing it safe" strategy might be a result of natural selection, providing an individual with an adaptation advantage over the individuals that lack it, at least in those cases where the discovered "ritual" indeed causes the desired outcome (Vyse, 1997). This strategy is particularly important if the ritual's cost to an animal is small but the reward it seeks is great. Like other evolutionarily inherited mechanisms (such as fear of the dark) in humans, this mechanism might become consciously processed and acquire the status of a theory (Pascal's wager hypothesis). The question is whether this theory excludes or does not exclude the possibility of magical causality. In my view, the Pascal's wager theory allows for the possibility of magic, because with all the rational calculations of the costs and benefits of living a Christian life, this theory admits that a prayer to God can affect the flow of natural events, such as one's health and well-being (mind-over-matter magic).

6

Culture and Magical Thinking

From a cross-cultural perspective, the existence of noninstitutionalized magical beliefs (NIMBs) in Western adults today can be viewed as a result of a historical change of fundamental beliefs about the relations between men and nature. One of these fundamental changes of beliefs occurred in Renaissance Europe, when the medieval cultural orientation that accommodated beliefs in both religion and magic was troubled by a major intruder—science (Losev, 1978; Tambiah, 1990). The scientific viewpoint is based on two main assumptions. The first assumption is that all natural events, without exception, are based on physical laws and governed by physical causality. The second assumption is that natural laws operate independently of the observer's mind (Kuhn, 1970; Lacatos, 1970). As long as magic implied the fusion of mind and nature, science rejected magic as a delusion. With the onset of scientific ideology, the ancient rivalry between religion and magic has finally been resolved. In this unexpected way, religion, which for centuries associated magic with the devil and paganism, has won in science a major ally. *Under the pressure of religion and science, magical beliefs were exiled in the domain of subconscious, and the phenomenon of subconscious NIMBs was born.*

PREACHING SCIENCE AND PRACTICING MAGIC:
A SANDWICH OF BELIEFS

As a result, beliefs about the relationship between man and nature became split. On a conscious level, the average Western individual strongly adheres to a belief in science. In the time before science, the human mind did not have a monopoly on consciousness: instead, consciousness was spread out in all natural things. Science takes consciousness out of natural things and concentrates it all in the mind. In the end, natural things became inanimate (soulless), and nature came to be viewed as indifferent to the person. According to science, humankind itself is a natural phenomenon, stranded on a small planet in the infinite void of the universe, destined to one day vanish. Religion provides a counterweight to this gloomy perspective by asserting beliefs in God, angels, paradise, and an immortal soul—yet it also demands a monopoly on magical beliefs. However, as the studies reviewed earlier in this book have shown, in their nonverbal responses and under certain conditions, adult participants exhibited behavior that indicated beliefs in mind-over-matter magic. There appears to be a "sandwich" of beliefs, with beliefs in science and religion being the "outer layers" of this sandwich and NIMBs providing the subconscious interior.

The sandwich of beliefs about man and nature is not a unique phenomenon. To a certain extent, the gap between adults' explicit disbelief in noninstitutionalized magic and their implicit magical beliefs echoes the coexistence of scientific theories and intuitive (or "folk") theories that has been shown to be present in many areas—physics, philosophy, biology, and psychology (Boyer, 1994; Carey, 1999; Christensen & Turner, 1993; Keil, 1989; Sperber, 1997). Another way to account for the distinction between "official" and "underground" beliefs about the world is to consider it as a difference between expert and novice views (Larkin, 1983). It has been argued, for instance, that until the middle of the 18th century, even scientists were unable to distinguish between concepts of heat and temperature (Wiser & Carey, 1983), and the confusion between physical properties of objects and their perceptual qualities is overwhelming among contemporary children and adults (Subbotsky, 1997b). This indicates that, in some areas of knowledge and beliefs, school education fails to create a scientific vision of the world in students' minds. The studies discussed in Chapter 5 suggest that this failure extends from beliefs about the nature of perceptual qualities to beliefs about the universal power of physical causality.

BELIEF IN SCIENCE: HOW DEEP UNDER THE SKIN?

Two main scenarios about the power of scientific ideology over the mind of a Western individual are possible: "deep penetration" and "partial penetration." According to the deep penetration scenario, physical laws exhaustively govern the world. In contrast, the partial penetration scenario asserts adherence to scientific rationality only to an extent; under certain conditions, however, individuals may believe that the world conforms to the laws of magical causality.

In the psychological literature, arguments in favor of both deep and partial penetration can be found. Thus, in developmental psychology, the mind of a child has been increasingly described as the mind of a "little scientist." It has been argued, for instance, that infants and even newborns can "understand" certain laws that are fundamental to contemporary science and rationality, such as object permanence and physical causality (Bower, 1974, 1989; Gelman & Baillargeon, 1983). In the area of perception, the work of the human perceptual system is presented as governed by rational laws (Gregory, 1980). In cognitive psychology, the "computer metaphor" is applied to the individual mind, which presents the mind as a rationally constructed "virtual machine" (Dennett, 1991; Dowling, 1998; Frawley, 1997; Jackendoff, 1987). Viewed in this way, the mind of an average Western individual is progressively approaching the image of a rationally working device, with any irrationality being viewed as a residue of the past.

As an alternative to this scenario, the idea of the pluralistic structure of the individual's mind has been worked out in contemporary writings on cultural psychology (Tulviste, 1991; Wertsch, 1991) and anthropology (Boyer, 1994; Tambiah, 1990). Thus, according to Tambiah (1990), scientific (rational) thinking has its necessary complement in the belief in participation (the belief that individuals or societies are magically "linked" to certain objects or animals), which is crucial for religious and communicative practices. Multiple studies have shown that beliefs in various forms of magic are still widespread among people living in cultural environments packed with computers and advanced technologies (Boyer, 1994; Jahoda, 1969; Lehman & Mayers, 1985; Vyse, 1997; Zusne, 1985; Zusne & Jones, 1982). These studies, however, do not explain why, despite being opposed by both science and religion, magic still survives in the modern world.

The hypothesis that, under the pressure of science and religion, in Western individuals magical beliefs are exiled to the domain of the subconscious (see Chapter 1) explains the resilience of magical beliefs in modern Western cultures. Being subconscious, NIMBs do not threaten the power of science and religion. As a result, dominant (science and religion) and subdominant (magic) beliefs can peacefully coexist in one mind.

A MAGICAL BRIDGE ACROSS THE ATLANTIC: FROM MEXICO TO BRITAIN

Taking on this hypothesis, one can expect that members of a rural community that have not received formal science education would consciously endorse magical beliefs to a significantly greater extent than would members of a more technologically advanced community. Indeed, while in modern cultures most people believe that science is the only way to account for natural events (issues such as the evolution versus creation debate notwithstanding), in some developing societies the pressure of scientific rationality on an individual is substantially less evident due to the inaccessibility of formal scientific education to much of the population. In addition, the abundance of pre-Christian magical beliefs in many developing societies makes the Catholic Church more tolerant toward magic there than it is in other societies. As a result, in many individuals from developing cultures, NIMBs remain in the domain of consciousness. In order to examine this prediction, the experiment reviewed in Chapter 5 was carried out in Mexico with participants who had received no formal science education.

Anthropological and ethnographic studies of Mexican culture and religion suggest that there exists a strong adherence to magical beliefs. The widespread belief in Nahual—a person who can occasionally turn into an animal—is a typical manifestation of NIMBs. Unlike monotheistic religions, NIMBs lack the idea that a human person is superior to natural things and subordinate only to gods. In traditional practices of ancient Mexico, every natural object or event was believed to have an individual will of its own, with which people with special powers (sorcerers) could identify. Importantly, note that it is not that a sorcerer, while imitating rain, is involved in some kind of symbolic activity of "pretending to be rain" (a typical modern rationalistic misinterpretation of magic); instead, the sorcerer *really becomes rain, without resembling rain physically* (Sejourne, 1976). The essence of magical beliefs is, therefore, the idea that a real metamorphosis of a person into a natural thing (such as an animal) can be achieved.[1] This kind of magical belief is still common in contemporary rural Mexican communities, and it coexists with the official Christian religious ideology. Thus, according to Selby (1974), in the modern Zapotec community, people believe that they have two souls: the Christian soul and "tono"—the soul of an animal. When a person's death is untimely, this is invariably explained by an accident that occurred with the person's tono. The belief in witchcraft is universal, even among locals who are progressive Protestants and have some education and experience of living in large Mexican cities and in the United States. One of the elements of traditional Mexican magical beliefs is that "certain persons can turn themselves into animals and in this form go about at night doing evil and indecent acts" (Redfield, 1968, pp. 307–308).

The method of the experiments conducted in Mexico was identical to that carried out in England (see Chapter 5). Participants were shown an unusual phenomenon (an unexpected destruction of an object in an apparently empty box), which was framed either in a scientific (an unknown physical device was switched on and off again) or a magical (the experimenter pronounced a magic spell) causal context. The study indicated that in their verbal judgments, British adults showed a higher degree of credulity toward scientific explanations than toward magical explanations. However, in their actions under the high-risk condition, British adults endorsed scientific and magical explanations to an equal extent. This result was in support of the main hypothesis: scientific education eliminates noninstitutionalized magical beliefs from adults' verbal thinking, yet in nonverbal behavioral responses, adults' NIMBs are still present.

Another result of the study was that, in their actions, adult participants showed a low degree of credulity toward magical explanations when the cost of disregarding such explanations was low (possible damage to the participants' driver's licenses that could result from the experimenter's magic spell). When the cost was high (participants' hands being badly scratched), a significantly larger number of adults behaved in a way that suggested they believed in magical causality.

The Mexican study was conducted with 28 male and female participants (Subbotsky & Quinteros, 2002) drawn from small rural communities located in the Morelos district in central Mexico, near the city of Cuernavaca. The results were compared to those obtained in the earlier study in Britain (Subbotsky, 2001). In the pretest interview, none of the British participants had acknowledged that a mythical creature (Centaurs) really existed; however, half of Mexican participants said that they believed in the existence of Nahual, and two of them claimed that they have actually seen the creature.[2]

The percentages of Mexican and British participants in the verbal trial who acknowledged that the effect had been caused by the accompanying action and the percentages of participants in the action trial who asked the experimenter not to reproduce the accompanying action under a low-risk condition (with their valuable documents under the threat of destruction) are shown in Figure 6.1.

As predicted, in the low-risk condition, Mexican participants showed equally strong beliefs in scientific and magical explanations, both in the verbal and action trials. They also believed in magical explanations to a

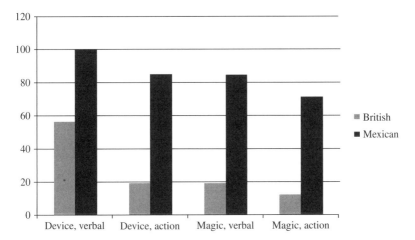

Figure 6.1. Percent of participants (British versus Mexican) who acknowledged that the effect had been caused by the experimenter's manipulation (verbal) and asked the experimenter not to repeat the manipulation (action) in the low-risk condition (valuable documents damaged).

significantly larger extent than did British participants. In the high-risk condition (when participants' hands, rather than their valuable documents, were put under the threat), in their verbal judgments Mexican participants again accepted magical explanations significantly more frequently than did British participants. Interestingly, in their nonverbal behavioral reactions in the high-risk condition, Mexican and British participants endorsed beliefs in the efficacy of the magic spell to an approximately equal extent (see Figure 6.2).

Overall, the results of the two experiments support the prediction that in an industrial culture today, science and religion exile NIMBs into the domain of the subconscious (Chapter 1). The adherence of participants from developed societies to the belief in the universal power of physical causality depends on the conditions in which the individuals' causal beliefs are tested. One of these conditions is the mode in which the beliefs are displayed: the individuals' verbal judgments as compared to their nonverbal behavioral responses. In their verbal judgments, individuals are prone to follow values and causal beliefs that prevail in the "upper culture" of their societies. Thus, in their explanations of the unusual causal effect, British participants were skeptical toward magic; rather, they believed in the causal role of a physical device (see Figures 5.2 and 6.1, verbal trial). In contrast, Mexican participants showed the same (and a high) degree of verbal credulity toward both scientific (device) and nonscientific (magic) explanations of the observed phenomenon.

As the results of this study show, participants' nonverbal responses are related to the demands of the "upper culture" in a more complex way than are

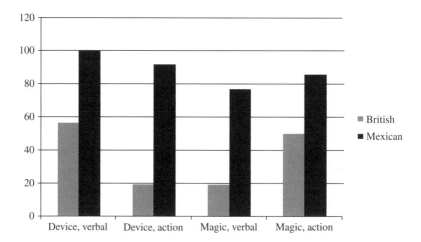

FIGURE 6.2. Percent of participants (British versus Mexican) who acknowledged that the effect had been caused by the experimenter's manipulation (verbal) and asked the experimenter not to repeat the manipulation (action) in the high-risk condition (participants' hands damaged).

participants' judgments. As in their judgments, in their actions British participants showed their adherence to the ideal of scientific rationality. This, however, was the case only when the risk of disregarding beliefs in magic was low. *When the risk was high, NIMBs ascended to the level of consciousness and British participants showed credulity toward magical beliefs to the same extent as did Mexican participants.*

It is safe to surmise that, at some point in history (in the druidic period and, later, in the time of Roman rule), British culture was as tolerant toward magical beliefs as Mexican culture is today. Later, with the onset of Christianity, religion separated itself from magic. If this indeed was the case, then the results of the experiment discussed in this chapter support my main hypothesis (Chapter 1). They suggest that, *at some point in history in Britain, magical and religious beliefs were the same and existed in the domain of consciousness. When religion separated from magic and science joined religion in its persecution of magic, NIMBs descended into the domain of the subconscious.* At the level of their subconscious, in regard to their magical beliefs, people today may be not different from their ancestors of thousands of years ago.

USES AND MISUSES OF MAGICAL BELIEFS

The aforementioned results are in accord with earlier reports showing the presence of magical thinking in individuals of modern industrial cultures.

Nemeroff and Rozin (2000) have accumulated a substantial amount of evidence that sympathetic magical thinking operates in disgust, contagion, and other domains of the mind of a contemporary educated person. Usually, mechanisms of sympathetic magical thinking are triggered in situations where the cost for disregarding this kind of thinking is relatively high—for instance, where there is the possibility of catching a dangerous disease like AIDS or hepatitis. Cross-cultural comparisons, too, highlighted the role of cost in sympathetic magical thinking. Both in America and in developing cultures (such as India or New Guinea), the effect of negative contagion proved to be more powerful than that of positive contagion (the belief that one may obtain some good quality from contacts with positive sources). It appears that it is more important to keep away from an incurable disease than to enhance one's self through contact with a personification of goodness and holiness.

But if the mind of a modern person is a pluralistic unity, which contains different, even alternative, causal beliefs, then educational and social practices in modern industrial societies should become more eclectic, taking into account the irrational as well as the rational areas of the mind. This would involve, for instance, a greater emphasis on imaginative pretend play in child development and education. As the study reviewed in Chapter 4 showed, watching a magical movie can enhance children's performance on creativity tasks. Recreation activities based on fantasy (movies, plays, art galleries, and so on) can be used for social and political management in contemporary industrial societies. The pluralistic nature of causal beliefs would explain why beliefs in extraordinary and paranormal phenomena, practices of magic and astrology, and other activities incompatible with scientific views are so widespread among individuals living in industrial cultures. It can also explain why in the state of a crisis (a war, a revolution), even in Western developed cultures people's magical beliefs are on the increase (Keinan, 1994; Subbotsky & Trommsdorff, 1992). Another important implication of acknowledging NIMBs would be in making realistic prognoses of cultural and ethnic conflicts (including suicidal terrorism) that often arise as a result of under-evaluating the role that mythical, magical, and other modes of irrational thinking play in the mind of modern individuals.

Let us take terrorism as an example. The success of *kamikaze* ("divine wind") in the Battle of Okinawa (April 1945), which strongly impacted the U.S. decision to use the atomic bomb in order to end the war, showed the power of magical beliefs, given that kamikaze were volunteers sacrificing their lives to their divine values. Indeed, anthropological research on suicidal terrorism suggests that at the core of this kind of terrorism are "sacred values" that supercede economic and other material considerations (Atran, Axelrod, & Davis, 2007). In the list of such values, a component that is particularly important is religion. It has been found that most Palestinian suicide bombers do not differ from the average member of their community in terms of education, well-being, or mental health—"Yet 'all were deeply religious,' believing their actions 'sanctioned by the divinely revealed religion of Islam'" (Atran, 2003, p. 1537). Another report on operatives of Al-Qaeda allies in Southeast Asia echoes the pattern: those men were not isolated or disenfranchised, had no psychopathology, and held normal, respectable jobs. But most of them "regarded religion as their most important personal value" (cited in Atran, 2003, p. 1537). It would be wrong to reduce the phenomenon of suicidal terrorism to religious belief only, yet the belief in a magical unity with God's will, and the belief in great rewards waiting in the afterlife, undoubtedly make the decision to commit a suicidal act of terror more psychologically acceptable.

Magic and Exploratory Behavior

As the aforementioned studies have shown (see Chapter 5), under the low-risk condition, adults from industrial Western cultures repeatedly denied the mind-over-matter magical explanations of an inexplicable change of an object in an apparently empty box. It is only when denial of noninstitutionalized magical beliefs (NIMBs) involved a relatively high risk that participants were prepared to accept magical explanations. I explain this result in terms of my main hypothesis. Since middle childhood, among participants from developed Western nations, beliefs in physical causality are dominant and deeply entrenched (see Chapter 3); at the same time, their NIMBs are repressed and ousted to the domain of the subconscious. When denying NIMBs becomes costly, participants, albeit reluctantly, allow their NIMBs into the domain of consciousness.

There is, however, another way to let NIMBs into the domain of consciousness: through making NIMBs an object of exploration. When people are engaged in exploration, a compromise can be achieved between their dominant beliefs (in physical causality) and their repressed beliefs (in magical causality). Exploring phenomena that people think they do not believe in does not overtly challenge their dominant beliefs, but instead allows them to play with a "forbidden reality."

WEIRD BUT INTERESTING: CURIOSITY TOWARD THE SUPERNATURAL

Interest in exploratory behavior, initiated by Pavlov (1927) in his studies of animal behavioral responses to novelty in stimulus situations has been increasing in developmental psychology. This interest has resulted in studies of curiosity and exploratory behavior in animals (Butler, 1954; Harlow, 1953), children (Cantor & Cantor, 1964; Comerford & Witryol, 1993), and adults (Berlyne, 1960; Pliner, Pelchat, & Grabski, 1993). These studies showed that the degree of novelty in a stimulus is a major factor in eliciting exploratory behavior (Mendel, 1965), and that the intrinsic motivational value of novelty is equivalent to that provided by material and edible rewards (Cahill-Solis & Witryol, 1994). Stimulus novelty on its own, however, is not a sufficient factor for evoking exploratory behavior; to elicit exploration, a stimulus, apart from being novel, must also be attractive (Henderson & Moore, 1980). Thus, novel foods that look unattractive or dangerous are unlikely to engage a participant in exploration (Nemeroff & Rozin, 1992; Pliner et al., 1993).

One particular feature that makes a stimulus intrinsically attractive for humans is the capacity of the stimulus to violate fundamental physical laws. By definition, magical events are counterintuitive, impossible to explain in terms of physical causality. Ghosts, witchcraft, astrology, psi, and other magical phenomena have always attracted considerable public interest (Bem & Honorton, 1994; Jahoda, 1969; Lundahl, 1993; Zusne & Jones, 1982). What remains unclear, however, is the reason for this attraction. Due to their very nature, magical phenomena are rarely observed and there is no hard proof that they are actually real, so they are inherently novel. Apart from being novel, they are also repressed (declared to be false, illegitimate, or evil) by modern science and religion. Along with magical events, a person can come across physical events that are not associated with the supernatural and yet are just as counterintuitive as magical events. Both magical and counterintuitive physical events are interesting to explore. Yet a magical event is also supernatural and repressed; it should therefore evoke a stronger interest than a counterintuitive physical event. This is expected because a counterintuitive physical event, even when recognized as impossible, does not directly challenge participants' belief in the universal power of physical causality, whereas a magical event does.

Indeed, a counterintuitive physical event can be explained by the failure of participants' memories, perceptions, or understandings (see Chapter 10 for more on this). However, a true magical event[1] presents a challenge to participants' dominant beliefs in science and rationality. In addition to curiosity elicited by the event's novelty, which the magical event shares with the counterintuitive physical event, the magical event also elicits curiosity because it is a part of the forbidden (repressed) magical reality. If the fact that NIMBs are repressed and exist in the domain of subconscious is indeed an additional factor that contributes toward eliciting curiosity and exploration, then the following effect should be observed: *participants' tendency to engage in exploratory behavior toward the magical event should be significantly stronger than toward the counterintuitive physical event.* I will refer to this effect as the "magical over counterintuitive physical" (the M/CP) effect.

MAGICAL VERSUS COUNTERINTUITIVE PHYSICAL: THE M/CP EFFECT

To examine this effect, it was necessary to provide a research study participant with a counterintuitive causal event framed either in the context of scientific views (a counterintuitive physical event) or in the context of NIMBs (a magical event). To rephrase, *the M/CP effect implies that, other conditions being equal, a counterintuitive causal event elicits stronger curiosity and exploratory behavior in participants if its suggested explanation includes an element of the supernatural (a magical event) than if it does not (a counter-intuitive physical event).*

Studies based on the "violation of expectation" paradigm have found that young infants show a higher degree of exploratory behavior toward displays that violate principles of physical causality than toward similar displays with no violation of these principles (Baillargeon, 1987; Leslie, 1982, 1984). These data suggest that for infants, the counterintuitive nature of a stimulus is an independent factor that evokes exploratory behavior. There is good reason to assume that the same is the case for older children and adults. Unlike infants, older children and adults acquire a more distinctive knowledge of what is possible and impossible in the physical world. Given that, seeing a counter-intuitive physical event should indeed be puzzling and interesting for children and adults. This, however, does not answer the question of whether seeing a magical event will be even more puzzling and interesting than seeing a counterintuitive physical event.

In order to examine whether the M/CP effect is indeed the case, in Experiment 1, children aged 4, 6, and 9 years were first interviewed for their capacity to understand the difference between magical and ordinary outcomes (Subbotsky, 2009b). For example, an ordinary outcome was presented as follows: "I put a postage stamp into this box, close it, wave a magic wand, then open the box and see that the postage stamp is still there. Can we say that the postage stamp appeared in the box by magic, or would there not be any magic in this?" The magical outcome was presented as follows: "Suppose I take an empty box, close it, wave a magic wand, and say, 'postage stamp—appear,' and then look into the box and see that the postage stamp appeared in it. Please, bear in mind that the stamp appeared because the magic wand made it appear, not because it was some kind of trick, OK? Now, can we say that the stamp appeared by magic or there is not any magic in this?"

The children who were able to tell magical outcomes from ordinary ones were then individually tested in two conditions of the *demonstration trial*, in which they were shown an unusual effect: the disappearance of a new postage stamp while in an apparently empty box. In the "magical condition" (MC), the phenomenon was caused by mind-over-matter magic. Children were given a wooden stick and told that it was a magic wand and that they could check whether it worked. The children were then encouraged to place the postage stamp into the box, close the box, wave the magic wand, and wish the stamp to disappear. Upon opening the box, the children found that it was empty.

In the "counterintuitive physical" condition (CPC), the procedure followed the same line, but no magic wand was given to the child. Children were encouraged to place the postage stamp in the box and close the box. They were then asked whether they believed that the stamp was still there or if it had disappeared. Next, the children were asked to open the box, and when they did they discovered that it was empty. In both conditions, children were thanked for their answers and given a nice postage stamp as a prize.

Next, children participated in the *action trial*. In the MC, the children were asked if they wanted to put their "prize" postage stamps into the box to see again how the magic wand worked, and in the CPC, how the trick box worked.[2]

We predicted that if children's exploratory behavior was triggered by the novelty of the counterintuitive phenomenon, then the number of participants encouraging the experimenter to reproduce the phenomenon would be approximately the same in both the MC and CPC conditions. If, however, in addition to the event's novelty, magic had a motivational value for children, then the number of children willing to put their valuable objects at risk in the MC would be significantly higher than that in the CPC. The results are shown in Figure 7.1.

In all age groups, a significantly larger number of children wanted to put their prize objects at risk in the MC than in the CPC. These results support the hypothesis that children will show a significantly stronger tendency to experiment with the magic wand than with the trick box, thus revealing the M/CP effect.

An alternative explanation of this discrepancy might be the greater amount of risk taken in the CPC, because it is easier to believe that a tricky box can destroy objects (CPC) than it is to believe that a magic wand can (MC). Indeed, in the demonstration trial of the MC, children may have thought that the postage stamp disappeared because the box made this happen, judging the magic wand manipulation as having been a distraction. However, if in the MC the children viewed the box, and not the magic wand, as the real cause of the

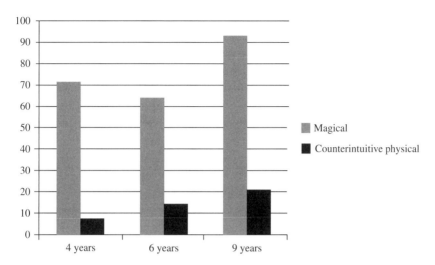

FIGURE 7.1. Percent of children who agreed to proceed with the testing using their valuable objects as a function of age (4, 6, and 9 years) and condition (magical versus counterintuitive physical).

postage stamp's disappearance, then in the action trial they would be reluctant to place their prize postage stamps in the box in the MC to the same extent as in the CPC. Yet this was not the case.

The results also showed a difference between curiosity toward magic and magical beliefs. Although many children were skeptical of the possibility of magic in the demonstration trial, in the action trial most of these children wanted to repeat the effect. Interestingly, children of all age groups showed the tendency to experiment with magic to an approximately equal extent. This shows that even though children's verbal magical beliefs decrease with age (Johnson & Harris, 1994; Piaget, 1927; Subbotsky, 2004; Woolley, 2000), their curiosity toward magic does not.

There remain, however, other possibile explanations of these results. The first is that, even though in the pretest interview all children called the counterintuitive event magical, it was not completely clear whether magic meant true magic (which involves the element of the supernatural) or stage magic (tricks). As was shown in earlier studies, when 4- and 5-year-olds were shown pictures with possible and impossible transformations of objects, they quite selectively called impossible transformations magical (Rosengren & Hickling, 1994). Yet the chance still remains that children viewed the magical transformations as tricks; children of preschool and school ages often label as magical the events for which they simply lack plausible scientific explanations (Phelps & Woolley, 1994). Indeed, Chandler and Lalonde (1994) showed 3- to 5-year-old children an impossible causal effect: a solid screen apparently passing through space already occupied by another solid object. Although initially most children called this event magical, a more thorough examination of their answers revealed that what they actually had meant was a trick. If, in the pretest interview of Experiment 1, while correctly distinguishing magical effects from the nonmagical ones children still viewed magical effects as magic tricks, then the statistical difference between conditions could result from the fact that children found a magic trick in the MC to be more interesting than the trick they observed in the CPC.

The second alternative explanation comes from the possibility that in Experiment 1, the children were not aware of the irreversibility of the postage stamp's disappearance. They may have been more willing to experiment with the magic wand (MC) than with the trick box (CPC) on a tacit assumption that they would be able to subsequently recover the stamp with the same magic wand—a possibility that would seem much less likely with a box that annihilates objects placed into it.

Finally, a third alternative explanation is that in the MC the observed effect was made to look like it had been caused by an external factor (by wishing and waving the magic wand), whereas in the CPC it was made to look as if it were happening inside of the box. Also, the child's "own agency" could play a role in the effect: the child did something to create an effect in the MC condition, but not in the CPC condition. This difference in the "causality vector" (external versus internal) and agency (doing versus not doing something) could also contribute to the fact that children were willing to repeat the experiment with their prize objects in the MC more frequently than in the CPC.

To examine the first and second alternative explanations, in Experiment 2, 32 adult participants (university graduates and undergraduates) were tested in the same two conditions. In contrast to children, the difference between true magic (involving an element of the supernatural) and stage magic (tricks) can be more clearly explained to adults. It can also be made clear to them that if they lose their valuable objects in any of the aforementioned conditions, this would be irreversible.

The procedure of this experiment followed the procedure of Experiment 1, with a few exceptions. First, in the verbal trial of the MC, instead of the participants using the magic wand, a magic spell pronounced by an experimenter was used as the magical setup for the phenomenon. This was done in order to equate the "own agency" factor: unlike in Experiment 1, in which the children, after placing the postage stamps into the box, waved the magic wand in the MC but not in the CPC, in this experiment in both conditions all that participants were required to do was to place the postage stamps into the box. Second, in order to prevent a direct association between the magical effects presented in the pretest interview and the main interview, the objects employed in the pretest interview were changed. Instead of the box and the postage stamp, a briefcase and a book were used. Third, with the aim of ensuring that the participants could distinguish between true magic and stage magic, in the questions with the impossible outcome these two possibilities were explicitly spelled out. For instance, after the unexpected emergence of the book in the briefcase was described, the experimenter continued as follows: "Now, consider two possibilities. Possibility 1: the book appeared in the briefcase because my magic spell made it appear from nothing; I simply thought hard about making the book appear, said my magic spell, and the book just appeared from thin air. Possibility 2: there was some trap compartment in the briefcase, and the book appeared from that compartment. Which of these two possibilities is a trick, and which is an instance of true magic?" Finally, instead of rewarding participants with the new postage stamps to provide them with valuable objects, participants were asked to have their driver's licenses at hand.

In the MC, after participants were asked to put a new postage stamp in the box and close the lid, the experimenter informed them that he was going to put a magic spell on the box, with the aim of destroying the stamp. The experimenter then pronounced a series of words that sounded like a magic spell. Next, participants were encouraged to open the box, discovering that the postage stamp was cut in half.

Participants were then encouraged to inspect the box and asked to explain the phenomenon. The experimenter asked whether participants believed that the experimenter was in command of magic powers and that he had just destroyed the postage stamp by putting a magic spell on the box. If the answer was "yes," the instruction was as follows: "OK. Yet, do you think that it is worth trying to test my magic spell on your driver's license right now, or do you think that it is not worth trying?"

If the answer to the suggested magical explanation was "no," the instruction was different. Indeed, if participants explicitly stated that they were nonbelievers in magic, then they might think that not encouraging the experimenter, to proceed with the magic spell would show that they actually believed in magic. As a result, the participants might be willing to reassure the experimenter to show that they are skeptical and, because of their skepticism, encourage the experimenter to proceed with the testing. In order to avoid confusion between the two different motives (the desire to explore magical effects and the wish to show that one does not believe in magic), the experimenter explicitly stressed that he was aware of the participants' disbelief in magic. He then said that he would not interpret their desire to repeat the experiment with their driver's licenses as a concession to magical beliefs. The next question was whether it was worth trying the magic spell on the participants' driver's licenses. The aim of this question was to find out whether the participants, though skeptical toward magic, would nevertheless be curious to try it again by putting their valuable object at risk.

The question about the possibility of further experimenting with magic was asked in a neutral way ("Do you think it is worth trying...") in order to avoid any tacit suggestion that the experimenter was interested in trying the magic spell on the participants' licenses. As a result, participants were assured that they were not viewed as believers in magic, and that the experimenter himself had no special interest in the continuation of the experiment. Under these circumstances, the only interest that would motivate participants to prompt the experimenter to proceed with the experiment was their curiosity to find out whether magic would work again, even if this time there might be a price to pay.

In the CPC, participants were simply shown the phenomenon of a postage stamp being cut in half in an empty box. They were then given the opportunity to inspect the box with the aim of coming up with an explanation. After failing on this task, the participants were asked, "Do you think it is worth trying to test this box by closing the box with your driver's license inside it, or do you think it is not worth trying?"

In both conditions, participants who agreed to place their driver's licenses into the box and to continue the experiment were explicitly warned that the experimenter takes no responsibility for the safety of their driver's licenses and that, if damaged, their licenses could not be restored.

The hypothesis in this experiment was the same as in Experiment 1. It was assumed that if specific interest in seeing the magical event (and not just a counterintuitive physical event) made the participants explore, then the number of curious participants in the MC would significantly exceed that in the CPC (the M/CP effect).

In both conditions, participants were asked why they encouraged (or did not encourage) the experimenter to proceed with testing . In the MC, they were also asked if they would be happy if magic had really worked.

The results of Experiment 2 confirmed the M/CP effect. In the MC, all 16 participants decided to put their driver's licenses at risk in order to see again how the magic worked. This happened even though the participants had a clear understanding that the effect they wanted to see was true magic and not a magic trick, and that if their driver's licenses were indeed damaged, then this would be irreversible.

Participants' answers to the follow-up questions showed that their reason for encouraging the experimenter to proceed with the magic spell was not to show their disbelief in magic, but rather to satisfy their curiosity toward the possibility that it might still work. The presence of the specific motivation—curiosity about magic—was confirmed by the fact that in the MC, all participants but one said they would be happy to discover that magic was real. Some participants were even more explicit on the topic, saying that if magic were real it would "make the world a more interesting place to live in."

In contrast, in the CPC, only 9 of 16 participants encouraged the experimenter to proceed with the testing, and only 4 of those justified their decisions by curiosity. As soon as the phenomenon demonstrated (cutting a postage stamp inside the empty box) was the same in both conditions, and the only difference between the conditions was the presence or absence of magic, this result clearly supported the M/CP effect. Altogether, the results of this experiment make the first alternative explanation (misunderstanding of what true magic is) and the second alternative explanation (not realizing that losing the valuable object would be irreversible) of the Experiment 1 results unlikely.

However, there remains a third alternative explanation of the participants' stronger curiosity about the effect they observed in the MC than in the CPC. This is the "causality vector" explanation, which postulates that participants will view an external cause in the MC—a magic spell—as inherently more interesting to investigate than the internal cause in the CPC—a mechanism inside the box. To examine this explanation, in Experiment 3, the causality vector was made external in both conditions.

Another hypothesis tested in Experiment 3 was that increasing irreversibility of the magical effect in the demonstration trial would decrease the number of participants willing to experiment with magic by using their valuable objects. This hypothesis is based on the assumption that, in the participants' view, making the magical effect more irreversible increases the probability of their valuable objects being damaged in the action trial, and thus raises the cost of exploratory behavior.

The procedure was the same as in Experiment 2, save for three differences. First, in the demonstration trial, the participants found that the postage stamp affected by the experimenter's manipulation became half-burned and not cut in half. This was done in order to make the "magical effect" look more irreversible. Indeed, if the driver's license is cut in half, one might tape it back together, but this would be impossible to do with the license half-burnt. Second, in the CPC, after a participant put the stamp in the box and closed the lid, the experimenter switched the unknown physical device on for a few seconds and then off again. This was done to make consistent the causality vector factor in both conditions, by making the causes of the unexplained phenomena look like external events (either the magic spell or the physical device). As in the MC, in the CPC, after the demonstration of the effect, participants were asked if they thought that the physical device had burned the postage stamp. Third, at the end of the experiment, the third (imaginative) trial was introduced. In this trial, participants were asked if they would be prepared to proceed with the testing if it were not their driver's licenses but their more valuable documents—passports—that were involved in the experiment. The purpose of this trial was to examine if the M/CP effect would remain when the cost of exploratory behavior was further increased.

If the alternative explanation of the Experiment 1 and 2 results by differences in the causality vectors between conditions (external in the MC versus internal in the CPC) were true, then in this experiment the number of participants willing to experiment with their driver's licenses in the MC and the CPC would be approximately the same. If, however, the number of participants who wished to put their valuable objects at risk in the MC was still higher than in the CPC, then this alternative explanation could be overruled.

We also expected that increasing the irreversibility of the magical effect (burning the stamp instead of cutting it in half) would significantly decrease the number of participants who wished to experiment with their driver's licenses in the MC, as compared with that number in Experiment 2.

Finally, we expected that in the imaginary trial, the M/CP effect should disappear. Indeed, in addition to increasing the cost of exploratory behavior by making the magical effect more irreversible in the demonstration trial, in the imaginary trial this cost was further increased by making the "objects at risk" more valuable (participants' passports instead of their driver's licenses). With such a high cost of exploratory behavior in the MC, participants' curiosity about seeing the magical event replicated would be overpowered by their concerns about the safety of their valuable objects, and this would eliminate the difference in curiosity between the conditions. The percentages of participants who opted for testing on their driver's licenses and passports are shown in Figure 7.2.

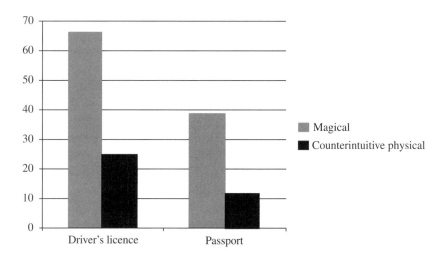

Figure 7.2. Percent of participants willing to experiment with their valuable objects as a function of cost (driver's licenses versus passports) and condition (magical versus counterintuitive physical).

The data did not support the proposal that the results of Experiment 1 were caused by the difference in the "causality vector" between conditions. In this experiment, the suggested causes of the phenomenon were external in both conditions (the magic spell in the MC and the physical device in the CPC). Yet, as in Experiments 1 and 2, in this experiment a significantly larger number of participants were willing to engage in exploratory behavior with their driver's licenses in the MC than in the CPC. This increases support for the hypothesis that a magical event is more interesting than an equally novel counterintuitive physical event, because the magical event involves an element of the supernatural whereas the counterintuitive physical event does not.

As expected, increasing the irreversibility of the magical effect inhibited exploratory behavior in the MC, presumably by increasing its potential cost. The number of participants who were willing to experiment with their licenses dropped significantly as compared to those in Experiment 2. In the CPC, the effect was in the same direction; however, as the total number of participants willing to experiment with their licenses in this condition was significantly smaller than in the MC, the effect did not reach a significant level.

Finally, the expectation was also supported that in the imaginary trial with the increased cost of exploratory behavior (participants' passports), the difference between the two conditions would drop to an insignificant level. This suggests that *the M/CP effect can only be observed under a certain "optimal" degree of cost, and when the cost becomes too high or too low, the M/CP effect disappears.* To test this hypothesis, the risk of exploratory behavior should be reduced to the minimum. If the hypothesis linking the M/CP effect with the "floor and ceiling" effect of the cost of exploration is valid, then in the low-cost trial, as in the high-cost trial, the M/CP effect should not be observed.

In addition, testing adults instead of children creates the possibility of one more "high-tech" alternative explanation of the M/CP effect. The problem is that most modern adults are very familiar with all sorts of sophisticated devices, such as the Clapper (the sound wave–sensitive light switch that directly responds to clapping) or cell phones and certain GPS devices that can be programmed to respond to voiced commands. Even though in this experiment the effect of the magic spell looked more authentic than in Experiment 2, there was no certainty as to whether participants did indeed view the effect as one that includes an element of the supernatural. Though small, the chance still exists for participants to interpret the magic spell as an auditory signal that triggers some remote-controlled device in the box and thus burns the object placed in the box. If this were the case, then in this experiment, as in Experiment 2, the M/CP effect could still be explained by the difference in the intrinsic interest toward the two counterintuitive physical events rather than by the difference between a magical and a counterintuitive physical event. Although one cannot completely overrule this explanation, one can reduce its likelihood by creating an explicit clash between the supernatural (magical) and the high-tech counterintuitive (nonmagical) explanations.

Experiment 4 tested these hypotheses. The procedure was the same as in Experiment 3, except for the following differences. First, in the action trial, instead of the participants' driver's licenses, the experimenter's business card was used. This was done in order to reduce the cost for exploratory behavior to a minimum and thus examine the hypothesis linking the M/CP effect with the optimal degree of cost of exploratory behavior. Second, after the participants responded to the question of whether they were willing to proceed with testing using the business card this time, in the MC condition the instruction was as follows: "It is quite clear that what happened to this postage stamp was either a high-tech trick, for example, a voice-censor device hidden in the box, or an instance of true magic—do you agree? In the beginning of this experiment, you and I agreed on what true magic was and what a trick was, didn't we? So, if it was my magic spell that burned part of this stamp, then was it an instance of true magic or a high-tech trick?"

After the participant answered, the instruction continued: "OK, now, my condition is as follows. If you are 100% sure that it was some kind of high-tech trick, then there is no point in trying my magic spell on this business card and this experiment ends. However, if you allow for the possibility that it was an instance of true magic, I will try my magic spell on this business card. As far as I am concerned, I don't care if you allow or do not allow for the possibility that it was an instance of true magic. It is for you to decide. So, are you 100% sure that this was a high-tech trick, or do you allow for the possibility that it was an instance of true magic?"

In the CPC, the procedure was the same as in the MC, except that instead of "magic spell," the words "physical device" were used.

As a result of this procedure, an explicit clash between the magical and the high-tech physical explanations was caused by making the rejection of the magical explanation costly. It was expected that if the participants wanted to satisfy their curiosity and proceed with testing in the action trial, they had to acknowledge that the cause of the effect shown in the demonstration trial was in fact true magic and not a high-tech trick.

Further, I assumed that if participants did indeed have subconscious magical beliefs, then they would be more likely to acknowledge this in the MC than in the CPC. Indeed, if participants strongly believed that the effect shown in the demonstration trial was a trick and not true magic (CPC), then they would stick to the nonmagical explanation even at the expense of not proceeding to the action trial and having their curiosity remain unsatisfied. This was expected because saying that the effect might be true magic when it is obvious that it is not would look like intentional lying, and most participants would not like to produce the impression that they are lying. However, if the effect implied even the smallest chance of having been caused by true magic (MC), then in this experiment participants should go for this explanation in order to proceed to the action trial and satisfy their curiosity.

Another expectation was that if the M/CP effect indeed occurred between the "floor and ceiling" of the cost of exploratory behavior, then in this experiment the number of participants willing to experiment with the business card in both conditions should be quite high and approximately the same.

The results of this experiment supported the expectation that lowering the cost of exploratory behavior down to zero eliminated the M/CP effect: 88% of participants in the MC and all participants in the CPC said that they wanted to proceed to the action trial. These numbers were significantly larger than in the same conditions of Experiment 3. The obvious explanation was that when there is no risk of losing their valuable object as a cost of their exploratory behavior, participants' curiosity becomes a dominant motivation for their actions in both conditions. Given that in the imaginary trial of Experiment 3 only a few participants in each condition expressed interest in proceeding to the action trial with their passports being at risk, the results of this experiment support the hypothesis that the M/CP effect occurs only when the cost of exploratory behavior is not too high or too low.

As expected, the number of participants who acknowledged the possibility that the effect in the demonstration trial was true magic and not a high-tech trick was significantly larger in the MC than in the CPC. This difference between conditions cannot be explained by participants' desire to meet the experimenter's expectations, since the instruction was the same in both conditions. This supports the assumption that in Experiments 2 and 3, participants viewed the magical event as including an element of the supernatural and not as another version of a counterintuitive physical event.

Altogether, Experiments 1 and 2 showed that both 4- to 9-year-old children and adults are more likely to engage in exploratory behavior if the target of this behavior is a magical event than if it is a counterintuitive physical event (the M/CP effect). Experiment 3 indicated that the M/CP effect remained when the magical phenomenon was made more irreversible (burning instead of cutting) and the causality vectors were made external in both conditions (magic spell in the MC and an unknown physical device in the CPC). This effect cannot be explained as an artifact of participants' mistaking the magical effect for yet another counterintuitive physical effect (Experiment 4). It was also found that the M/CP effect appears only in the conditions in which the cost of exploratory behavior is moderate (a threat to the safety of the participants' driver's licenses). If the cost is too high or too low, participants' exploratory behavior holds on or boosts up to the extent that the M/CP effect is eliminated.

The question arises as to what causes the M/CP effect. Why are children and adults attracted to explore phenomena that they (and their social environment) view as supernatural? Regarding children, this can be explained by the fact that adults purposefully encourage magical thinking in children by maintaining a special "culture of magic" in the form of traditional magical characters (Santa Claus, the Tooth Fairy) or by using magical explanations of events (Johnson & Harris, 1994; Rosengren & Hickling, 2000; Woolley, 1997). But why would adults exhibit the M/CP effect?

A likely explanation is that the M/CP effect is a manifestation of the fact that NIMBs exist in the domain of the subconscious (see Chapter 1). As the studies reviewed in Chapters 5 and 6 have shown, in Western developed cultures, adult participants are reluctant to explicitly acknowledge their NIMBs unless not acknowledging them involves a relatively high risk. However, when participants are offered the opportunity to explore phenomena based on mind-over-mind magic, they are enthusiastic, because in a situation of exploration, subconscious magical beliefs can surface into the area of conscious activity without forcing participants to explicitly acknowledge that they actually believe in magic.

One might argue against this explanation on the grounds that participants were more interested in exploring magical effects than counterintuitive physical effects simply because *magical effects looked to them counterintuitive to a larger extent than did counterintuitive physical effects.* However, this interpretation is unlikely to be correct, because the effect of the unknown physical device violated participants' intuitive expectations and knowledge about causal links to the same extent as the magic spell did. This becomes clear if we compare the percent of participants who were willing to put their driver's licenses at risk in order to prove their disbelief of the physical device and magic spell's ability to affect their licenses (Chapter 5, Figure 5.2) with the percent of participants who wanted to put their licenses at risk in order to satisfy their curiosity toward the same two effects (see Figure 7.3).

As Figure 7.3 shows, approximately equal numbers of participants were prepared to risk their driver's licenses in order to demonstrate their disbelief that the effects of either the device or the magic spell on the object in the box were possible. This means that participants viewed both of these effects as counterintuitive (contradicting their intuitive expectations and explicit knowledge about physical causality) to an equal extent. Yet, when the motivation was to satisfy curiosity, a significantly larger number of participants went for the risky option in the magic condition than in the device condition. The same pattern can be seen when denial of the belief in the effects of magic or device and satisfaction of curiosity toward the same effects involved a relatively high risk (damaging participants' hands or passports; see Figure 7.4).

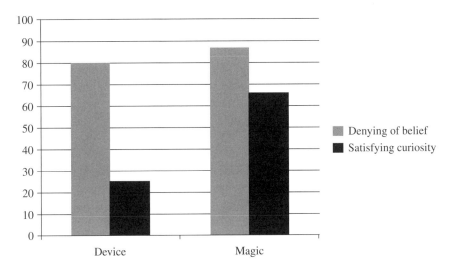

FIGURE 7.3. Percent of adult participants who agreed to put their driver's licenses at risk in order to deny their belief in the effect having been caused by the physical device or the magic spell and in order to satisfy their curiosity toward the same possibilities.

This suggests that in the curiosity experiment, the levels of motivation that powered exploration of the effects of magic and device were unequal. The motivation for exploring the effect of the physical device could only be fueled by participants' conscious knowledge that such effects contradict physical

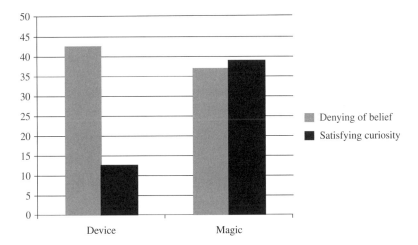

FIGURE 7.4. Percent of adult participants who agreed to put their hands or passports at risk in order to deny their belief in the effect having been caused by the physical device or the magic spell and in order to satisfy their curiosity toward the same possibilities.

causality. *In contrast, the motivation to explore the effect of the magic spell could receive additional energy from the participants' subconscious and suppressed belief in mind-over-matter magic.*

The M/CP effect supports the main hypothesis of this book concerning the origins of NIMBs (see Chapter 1). In addition, this effect can explain the success that fantastic characters with magical powers enjoy in the domains of fiction, entertainment, and commercial advertising, as well as the public appeal of the individuals with "special powers." People may express a certain amount of interest to be able to see how a spoon is bent remotely by an unknown physical device, yet they are likely to be a lot more captivated by viewing a person bending a spoon with his or her look or a slight touch only, if such a person really existed.

8

Magical Thinking and Imagination

The studies reviewed in the previous chapters employed only the mind-over-matter type of noninstitutionalized magical beliefs (NIMBs). In all the demonstrations of magical effects, a mental effort (a wish, a magic spell, or a magic gesture) affected a perceived physical object (a postage stamp, a driver's license, a participant's hand). But participants' imaginary, rather than perceived, objects may also be affected by magical causation. In Chapter 1, this type of magic was introduced as mind-over-mind magic. The studies that will be reviewed in this chapter explored the belief that magic can affect the objects in our imagination.

One feature that distinguishes imaginary objects (a tree that I am imagining) from perceived ones (a tree that I am seeing) is that most perceived objects are permanent. Following Kant (1929), Piaget (1954) defined the concept of object permanence as the belief that a physical object continues to exist after it disappears from the perceptual field. Piaget argued that children understand object permanence by the age of 2 years. Having this capacity enables children to represent physical objects in a mental form (as images in memory). In later years, children's imagination is amplified by the emergence of pretend play and verbal representations (Harris, 2000; Piaget, 1962).

Children's developing beliefs in object permanence have been studied in great depth by a number of researchers (for reviews, see Baillargeon, 1987;

Bower, 1971; Subbotsky, 1991b), and this has led to clarification of the concept. For instance, Johnson and Harris (1994) have proposed that children are likely to know of a number of related constraints, including constancy (inanimate objects do not spontaneously change shape or identity), permanence (inanimate objects do not spontaneously disappear or cease to exist), and noncreation (inanimate objects do not spontaneously come into existence). In most cases, these constraints relate to animate objects as well. Thus, it can be assumed that people view an object as permanent if they believe that (*1*) the object cannot instantly vanish without leaving any tangible traces, (*2*) the object cannot instantly change into a different one, and (*3*) the object cannot be changed by thinking or wishing it to happen without the use of physical force, tools, or actions. Importantly, the last rule protects permanent physical objects from the mind-over-matter magic (see Chapter 1).

ARE MENTAL OBJECTS PERMANENT?

A common view is that the laws of physics apply only to perceived objects, whereas imagined objects are free from physical constraints. For instance, perceived objects are supposed to be permanent and to conform to physical causality. In contrast, imagined objects are viewed as nonpermanent and capable of magical transformations. Dreams, art, and fiction provide ample evidence of imagined objects' independence from physical constraints. In dreams, objects can alter their shapes, animals can turn into humans, and inanimate objects can turn into animals (Rittenhouse, Stickgold, & Hobson, 1994). In magical worlds described in fictional accounts, people can fly and rocks can be moved by magical powers. In psychological research, imagined objects are assumed to be nonpermanent, or "inconsistent." For instance, Wellman and Estes (1986) claim that, unlike real physical objects, mental entities "are 'there' only when one is actively representing them" (p. 912).

   Yet, even imagined objects must be subject to certain constraints: if imagined objects were totally nonpermanent, they would be impossible to conceive. Even in dreams inanimate objects do not typically change into humans (Rittenhouse et al., 1994), and in fiction magic does not always work and magical events are mixed with ordinary physical events. In myths and fairy tales, transformations of objects into other objects are constrained by the ontological proximity between these objects. For instance, Kelly and Keil (1985) demonstrated that in Ovid's *Metamorphoses* and Grimm's' *Fairy Tales,* conscious beings were much more likely to be transformed into animals than into plants or inanimate objects. The fact that imagined objects are nevertheless subject to certain constraints has been reported in past research. Undergraduate students systematically applied anthropomorphic constraints to the imagined psychological characteristics of God (such as the ability to concentrate on only one object at a time), despite the fact that they ascribed to God omnipotent properties that would necessarily be free of such constraints (Barrett & Keil, 1996). In research with children, Woolley, Browne, and Boerger (2006) found that 6-year-olds, and to a lesser extent 5-year-olds, treated magical causal events as constrained by parameters of ordinary causality, which included priority (a cause precedes an effect) and exclusivity (an event cannot be caused by two alternative causes simultaneously). At the same time, children are not bound to apply the constraints of ordinary reality to all aspects of imagined reality. For example, 5- and 6-year-old American children (Barrett, Richert, & Driesenga, 2001) and 7-year-old Yukatek Mayan children (Knight, Sousa, Barrett, & Atran, 2004) attributed false beliefs to humans and to some nonhuman agents (such as animals and trees), yet did not attribute them to God.

PHYSICAL VERSUS FICTIONAL: DOMAINS OF IMAGINARY REALITY

When contrasting perceived reality with imagined reality, I distinguish between two ontologically different domains of imagined reality: imagined physical reality and fictional reality domains.[1] Within *imagined physical reality*, objects and events exist that comply with the same physical and causal constraints as their perceived counterparts. For instance, if I imagine a physical item that I see in a catalog and want to buy (such as a particular painting by a favorite artist), then the imagined item has the same properties of shape, color, solidity, and permanence as its real equivalent. Even if my thinking about the item is interrupted, on resumption I am likely to think of the item as having continued to exist and not as being recreated a second time. In contrast, within *fictional reality*, principles of the perceived physical world can be suspended. In this world, we can dream of impossible and fantastic objects (such as a flying dog), irregular physical objects made of nonpermanent substances (an elephant made of steam, a pencil made of smoke, a person made of shadows). The common feature that unites these classes of fictional objects is that they do not have matching prototypes in the perceived world.

Research has shown that even 3-year-olds can distinguish between imagined and perceived physical objects (Estes, Wellman, & Woolley, 1989; Wellman & Estes, 1986).[2] Harris, Brown, Marriot, Whittal, and Harmer (1991) reported that 4- and 6-year-olds can distinguish between perceived objects (a perceived cup), imagined physical objects (an imagined cup), and fantastic objects (a witch flying in the sky). Five-year-olds are as good as adults are at differentiating between properties of fantastic and nonfantastic characters (Sharon & Woolley, 2004). Three-year-old children understand that, unlike perceived physical objects, imagined entities cannot be touched or seen by other people and can also be fantastic (Wellman & Estes, 1986).

Yet whether children view mental entities as permanent or nonpermanent to the same extent as perceived physical objects is unknown. Specifically, do children (and, for that matter, adults) distinguish between different types of mental entities, such as imagined physical objects and fantastic objects, in terms of object permanence? Researchers have examined similarities between imagined and perceived objects (Attneave & Pierce, 1978; Belli, Schuman, & Jackson, 1997; Ceci, Huffman, Smith, & Loftus, 1994; Freyd & Finke, 1984; Henkel & Franklin, 1998; Johnson, 1988; Johnson, Foley, Suengas, & Raye, 1988). However, in general, little is known about how imagined objects compare with perceived objects in terms of permanence or stability.

CAN MAGICAL SUGGESTION CHANGE IMAGINATION?
MIND-OVER-MIND MAGIC

As the studies reviewed in preceding chapters have shown, under certain conditions, children and adults are prepared to suspend initially strong beliefs in the permanence of perceived objects and start believing in mind-over-matter magic. The question arises of whether a similar suspension of beliefs in object permanence can affect imagined rather than perceived objects. Asking this question means replacing mind-over-matter magic with its social offshoot—mind-over-mind magic—because changing imagined objects means changing people's minds rather than altering real physical objects that exist outside of the mind. Characteristically, most objects with which existing magical practices operate are imagined and not perceived— astrology, fortune telling, palm reading, and magical healing deal with objects and events that (may) exist in the future and not in reality. Art and entertainment, too, appeal to our magical thinking by creating fantastic objects and scenarios on a mass scale. Knowledge of how magical manipulations, such as spells and rituals, affect imagined objects can help to assess the role that magical thinking plays in determining the success of these kinds of manipulative techniques.

In research, there is evidence that preschool children treat wishing as a force that can affect (change or materialize) physical objects. Some children aged 3 to 6 years believe that imagining an object in an empty container and wishing it to appear can actually create the object (Woolley & Wellman, 1993; Woolley, Phelps, Davis, & Mandel, 1999). Furthermore, children believe that their wish can affect other people's minds. In one study, 4- to 6-year-old children believed that they were able to influence another person's behavior by simply wishing the person to do something (Vikan & Clausen, 1993).

To summarize, the question to be answered is, *to what extent do imagined objects succumb to or resist magical causation compared with perceived objects?* In addition to advancing our knowledge of the development of object permanence in children, exploring the permanence of perceived, imagined, and fantastic objects adds to our knowledge of children's understanding of theory of mind. Researchers have argued that children younger than 4 years have a limited capacity for understanding how the mind works. For example, young children often fail to understand false beliefs (Gopnik & Astington, 1988; Lewis & Mitchell, 1994; Perner, 1991; Wimmer & Perner, 1983), and in certain conditions, even adults make "realist errors" in judging about the mind (Mitchell, Robinson, Isaacs, & Nye, 1996). To date, research into children's understanding of the mind has been confined to exploring its cognitive operational functions, such as the capacity to act on the basis of insufficient information and to hold false beliefs. Clearly, there is more to understand about the mind. For instance, do children understand that the mind can create both accurate and distorted images of perceived objects or, indeed, completely fictional objects? Do they understand that, given differences between imagined physical objects and fictional objects, imagined physical objects are permanent whereas fictional objects are not? If children believe that mental efforts, such as a wish or a magic spell, cannot affect perceived objects, do they believe at the same time that magical causation can affect various types of imagined objects, and to what extent? In other words, along with the cognitive tasks examined within theory-of-mind research, the mind also has to undertake ontological tasks (see, for example, Boyer & Walker, 2000). Ontologically, imagined reality can be fundamentally different from perceived physical reality and contain nonpermanent fictional objects. Imagined reality can also be similar to perceived reality, in containing permanent imagined physical objects. In this sense, along with a cognitive theory of mind, children also develop an ontological theory of mind.

To a considerable extent, studying the permanence of perceived and imagined objects in older children and adults has been impeded by the absence of a suitable method. Traditionally, nonverbal tests were used for studying permanence of perceived objects in infants, with displays such as obstruction of perceived objects by other objects, invisible displacement, or replacing one object with another one behind a screen (Baillargeon, 1987; Bower, 1971; Piaget, 1937). Clearly, this method is inappropriate for older children and adults. Unlike infants, older children and adults do not view these kinds of displays as challenges to their beliefs in object permanence; rather, they view them as tricks. For example, Chandler and Lalonde (1994) showed preschoolers aged 3 to 5 years a display similar to that earlier employed in Baillargeon's (1987) study, in which one solid object was shown passing unhindered through a space occupied by another solid object. Only half of the children called the event magical, and even these children, after further questioning, said they had meant that the event was actually a trick.

To overcome this difficulty, an alternative method was used here to test beliefs about object permanence in older children and adults. This method is a version of the invisible replacement task (Bower, 1971). It employs a trick box that causes a physical object's disappearance or transformation in such a way that these manipulations are extremely hard to explain in terms of known mechanical and other causal factors (as described in Chapter 2). Unlike stage tricks that are shown at a distance, the effects happen in participants' own hands within a simple wooden box after participants have thoroughly examined the box and acknowledged that it is empty. In addition, participants are encouraged to search in the box for the disappeared object as much as they want to. This creates the impression in participants that the effects they observed indeed violate the physical principle of object permanence.

TURNING A RABBIT INTO A FISH: THE MIND-OVER-MIND MAGIC EXPERIMENT

The study reviewed in this chapter (Subbotsky, 2005) addressed two related issues. First, the baseline permanence of imaginary and perceived objects was assessed. Unlike earlier studies (Subbotsky, 1997a, 2001; Subbotsky & Quinteros, 2002; Subbotsky & Trommsdorff, 1992), in which an object's concealed replacement was accompanied by the experimenter's suggestive manipulations (an effort of will or a magic spell), in the current study baseline permanence was assessed via a demonstration of the object's change without any suggestive context. Second, the extent to which mental-physical causality (magic spell or wishing) affects the permanence of different types of objects was studied. In Experiment 1, these issues were examined on imagined physical objects (an imagined piece of paper) and perceived objects (a perceived piece of paper). In Experiment 2, the same procedures were applied to test the permanence of a fantastic object (a flying dog) compared with a perceived object (a figure of a rabbit cut out of a card). In Experiment 3, the permanence of perceived objects, imagined physical objects, and fantastic objects were compared using a different type of mind-over-mind causation: instead of trying to affect an object with a magic spell, the experimenter encouraged participants to affect the object by wishing it to happen. Experiment 4 assessed the sensitivity to magical causation of imagined objects that were personally important (participants' mental images of their future lives).

Two pretest interviews accompanied the experiments. One of the interviews assessed participants' ability to distinguish between magical events and tricks. Indeed, Woolley and colleagues (1999) reported that most 6-year-olds who judged materialization of their wishes to be magical events actually meant that they were tricks. In order to minimize the ambiguity in the interpretation of participants' answers that contained references to magic, the interview aimed to ensure that participants who gave nonpermanent answers did indeed mean a magical change of an object, and not a "trick change" involving an explicable though hidden mechanical effect such as a sleight of hand. This interview was the same as the "two wizards" interview described in Chapter 3. The second pretest interview examined whether participants could understand the difference between imagined and perceived objects. The criteria for this distinction were externality (perceived objects are "out there," whereas imagined ones are "in the mind"), accessibility to sensations (perceived objects can be touched and seen, and imagined ones cannot), and intersubjectivity (perceived objects can be seen by other people, and objects that we imagine cannot). Wellman and Estes (1986) reported that young children are aware of these constraints.

In order to test the permanence of perceived and imagined physical objects, in the *imaginary physical object trial* of Experiment 1 of this study, participants (6- and 9-year-old children and university graduates and undergraduates) were shown an empty wooden box and a clean square of paper (5 × 9 cm), which was immediately taken from view. They were then asked to imagine putting this square of paper in the box. Next, participants were instructed to imagine opening the box and taking the square of paper out. At this moment, participants were asked to imagine that a new element—a picture of a rabbit—had appeared on the square of paper. They were then questioned with the purpose of determining whether they treated the square of paper as a permanent or nonpermanent object. The answers were scored for attributing the imagined object with permanence, from 2 (full permanence) to 0 (nonpermanence).

In the *perceived object trial,* the same manipulations were done with the real square of paper. Unbeknownst to the participants, in this condition the original square was replaced by another square of paper by flapping the trap door inside the box. There were also two conditions in the experiment. In the *baseline condition*, the aforementioned manipulations did not involve references to magic, and in the *magic condition,* the change in the objects was presented as a result of the experimenter's magic spell. The aim of the experiment was to find out if participants would treat imaginary physical objects as more vulnerable to magical causation than real physical objects. We predicted that (*1*) children would treat the objects (both imaginary and perceived) as less permanent than would adults, (*2*) in the magical condition participants would treat objects as less permanent than in the baseline condition, and (*3*) imagined objects would be treated as less permanent than perceived objects. The results are shown in Figure 8.1.

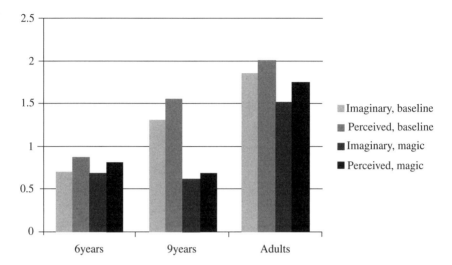

FIGURE 8.1. Mean permanence scores as a function of age, trial (imaginary physical versus perceived), and condition (magic versus baseline).

The prediction was supported that 6- and 9-year-olds would be more likely than adults to suspend their belief in object permanence in a situation where a concealed replacement was made that was difficult to explain in a rational way. This result is in accord with earlier observations that the developmental phase of establishing belief in permanence of physical objects extends far beyond the age of 2 years (Subbotsky, 1991a,b).

The results also supported the prediction that the magic manipulation would move permanence scores below the baseline. Since in 6-year-olds baseline permanence scores were low, the effect of the magic spell was not evident, yet this effect was salient in 9-year-olds and adults. The data from this experiment are consistent with earlier observations that the beliefs in the efficacy of wishing on matter decline with age (Phelps & Woolley, 1994; Rosengren & Hickling, 1994; Woolley, 2000). The data are also in accord with the experiments reported in Chapter 3 (see Figure 3.4), which showed that most 5-year-olds and half of 9-year-olds drop their nonmagical explanations and return to magical explanations if shown an anomalous causal effect. Yet the data of this experiment, as well as those reviewed in Chapter 3, suggest that the decline in children's verbal magical beliefs occurs slower than it was thought, as long as many 9-year-olds, and to a smaller extent adults, were prepared to believe that a magic spell changed perceived or imagined objects.

The prediction that imagined objects would be treated as less permanent than perceived objects was not supported by the results. Instead, the results showed a considerable similarity between imagined physical and perceived objects in terms of their degree of permanence. How might this similarity be explained?

Imagined physical objects can serve *the function of representing perceived objects* that temporarily move out of the perceptual field. For instance, my house is temporarily out of sight when I go to my office, but an image of my house can be used to complete a mental activity such as wondering where I might have left some important papers. This requires imagined physical objects to have a degree of permanence comparable with that of perceived objects.

One way of examining this explanation would be to replace imagined physical objects with fantastic objects. Indeed, fantastic objects do not stand for any perceived object. *If the permanence of imagined physical objects can be explained by their representational function, then fantastic objects should be treated as less permanent than both imagined physical and perceived objects.* Experiment 2 tested this expectation. A second aim of Experiment 2 was to examine whether a large degree of object transformation (changing three features of a perceived object—shape, size, and color) would result in larger mean scores of permanence than the small degree of transformation tested in Experiment 1 (altering just one feature—a picture appeared on a blank piece of paper). The rationale for this manipulation is based on earlier studies of phenomenalistic causal judgments in adults. Michotte (1962) reported that participants judged an object presented as a display on a screen as the same if only one of four features (shape, size, color, or spatial location) was changed. If, however, two or more features were changed simultaneously, participants believed that the object had been replaced with another. Thus, it was predicted that *in Experiment 2, participants would treat imagined and perceived objects as more permanent than participants in Experiment 1 had treated the objects that varied in only one feature.*

The procedure of Experiment 2 was the same as in Experiment 1, except for two differences. First, in the imaginary object trial, instead of imagining a piece of paper, participants were asked to imagine a fantastic animal (a small flying dog with wings) that transformed into another fantastic animal (a small cat with the tail of a fish).

Second, in the perceived object trial, instead of a blank piece of paper developing a picture on it, a small rabbit-shaped piece of green card stock was converted into a much larger fish shape cut out of orange card stock. This was done in order to approximately equate the degrees of change observed in both trials (one animal changed into another animal).

Results supported the expectation that fantastic objects would be treated as significantly less permanent than perceived objects (see Figure 8.2).

In all age groups, fantastic objects scored significantly lower on permanence scores than did perceived objects. Unlike in Experiment 1, in this

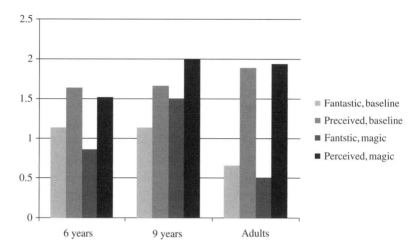

FIGURE 8.2. Mean permanence scores as a function of age, trial (fantastic versus perceived), and condition (magic versus baseline).

experiment there was no difference between the magic and baseline conditions. It appears that the degree of object transformation in this experiment
(one animal turning into another animal) was too strong for the magic spell to
be able to move the objects' permanence below the baseline. There was no
difference between age groups either. This suggests that, when a degree of
transformation is big, children and adults are equally likely to treat objects as
permanent or nonpermanent regardless of type. The comparisons between the
results of this experiment and those of Experiment 1 supported the prediction
that permanence of perceived objects would increase if the degree of transformation were increased. In the baseline condition, 6-year-olds treated perceived objects that underwent a big change (size, shape, and color, this
experiment) as significantly more permanent than perceived objects that
underwent a small change (a blank piece of paper upon which a picture
appeared, Experiment 1), and in the magic condition 6- and 9-year-olds did
the same. This suggests that, generally, children were prepared to accept that a
small change in a perceived object could happen or be done in a magical way
(Experiment 1). Yet when the change was big (Experiment 2), children
viewed it as a stronger challenge to their intuitive experience that physical
objects are permanent and cannot be altered by a nonphysical force. Due to a
ceiling effect, in adults, a "degree of transformation" manipulation yielded no
significant increase in permanence for perceived objects.

It has been reported in earlier research that even 3-year-olds exhibit some
realization that fantastic objects are less real than perceived or imagined physical
objects (Harris et al., 1991; Wellman & Estes, 1986). Contrary to the a priori
assumption that in this experiment fantastic objects would be treated

as significantly less permanent than imagined physical objects, children of both age groups did not show this effect; in fact, in the magic condition, 9-year-olds treated fantastic objects as more permanent than imagined physical objects. This can be explained by the difference between conceptual and onto-logical judgments (see Chapter 3). While being able to distinguish between concepts of fantastic and imaginary physical objects (for instance, by saying that imagined physical objects exist whereas fantastic objects do not), children may fail to realize that fantastic objects are less permanent than imagined physical objects.

Unlike children, adults did treat fantastic objects as significantly less permanent than imagined physical objects. At least two explanations of this contrast between children's and adults' views on permanence of fantastic objects are possible. First, it can be assumed that it is only in adults that the divide appears between the two domains of imagined reality: imagined phy-sical reality and fictional reality (as discussed earlier in this chapter). Like children, adults viewed imagined physical objects as similar to their perceived counterparts; consequently, they attributed imagined physical objects with the same degree of permanence that they did perceived objects. Unlike children, adults viewed fantastic objects as a part of fictional reality, and therefore treated them as significantly less permanent than imagined physical objects.

An alternative explanation of the contrast between fantastic and imagined physical objects in adults would be to assume that adults selectively associated fantastic objects with magic (a phenomenon that most adults consider a product of fantasy), whereas children made no such association. Evidence for this explanation comes from explanations that some adults gave to the fact that one fantastic animal had turned into another one ("This is such a crazy animal that, probably, it can do such things," "Because this flying dog does not exist anyway, it could have just changed into the cat with a fish tail"). Due to this selective association between fantastic objects and magic in adults, permanence of fantastic objects may have been undermined, whereas perma-nence of imagined physical objects remained unaffected by the magic spell.

In order to test the alternative explanation, in Experiment 3, children and adults were encouraged to change both types of imagined objects with the power of their own wish. For example, in the imagined physical object trial, the instruction was as follows: "Now I'd like to ask you to try and think hard that a picture of a rose flower appears on the piece of paper that you are imagining in the box." Unlike a magic spell, which is traditionally associated with magic and fantastic things, wishing does not necessarily bear a magical connotation. Indeed, we can reject the idea that somebody else's magic spell can change physical objects that we are imagining, yet find it quite natural that our own wish can. If in Experiment 2 adults selectively associated fantastic objects with magic and on this ground treated fantastic objects as nonpermanent, then in this experiment, in which the possibility of such an association was eliminated (participants attempted to change imagined objects by the power of their wish), adults would view fantastic objects to be as permanent as either perceived or nonfantastic imagined objects.

The results of this experiment (see Figure 8.3) did not support the idea that in Experiment 2 adults selectively associated fantastic objects with magic and on this ground treated fantastic objects as nonpermanent. In this experiment, as in Experiment 2, adults treated fantastic objects as significantly less permanent than either perceived or nonfantastic imagined objects, and children did not. Justifications of successful attempts in this experiment were similar to those given in Experiment 2: most adults said they had changed fantastic objects by the efforts of their mind, will, or imagination and qualified the change to be true magic and not a trick. *This outcome supports the idea that for adults, but not for children, fantastic objects are a special type of object. For adults, fantastic objects, but not perceived or imagined physical objects, can spontaneously change or be magically converted into other objects.*

To summarize, the results of this experiment support the view that, while permanence of perceived and imagined physical objects increases with age, fantastic objects remain largely nonpermanent throughout the age span explored in this study. Whereas 6- and 9-year-old children did not draw a line between fantastic and imagined physical types of objects in terms of their freedom from physical constraints, adults did. Adults believed that, whereas perceived and imagined physical objects cannot magically change into other objects, fantastic objects can.

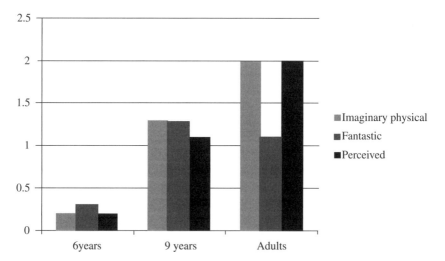

FIGURE 8.3. Mean permanence scores as a function of age and trial (imagined physical, fantastic, and perceived objects).

The question arises as to what was special about fantastic objects that made adults treat them as more nonpermanent than either perceived objects or imagined physical objects. It may be the case that, with adults, there is a general understanding that imagined reality is divided into two ontologically different domains: *the domain of imagined physical reality and the domain of fictional reality.*

One feature that distinguishes fictional objects from imagined physical objects is that fictional objects have no representatives in the perceptual world. Even if illustrated in movies or objects of art, fictional objects are still sheer products of the creative imagination. To put it another way, *the ontological status of fictional objects, by definition, is weaker than that of perceived objects or imagined physical objects.* When two objects with a priori different ontological statuses are presented to participants, participants' reactions to these objects can show whether they can or cannot distinguish between them. Thus, *a diminished ontological status of fantastic objects may explain why adults view these objects as significantly less permanent than either perceived or imagined physical objects.*

As argued previously in this chapter, the domain of fictional reality includes two kinds of objects: fantastic objects (a flying dog) and irregular imagined physical objects (an elephant made of smoke). Imagined future events (a future trajectory of the flight of a butterfly) can also be included in this domain. Although a future event can become real, it is not possible to predict with certainty which of the multiple versions of this event might come true, and when it occurs, it stops being a future event. This makes an image of a future event ontologically the same as that of a fictional event.

CURSING ONE'S FUTURE: MAGIC AND PERSONAL DESTINY

A special kind of imagining is a person's thoughts about his or her own future or destiny. Indeed, whatever plans we create about our future, we know that these plans can be suddenly interrupted by unforeseen circumstances. I refer to these kinds of events as "personally significant imagined" (PERSIM) objects. *In addition to an individual's future life, PERSIM objects include thoughts about the future lives of close ones, the future of personally significant environments (a house, a homeland, the planet), future outcomes of risky and meaningful activities (in gambling, business, politics, war, pregnancy, marriage), and other future events closely related to an individual's health and well-being.* Unlike other imagined future objects (tomorrow's weather, a TV program, or the approaching Christmas), PERSIM objects are filled with emotional significance and personal value, and this makes them ontologically weak and vulnerable to magical manipulations. Whereas fantastic objects are generally conceived in the arts and mass entertainment, *practices and persuasion techniques used in magic, religion, psychotherapy, politics, and commercial advertising target PERSIM objects.* It is also an established fact that, when thinking of events or making important decisions that might affect their future lives, many otherwise rational individuals become superstitious (Jahoda, 1969; Vyse, 1997).

In order to examine whether PERSIM objects can be affected by magical causation, in Experiment 4 of this study, in the personal involvement condition, adult participants were asked to imagine that a witch had approached them in the street and said that she wanted to put a good spell on their future lives, which would make them happy and rich for life. But in order for this spell to work, they had to give their permission for the spell to be put on their future lives; without their permission, the spell would not work. The key question then followed: "If you were in this situation, would you allow the witch to put the spell on your life, or would you not? Why?" After participants answered and justified their answers, the experimenter asked them to imagine a different scenario. In this scenario, the witch was a servant to the devil and wanted to put a spell on their future lives in order to make them serve the devil as well. After this, the key question followed as before. For half of participants, the order of the questions about the good and mean spells was reversed.

In the no personal involvement condition, participants were told the same story, only this time it was happening to another person. That other person was introduced as a scientist, a rational person, and a nonbeliever in magic. Participants were then asked if the character should have said "yes" or "no" to the good and mean witches. Since in this condition someone else's PERSIM objects, and not the participants', were under the spell, participants were expected to judge the character's behavior on rational grounds only. In addition, after participants answered the questions about what the scientist should have said, they were asked what they would have said if they were in the scientist's place. This was done in order to check if making participants personally involved would make them react to the possibility of the mean spell in the same way, as did participants in the Personal involvement condition.

It was predicted that if the participants were skeptical toward magic, they would treat the magic spells as not affecting the course of their future lives—in other words, they would treat their own future lives as if they were permanent imaginary objects. For such participants, their future lives would depend on factors such as heredity and environment, and not on magic forces. As a result, these participants would be willing or not willing to allow both kinds of witches to proceed with their spells to an equal extent. Because a variety of motives can affect participants' judgments (wanting to comply with the women's request, to prove their skepticism toward magic, to avoid interfering with magic forces), these participants would be expected to give "yes" and "no" answers in about equal numbers.

But if despite conscious skepticism toward magic, subconsciously participants did believe in the effect of the magic spell on their lives, then their responses in the two conditions would diverge. Regarding the good spell, some participants might be motivated to say "yes" in order to benefit from magic forces, or to comply with the woman's request. Other participants might be nervous about interfering with magic forces. As a result, frequencies of "yes" and "no" answers would still be split 50/50. Regarding the mean spell, while participants may not consciously believe that a magic spell can affect their future lives, subconsciously they might give this possibility some credit. This would make participants go against their rational views and make them inclined to say "no" to the mean spell with a frequency significantly above 50%. Consequently, in the personal involvement condition, the "disbelief in magic" hypothesis would predict no difference between mean and good spells, whereas the "belief in magic" hypothesis would predict a significant difference.

The results (see Figure 8.4) supported the "belief in magic" hypothesis: in the good spell condition, 10 out of 17 participants (59%) said that they would go for a spell, either to prove that they did not believe in magic or to benefit from the spell. In the bad spell condition, all 17 participants (100%) said "no," and justified their answers by the fear that the spell might actually affect their future lives.

In the no personal involvement condition, about half of participants said that the scientist should say "yes" to both good and mean spells. The reasons

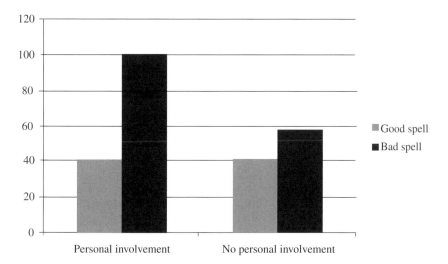

FIGURE 8.4. Percent of participants who said "no" to the offer of the magic spell as a function of trial (good versus bad spell) and condition (personal versus no personal involvement).

for allowing the mean spell were justified by pointing out that the scientist is a rational person and so should not give any credit to the mean spell ("Because if she did not believe in magic, this would not do any harm to her anyway," "If she is a rational person, she should check it out," "To show the witch that she did not care what she does"). Interestingly, when participants were then asked what they themselves would say to the good spell offer if they were in the scientist's place, half of them said this would be "yes" and the other half said this would be "no." Yet, in regard to the mean spell offer, all participants who said that the scientist should have said "no" thought they also would have said "no," and all participants who said that the scientist should have said "yes" thought that they personally would have said "no" and justified their answers with reasons suggesting that they believed that the spell could actually work on their future lives. In other words, *when someone else's PERSIM objects were subjected to magical manipulations (no personal involvement condition), participants exhibited rational behavior and a disbelief in magic. Yet, when participants' own PERSIM objects were involved (personal involvement condition), participants exhibited superstitious magical behavior.*

Altogether, the results of this study show the tendency of older children and adults to view perceived and imagined physical objects as increasingly permanent. This confirms the general age trend of a decrease in verbal magical beliefs in older children and adults (see works reviewed in Chapters 2 through 5). However, participants of all three age groups involved in this study viewed fantastic objects as nonpermanent. Moreover, in Experiments 2 and 3, adults treated fantastic objects as significantly less permanent than imagined physical objects, and children did not. It is hard to assume that adults simply failed to develop the view that fantastic objects are permanent, a view that they adopted regarding perceived and imagined physical objects. Rather, it is more likely that adults adopt the idea that fantastic objects are fundamentally nonpermanent. While in children the line between fictional and physical domains of imaginary reality is blurred, adults develop the view that, in the realm of fictional (but not physical) imagined reality, objects are free from physical constraints such as permanence and physical causality.

The results also suggest that magical causality has different meanings for children and adults. Children do not associate magical causality with fictional objects only; rather, they believe that magic can affect fictional, imagined physical, and perceived objects to an equal extent. For adults, magical causality becomes object specific. *In regard to perceived and imagined physical objects, adults are skeptical toward the mind-over-matter and mind-over-mind magic; they nevertheless endorse the mind-over-mind magic in regard to fantastic and PERSIM objects.* Looking ahead, in Chapter 11, I will be referring to the former class of objects as belonging to ordinary reality and to the latter class of objects as belonging to magical reality.

The fact that adults endorse the mind-over-mind magic in regard to their PERSIM objects may shed additional light on why religious and magical practices persist in Western societies. Usually, such practices target PERSIM objects: people's representations about their future destiny, health, outcomes of important activities, and so forth. As long as PERSIM objects, unlike ghosts or UFOs, are undeniably real and yet vulnerable to magical causation, there will always be individuals who claim to be able to affect such objects with their magical powers. These individuals' personal intentions can vary (from an altruistic desire to "improve the world" to a more pragmatic interest of extracting financial or psychological profit), yet their methods of manipulating with people's PERSIM objects are similar. As I will argue in the next chapter, these methods are based on a special psychological mechanism—participation.

To summarize, the results of this study support the prediction of the book's main hypothesis: while, consciously, modern Western adults deny their magical beliefs, subconsciously, they believe in noninstitutionalized magic.

9

Magic and Human Communication

The studies presented in Chapters 5 and 8 indicated that when participants' personally significant imagined (PERSIM) objects were not involved (when magical manipulations could affect the future condition of participants' driver's licenses, or someone else's life), adults exhibited rational behavior and denied their belief in magic. Yet when participants' PERSIM objects (the future of their hands or lives) were at risk of being affected by magic, participants exhibited magical behavior. Since PERSIM objects exist in imagination, mind-over-mind magic deals with them.

As I argued in Chapter 1, magic spells or rituals can affect other people's thoughts, feelings, or desires, as long as these people know that their minds are targeted by magical intervention. Indeed, some researchers have claimed that magic can affect minds via the mechanisms of suggestion and autosuggestion (Boyer, 1994; Freska & Kulcsar, 1989; Nemeroff & Rozin, 2000). Indirectly, the sensitivity of one's thoughts to magical influence is demonstrated in the phenomenon of "magical contagion." This effect showed that even imagining putting on a sweater worn for a day by someone with AIDS (and then washed) was rated as less desirable than imagining putting on a sweater owned, but never worn, by someone with AIDS (Rozin, Markwith, & McCauley, 1994). Similarly, participants felt sicker if imagined germs supposedly came from a morally bad person than from a morally good person (Nemeroff, 1995). And in certain circumstances, individuals are likely to assume that their prayers can affect other people psychologically (Barrett, 2001).

In developmental research, there is also some indirect evidence supporting the notion that mind-over-mind magic works via suggestion. For example, preschool and elementary school children have been shown to be more likely to investigate an empty box in which they had been invited to imagine an object than they were to investigate boxes in which they had imagined nothing at all (Harris, Brown, Marriot, Whittal, & Harmer, 1991; Johnson & Harris, 1994). Preschool children who were "visited" by a novel fantastic entity, the Candy Witch, exhibited stronger beliefs in this entity's reality than did those who were not (Woolley, Boerger, & Markman, 2004). Yet, *it is still unknown how people will react when their thoughts and feelings are directly affected in a magical way via suggestion.*

MAGICAL AND ORDINARY SUGGESTION: ARE THEY CLOSE RELATIVES?

The importance of this question stems from the fact that in contemporary society, suggestion, along with logical persuasion, is a major mechanism of manipulation of mass consciousness. Research has shown that individuals' susceptibility to suggestion (known as suggestibility) is positively related to compliance, their ability to be hypnotized, and their belief in paranormal phenomena (Hergovich, 2003; Kisch & Braffman, 2001; Richardson & Kelly, 2004). The effects of conformity and group pressure in social relations are also based on suggestibility. Brehm and Kassin (1996) refer to an individual's conformity to group norms (see Asch, 1951; Sherif, 1966) as a classic case of suggestibility. In their American Psychological Association report on deceptive and indirect techniques of persuasion and control, Singer and colleagues (1986) argue that many of the persuasion practices used in religion, politics, and psychotherapy rely on compliance tactics and hypnosis. Such techniques aim to induce authoritarian messages in the minds of clients or followers by reducing their capacities of conscious critical control. In developmental psychology, suggestibility is widely understood as "...the degree to which children's encoding, storage, retrieval, and reporting of events can be influenced by a range of social and psychological factors" (Ceci & Bruck, 1993, p. 404). Although magical suggestion can be one of these factors, little is known about how magical suggestion, compared to ordinary suggestion, can influence individuals' cognitive processes. *Can ordinary suggestion be viewed as a version of magical suggestion that has historically and culturally evolved to fit the dominant scientific orientation in Western societies?*

Although most contemporary suggestive techniques do not use manipulations like magic spells or sacred rituals, with regard to their underlying psychological mechanisms, these techniques can be similar to magical suggestion. Indeed, it has long been proposed that psychological links exist between magical and ordinary types of suggestion. Thus, Needham (1925) emphasizes psychological unity between suggestion, autosuggestion, and religious faith. All three phenomena are perceived as different versions of a transition from passively keeping an idea in mind to asserting the idea with reality. In his analysis of Trobriand magic, Malinowski (1935) emphasized psychological similarities between magical speech and rituals in traditional societies, and persuasion techniques used in industrial societies for commercial advertisements and political rhetoric. But what psychological mechanism could explain the similarity between the ordinary and magical types of suggestion?

THE MECHANISM OF MAGICAL INFLUENCE: PARTICIPATION

One tempting hypothesis is to view this mechanism as "participation". Lévy-Brühl (1966) introduced the concept of participation to refer to a mechanism that underlies belief in magical causality. In "traditional cultures," thinking has a tendency to merge entities that, from a rational point of view, should be treated as separate. For instance, to the natives of New Guinea, a wizard (a person) is at the same time perceived as a crocodile (an animal) without being physically fused with the crocodile. Clearly, from the point of view of rational logic, such connections should be treated as abnormal. Unlike physical causality, magical causality implies that mental processes (wishing, imagining, chanting spells) can directly affect ("participate in" or "be a part of") physical processes (such as the weather or crops), thus bridging the gap between mental and physical realities.

Piaget (1971) and some contemporary scholars (Nemeroff & Rozin, 2000; Tambiah, 1990) have adopted this view. For example, Tambiah (1990) distinguished two "contrasting and complementary" orientations to the world: participation and causality. Causality is the realm of positive science and logical reasoning, whereas participation involves holistic thinking, magic, myths, rituals, and religion. An example of participation-based thinking is "nominal realism," in which the name of an entity merges with the entity's physical substance. As discussed earlier, research has shown that if adult participants are given two labels, one bearing the word "sucrose" and the other "sodium cyanide, poison," and are instructed to attach them to empty clean bottles, the bottle with the "cyanide" label acquires a negative connotation to the participants. The participants saw that sugar water from the same container was poured into both bottles, yet they preferred to taste a drink made from the sugar-labeled bottle when compared with the drink made from the bottle labeled "cyanide" (Rozin, Markwith, & Ross, 1990; Rozin, Millman, & Nemeroff, 1986). In other words, participants' subconscious attitudes toward the substance in the bottles were based on the message suggested by the label (the bottle contains cyanide) and not on their rational understanding (the bottle contains sugar water).

It is important to emphasize that an action based on the mechanism of participation is different from an automatic "reflex-type" response (such as blinking or sneezing). The individual is acting consciously and has a free choice. However, the individual's decisions are made on a subconscious level and are in contradiction with the individual's conscious view. Participation-based behavior is also different from *emotionally driven* cognitive functioning. Reasoning and other cognitive functions can also be affected by emotional attitudes (Clore, Schwarz, & Conway, 1994; Forgas, 1995, 2002; Gasper, 2004). However, the characteristic feature of participation that distinguishes it from "emotionally driven" responses is that, while affecting an individual's actions, participation does not affect the individual's critical reasoning capacities. As a result, when acting on the basis of participation, individuals are aware that what they do is "not right" and therefore contradicts their consciously adopted views or interests.

COMMUNICATIVE MAGIC: THE STUDY

The study discussed in the previous chapter attempted to affect participants' imagined objects by a magic spell indirectly: participants' opinions were asked about their imaginary objects that had been (or might be) changed by a magic spell. In the study presented in this chapter, an attempt was made to directly affect objects that participants were imagining by either magical or ordinary suggestion. This kind of magical manipulation will be referred to as *communicative magic*. Communicative magic is a special kind of mind-over-mind magic. As will be argued later in this chapter, communicative magic can be viewed as a historic predecessor of certain types of influence techniques used in communication today—suggestion and persuasion.

In everyday speech, people often use expressions such as "the magic of words," "the magic of art," "the magic of love," and "the magic of human communication." Usually, these expressions are used metaphorically and emphasize the suggestive power of speech, art, love, and communication. The idea behind this study originated from the supposition that there could be more to these expressions than poetic association. Specifically, the hypothesis was tested that both magical and ordinary suggestions are based on the same psychological mechanism—participation.

I assumed that the way participation works in communicative magic is as follows: if an idea is suggested to individuals, it is adopted on a subconscious level and acted upon at that level even though the individuals' rational judgments may indicate that the idea is untrue or contrary to their personal interests. The difference between participation in mind-over-matter magic and participation in communicative magic is that in the former, a connection is made between a suggestive mental action (a magic spell or ritual) and a physical event (the sun rising or rain coming), and in the latter, the connection is made between a suggested idea and the recipient's mental/physical state. For example, suggesting that an individual becomes ill after a magic curse is cast on him or her (the idea) can indeed have the effect of influencing the person's mental/physical state. The important characteristic of participation is that a recipient unconsciously adopts the agent's message while consciously disagrees with the message and rejects it. Speaking in operational terms, *the participation-based behavioral pattern is observed when two criteria are met: (1) individuals act in accord with the suggested idea and (2) they are aware that the idea is wrong and/or is of no personal benefit to them.*

A type of communicative causation alternative to the one based on participation is causation based on *rationality*. An instance of rationality-based communicative causation is *logical persuasion*: an individual who adopts a suggested message *does it because he or she has logical reasons to believe that the message is true and/or beneficial to him or her, albeit indirectly, in the long term.* For example, a scientist can be persuaded that his or her theory is wrong, even if in the short term losing the dispute may be painful to the scientist's self-respect. Another instance of communicative causation based on rationality is *a direct request for compliance*. In this case, *people can consciously accept or reject the request depending on whether or not they see it as true and/or beneficial for themselves.* For instance, advertising a commercial product often involves the advertiser providing rational reasons why the consumer might benefit from buying the product.

On the basis of these theoretical distinctions, it can be assumed that *magical suggestion and logical persuasion are based on different psychological mechanisms*. Magical suggestion (like magical healing or cursing) is based on the mechanism of participation, whereas logical persuasion is based on the mechanism of rationality. When a medicine man heals a sick person by performing healing rituals on his own body, the result is achieved due to the patient's belief that a supernatural unity exists between the medicine man and the patient's illness. Conversely, a medical doctor is supposed to be able to logically persuade a patient to take certain drugs by explaining to the patient why taking these drugs may result in a positive healing effect.

Similar to the original definition of participation in terms of shared or blended "essences" (the shaman who is also a crocodile is truly a crocodile even though he looks just like a man), in communicative magic the person shares (or blends with) the essence of the suggested message even though this message seems incorrect or even harmful to the person. However, often overlooked is that, in addition to "sharing essences," participation includes another feature—not sharing appearances. Indeed, in the Lévy-Brühl's example, traditional people who identified their wizard with a crocodile did not actually believe that the wizard was a crocodile in terms of appearance. That is why participation is defined as involving two features: (*1*) essences between two different kinds are shared (the wizard is essentially a crocodile) and (*2*) appearances of these different kinds are kept separate (the wizard is a man, and the crocodile is an animal). When projected into the domain of communication, this understanding of participation produces the same features: a recipient to whom a message is magically suggested accepts the essence of this message (makes it a part of his or her life by doing what the message tells him or her to do), but consciously rejects the "wrapping" of this message (the messenger's implicit assumption or explicit statement that the message is true and/or that accepting the message is for the recipient's own good). In contrast, when the person rationally accepts or rejects the message, both sides of the message (its essence and its appearance) are treated in the same way: they are either both accepted (the person follows the message and thinks that the message is true and/or that accepting the message is beneficial for him or her) or rejected (the person doesn't follow the message and understands that the message is false and/or that accepting the message would do no good to him or her). In other words, *participation-based suggestion results in manipulation, whereas rationality-based persuasion results in cooperation.*[1]

The question arises as to whether *ordinary suggestion* is also based on the mechanism of participation. In the *Cambridge International Dictionary of English*, the term "suggest" is defined as "to communicate or show (an idea or feeling) without stating it directly or giving proof" (Procter, 1995, p. 1457). This implies that suggestion might be a type of communicative causation that is not based on rationality. For instance, one of the suggestive techniques used in commercial advertising is "product placement"—placing products within popular movies or magazine articles. Although this technique does not rationally persuade consumers that buying the product is beneficial for them, product placement can indeed facilitate people's choices of the product. This is achieved via the consumers' subconscious identification with favorite movie characters that are wearing or using the product in the advertisement (Babin & Garder, 1996; Gupta & Lord, 1998; Karrh, 1998). But if ordinary suggestion is not based on rational reasoning, can it be based on participation? In history and anthropology, viewing suggestive techniques used in medicine and politics today as historically evolved from magic is not a new idea (Castiglioni, 1946; Coriat, 1923; Malinowski, 1935; Tambiah, 1990). The problem is *whether empirical evidence can be found for the hypothesis that magical and ordinary types of suggestion are based on the same psychological mechanism—participation.*

One empirically verifiable implication of this hypothesis is that *ordinary suggestion, like magical suggestion, should meet both operational criteria of participation: (1) individuals act in accord with the suggested idea and (2) they are conscious that the idea is wrong and/or of no personal benefit to them.* Another verifiable implication is that *both magical and ordinary suggestions should be equally effective in their attempts to influence mental reality.* If, however, magical suggestion and ordinary suggestion are based on different psychological mechanisms, their effects are likely to be different. For example, if magical suggestion was based on participation and ordinary suggestion based on rationality, in the situation where individuals are not interested in adopting a message, with other conditions being equal, the effect of magical suggestion should be significantly stronger than that of ordinary suggestion. This is expected because individuals are more likely to reject a nonattractive suggested idea if they are in control of their actions (rationality mechanism) than if they are not (participation mechanism).[2]

When examining these implications, precautions should be taken against the possibility that differences in effects of magical and ordinary types of suggestion, if found, could be explained by factors other than differences in the underlying psychological mechanisms—for example, by simply assuming that magical suggestion is inherently more or less powerful than ordinary suggestion. In order to make sure that both magical and ordinary suggestions are inherently equally powerful, the following conditions should be met. First, the same person should do the instruction in both magical and ordinary conditions. Second, the wording of the instruction in both conditions should be exactly the same, save the reference to the magic spell in the magical suggestion condition. Third, scoring should also be the same in both conditions. Under such circumstances, the only factor that could make the power of suggestion in the two conditions different is the magic spell in the magical suggestion condition.

The developmental aspect in this study compared the effects of magical and ordinary types of suggestion on children with those on adults. This comparison can shed extra light on whether magical and ordinary suggestions are based on the same or different psychological mechanisms. It has been established that children are generally stronger believers in magic than are adults (Subbotsky, 2004; Woolley, 1997, 2000). Given that, if magical and ordinary suggestions are based on different psychological mechanisms, then adults' and children's reactions to these types of suggestion should differ. Adults might treat both types of suggestion as similar (because they do not believe in magic and treat magical suggestion as ordinary suggestion), whereas children should succumb to magical suggestion to a significantly greater degree than to ordinary suggestion. If, however, magical and ordinary types of suggestion are based on the same psychological mechanism, then they should have the same effects on children as they do on adults. Six- and nine-year-old children were selected on the grounds that at these ages, children are still prone to magical beliefs yet, unlike younger children, are able to understand relatively complex instructions (Subbotsky, 2004).

A related but separate issue arises in examining at what age magical and nonmagical communicative causations separate. In order to test this, a direct request for compliance was introduced, which a priori was based on the rationality mechanism. Since participants had no reason to refuse changing the object that they were imagining if directly asked to do so, it was expected that the efficacy of the direct request would be significantly stronger than that of magical suggestion. This, however, could occur only if the mechanisms of communicative causation (rationality and participation) were separated. The question therefore was whether this separation exists in adults only, or if it is an earlier developmental achievement that can be observed in 6- and/or 9-year-old children.

To summarize, *the aim of this study was to examine the hypothesis that ordinary suggestion is based on the same mechanism as magical suggestion— participation.* To reiterate, if ordinary suggestion, like magical suggestion, is based on the psychological mechanism of participation, then magical and ordinary types of suggestion should be equally effective in their attempts to affect mental reality. If, however, magical suggestion is based on participation and ordinary suggestion based on rationality, in the situation where individuals are not interested in adopting a message, with other conditions being equal, the effect of magical suggestion should be significantly stronger than that of ordinary suggestion.

In order to test this hypothesis, in Experiment 1 of the reviewed study (Subbotsky, 2007), participants were first interviewed about their understanding of the difference between proper magical events versus magic tricks (see Chapters 2 and 5). After that they were asked to imagine various objects and to try to concentrate on these objects while the experimenter was attempting to alter these objects, against the participants' effort not to change the objects, by suggesting other objects to the participants. The imagined objects were visual representations of objects both physical (an imagined pencil) and fantastic (a flying dog with wings). In the *suggestion trial*, the suggestion was either accompanied by a magic spell (the *magical suggestion condition*) or it was not (the *ordinary suggestion condition*).

In the *magical suggestion condition*, participants were asked to imagine that a physical object (a blue pencil) was on the table in front of them. They were then instructed: "Now, I am going to say a magic spell that may turn the blue pencil that you are imagining into an imaginary steel spoon. When I say my magic spell, I hope that the blue pencil that you are imagining on the table will turn into an image of a spoon, even if you don't want this to happen. Please, bear in mind that I am not asking you to turn the pencil into a spoon; you are supposed to focus on the pencil. I just want to check if my magic spell might still work."

The experimenter then repeated a number of nonwords that sounded like a magic spell and asked the key question that assessed efficacy of magical suggestion: "So, has the blue pencil turned into the imagined spoon or has it not?" Next, questions assessing the magical status of the communicative causation were asked: "Was this magic or not?" "Was it true magic or fake magic?"

In the *ordinary suggestion condition*, the experimenter did not cast a magic spell. Instead, the experimenter suggested to participants that the objects they were imagining could change spontaneously into other objects even though they were supposed to focus on the original objects. Next, the alternative objects were suggested. This suggestion was perceived as ordinary for the following reasons. First, although in the physical world it is impossible for one physical object (a pencil) to change into another physical object (a steel spoon), such transformation could easily happen in the world of imagination. Second, the ability to control one's thoughts (for instance, avoiding thinking of an unpleasant object) is not uncommon in the everyday life of children and adults. Studies on thought control have revealed that people, though with some difficulty, were able to control their thoughts (Wegner & Erskine, 2003; Wegner, Schneider, Carter, & White, 1987). The results are shown in Figure 9.1.

Results indicated that, for both types of suggestion, many participants acknowledged that their imagined objects changed despite their effort to

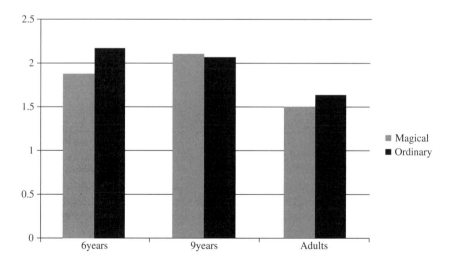

FIGURE 9.1. Mean scores indicating that suggestion changed the object that participants were imagining as a function of age and type of suggestion (magical versus ordinary).

retain them in their imagination. This is in concordance with both criteria of participation: (*1*) participants accepted the suggested message (changed the objects they were imagining in the direction that had been suggested) and (*2*) they were aware that this change occurred involuntarily and despite their conscious effort to keep in mind the original objects. Furthermore, both types of suggestion proved to be equally effective at changing the participants' imaginary objects. The results therefore favor the hypothesis that both magical and ordinary types of suggestion are based on the same psychological mechanism—participation. Indirectly, the conclusion that both types of suggestion were based on participation is supported by the fact that in children and adults, the difference between the efficacy of magical and ordinary suggestion was not significant, though children are known to be stronger believers in magic than are adults.

In the *direct request for compliance trial*, the experimenter asked participants to imagine that another object (a little ball) was on the table. He instructed participants as follows: "Now, can I ask you to do me a favor and turn this little ball into a sheet of paper for me please? Can you imagine that the little ball has turned into a sheet of paper?" The same follow-up questions were then asked as in the suggestion trial. Results (Figure 9.2) indicated that in adults, but not in children, the direct request for compliance produced a significantly greater effect than magical suggestion. This indicates that there is an age-related trend in the relationship between rationality-based and participation-based types of communicative causation.

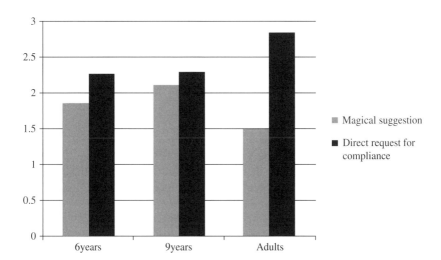

FIGURE 9.2. Mean scores indicating that communicative causation changed the object that participants were imagining as a function of age and type of causation (magical suggestion versus direct request for compliance).

In children, both types of communication are not yet separated. A possible explanation for this is that 6- and 9-year-olds' capacity to resist magical suggestion was limited, and this made magical suggestion as effective as was a direct request for compliance. In contrast, adults were able to resist magical suggestion to a larger extent than were children, yet they were prepared to convert their imagined objects into other objects if asked to do so as a favor to the experimenter. It is also possible that adults are generally more compliant than children, and this accounts for the developmental effect.

There could be, however, alternative explanations for the absence of a type of suggestion effect in this experiment. It could be argued that similarity between the effects of magical and ordinary types of suggestion was due to the specific nature of imagined objects used in this experiment. Indeed, the objects used were artificially implanted and situational imagined objects. First, participants may not have believed that a magic spell could change these objects in their minds, and for participation to work, such belief is necessary. If this were the case, then magical suggestion was in fact downgraded to the level of ordinary suggestion, and this explains the absence of a difference between magical and ordinary types of suggestion. The second alternative explanation is based on the fact that imagined objects suggested to participants by the experimenter (such as an imagined apple or a flying dog) were arbitrary and not anchored in participants' lives. As a result, participants' ability to consciously control these objects in their imagination was limited. Due to the arbitrary nature of the imagined objects, these objects could easily (without conscious intention) transform into ones suggested by the experimenter. As the literature on thought suppression and thought control has shown, participants usually find it difficult to suppress a thought that was suggested to them (Wegner, 1994; Wegner et al., 1987). Even if ordinary suggestion were based on the mechanism of rationality, the nature of imagined objects made it difficult for participants to exercise their capacity of conscious control over these types of objects. This masks the difference between ordinary and magical types of suggestion and makes ordinary suggestion as effective as magical suggestion.

In order to rule out the alternative explanations, imagined objects to be affected by suggestive causation should meet the following criteria: (1) it must be established that participants do believe that magical suggestion can affect these imagined objects; (2) with regard to these imagined objects, magical suggestion should produce a predictable pattern of results based on the mechanism of participation; and (3) these imagined objects should be anchored in participants' lives and not be randomly suggested objects as in Experiment 1. This would make participants able to consciously control their actions with regard to these imagined objects, thus eliminating the possibility that the objects changed involuntarily and independently from the experimenter's suggestion.

Participants' PERSIM objects meet all of these criteria. As the study reported in the previous chapter showed, *participants believed that their PERSIM objects (their future lives) could be affected by a magic spell, because they unanimously rejected the undesirable spell and acknowledged that the spell might actually work on their lives;* this meets the first of the aforementioned criteria. The study also showed that magical suggestion produces a predictable pattern of results based on participation: the subjects believed the possibility that the bad spell might affect their future lives while being aware at the same time that such belief was irrational and untrue, which meets the second criterion. Indeed, by saying in the "no personal involvement" condition that a rational person should disregard such belief and allow the mean spell to be cast, in the "personal involvement" condition the same participants took this belief on board and prohibited the spell. Finally, because PERSIM objects are not arbitrary but are anchored in participants' lives, participants are in full control of their reactions in regard to these objects, and this meets the third of the aforementioned criteria.

On these grounds, in Experiment 2 of this study, adult participants' PERSIM objects were targeted by magical and ordinary suggestion. The *magical suggestion condition* in this experiment involved a witch putting a good or a mean spell on the participant's future life and was identical to the one in the study reported earlier (see Chapter 8). In the *ordinary suggestion condition,* participants were shown a numeric pattern consisting of a row of either six or three ones on a laptop screen. It was suggested to them that if the experimenter decreased (changing 111111 to 111) or increased (changing 111 to 111111) a number of ones on a computer screen, their future lives would be affected in a desirable (half of the problems in their future life would disappear) or undesirable (the number of their future problems would double) way, respectively. Note that the numeric pattern employed here was just a row of ones and had nothing to do with the ancient practice of numerology, which assigned magical powers to certain combinations of numbers.[3]

In terms of the examined hypotheses, it was expected that in the magical suggestion condition, participants' reactions would conform to the pattern based on participation (see Chapter 8). In response to the good spell (the *desirable outcome trial*), participants' motivations would be mixed. On one hand, participants would be tempted to allow the experimenter to cast the good spell in order to comply with the experimenter's request and/or benefit from the spell. On the other hand, they may have been unwilling to interfere with magical forces on the basis that there may have been a price to pay. In this trial, the proportion of participants responding "yes" and "no" would be equal.[4]

In response to the mean spell (the *undesirable outcome trial*), the expectation was that the number of participants rejecting this offer would be significantly above 50%. The motivation for not allowing the spell would increase because the balance between the positive and negative poles of the motivational spectrum would be broken: the opportunity to benefit from the spell would no longer exist while the fear that the mean spell could actually affect the participants' futures in an undesirable way would add to the negative pole.

Of particular importance was to find out how participants would react in the ordinary suggestion condition. If their responses were based on the mechanism of rationality, this type of suggestion should produce results as in the no personal involvement condition of the earlier experiment (see Chapter 8), in which participants responded "yes" and "no" about equally in both the desirable and undesirable outcome trials. Indeed, if participants treated ordinary suggestion in a rational and logical way, they would realize that changing a numerical pattern on a computer screen has no causal relation to their futures. They would therefore have a mixture of motives to say "yes" and "no" to both outcomes. For example, certain participants might respond with a "yes" to the undesirable outcome in order to comply with the experimenter's request or to show that they did not believe that the suggested effect might come true. Other participants might respond with a "no" to the desirable outcome on the grounds that there was no reason to do something that cannot possibly have any effect.

If, however, ordinary suggestion were based on participation, the pattern of participants' answers would be as in the magical suggestion condition: in the desirable outcome trial, participants would say "no" 50% of the time. In the undesirable outcome trial, the frequency of "no" responses would be significantly above 50% and significantly higher than in the desirable outcome trial.

Results of this experiment showed that 38 out of 40 (95%) answers to the question about whether changing a pattern on a computer screen would affect participants' future lives were "no." This indicates that participants were explicitly aware that there was no causal connection between the changing of a numerical pattern on a computer screen and their futures. Yet, in their behavioral responses,[5] participants demonstrated the same pattern of behavior as the one they showed in the magical suggestion condition: in the desirable outcome trial, the number of participants who allowed and did not allow the change on the screen to be made was distributed equally, whereas in the undesirable outcome trial, the number of participants who prohibited the change was at a level significantly above 50% (see Figure 9.3).

Reasons that participants gave for their "no" responses with regard to the suggestion with the undesirable outcome were similar to those given in the magical suggestion condition: 15 out of 16 participants who said "no" to the

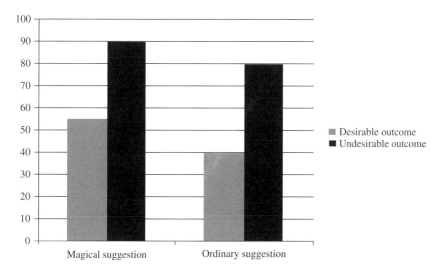

FIGURE 9.3. Percent of participants who said "no" to the suggested offer as a function of the type of suggestion (magical versus ordinary) and type of outcome (desirable versus undesirable).

offer of increasing the number on the screen justified their responses by suggesting that this action might in fact increase the number of problems in their lives. In contradiction with themselves, when asked a more general question of whether they thought that changing the pattern on the screen would have any effect on their future lives, only one of these participants also said "yes," with the rest 14 participants being sure that the manipulation, if performed, would not change anything in their lives. This indicated that participants were aware of the contradiction between their conscious beliefs (changing the pattern on the screen would change nothing) and their sub-conscious beliefs (changing the pattern on the screen could change their lives), yet this awareness did not affect their actions. Despite the fact that participants' actions represented their own free choices, they conformed to their subconscious beliefs and not to their conscious beliefs.

The results of this experiment further support the hypothesis that ordinary suggestion meets both criteria of participation: (*1*) individuals act in accord with the suggested idea (that changing a numeric pattern on the screen will change their future lives) and (2) they are conscious that the idea is wrong. Altogether, the results confirm the hypothesis that ordinary suggestion, like magical suggestion, is based on participation and not on rationality. These results have implications for our understanding of the role that magical thinking plays in Western societies today.

THE MAGIC OF TODAY: COMMUNICATIVE MAGIC AND INDIRECT PERSUASION TECHNIQUES

As argued in the previous chapters, beliefs in magic and everyday super-stitions are still common (Jahoda, 1969; Vyse, 1997). In psychological research, it has been shown that in certain domains, sympathetic magical thinking operates on the basis of laws of contagion ("once in contact, always in contact") and similarity ("the image equals the object") (Frazer, 1923; Nemeroff & Rozin, 2000). The results of the study reviewed previously in this chapter imply that *effects of participation-based thinking in modern societies may go beyond these special phenomena, to include one of the most powerful tools of modern mass communication—suggestion and indirect persuasion.*

For example, Petty and Cacioppo (1986) distinguished between the two "routes" to persuasion. The *central route* implies conscious consideration of the arguments: the receiver finds the message persuasive if he or she finds the rational arguments of this message to be solid and grounded. In contrast, the *peripheral route* to persuasion occurs when the listener relies on cues other than the strength of the rational argument, for example, when he or she finds the source of the message attractive. Although the authors do not refer to the concept of participation in regard to the peripheral route to persuasion, the parallel between this route and the participation-based suggestion is obvious. As one of the aforementioned experiments has shown, even when participants were rationally convinced that changing a numeric pattern on the computer screen would not affect their future lives, subconsciously they still believed that it would and prohibited this change from being made, thus revealing their participation with the experimenter's message.

In his classic book on influence, Cialdini (2007) explores various psycho-logical mechanisms that evoke compliance via the peripheral route, such as the rule of reciprocation, the attractiveness of the source of influence, its similarity with the target of influence, and others. He describes the case of an 11-year-old boy who persuaded him to buy two unwanted $1 chocolate bars after the man had declined to buy a $5 ticket to the annual Boy Scout circus. Although Cialdini does not employ such terms as participation and magical thinking, his example is a clear case of participation-based behavior. Indeed, the interests of the man (not to buy the chocolate bars that he did not like) and the boy (that the man buy the chocolate bars) were incompatible and in fact directly opposed. Suddenly the man gives up his interest and does what the boy wants him to do (criterion 1 of the participation), while realizing at the same time that what he is doing is not to his benefit (criterion 2 of the participation). But what could make an intelligent and educated adult suc-cumb to the request of a child during this casual interaction in the street?

Certainly it was not the boy who made the man comply—but if it was not the boy, then what was it? It was the way that the Boy Scout put his request: he framed his request (that the man purchase the chocolate bars) in the form of a concession on his part. The purchase was presented as a retreat from his initial request that the man buy (more expensive) tickets to the circus show. "It was a classic example of how a weapon of automatic influence can infuse a compliance request with its power. I had been moved to buy something not because of any favorable feelings toward the item, but because the purchase request had been presented in a way that drew force from the reciprocity rule" (Cialdini, 2007, p. 37). In other words, according to Cialdini, the "refuse then reciprocate" rule is one of the mechanisms developed by society to make people reciprocate to a concession, because such behavior benefits the society. It was not the boy, but the powerful demand of society built into the man's mind that made him comply. Research has confirmed that the "reciprocate to a concession" rule is indeed a reliable predictor of an individual's behavior (Cialdini, 2007).

One might ask what this has to do with magical thinking. The answer rests in the historic origins of this kind of participation-based "module" in our social minds. Indeed, suppose that in early humans, such mechanisms as reciprocation to a concession were absent. How, then, could society make a person do something that the person did not want to do—and do it willingly? We need to bear in mind that in early human groups, there were no police or other external social incentives to maintain surveillance and control over individuals' behavior. One possible way to compel people to follow certain rules was to claim that such rules had divine origin. For example, a person was made to believe that if he or she did not reciprocate to a concession, this would enrage ancestral spirits who would then exact punishment. Presenting this rule as a command from the gods would sanction the rule by the gods' magical power, such as the power to see into people's minds and supervise their everyday behavior. Through time, *the rule's "magical masters" were abandoned and replaced with a secular term, "society." Yet the rule's mind-over-mind magic mechanism—participation—has remained in people's subconscious.*

Do we have any evidence for this idea? Yes, we do. In the Judeo-Christian cultural tradition, Moses accepted the code of our modern moral rules directly from God, yet today we view these rules (the Ten Commandments) not as divinely given, but as a set of useful conventions worked out by our societies. More evidence comes from the history of political power. Early forms of political control relied on magical beliefs (Frazer, 1923; Jaynes, 1976; Lévy-Brühl, 1985; Malinowski, 1935; Tambiah, 1990). For instance, in Egypt the power of the pharaoh took its legitimacy from the mass belief in the pharaoh's divine origins. In the common view today, in modern industrial societies political power (at least as it is presented by its ideologists) is based on rationally controlled electoral processes, and not on magical beliefs. Nevertheless, psychological mechanisms that make many people collaborate with the political power retain features of worshiping the gods. For example, in World War II Germany, many people collaborated with the Nazi regime willingly and even in circumstances under which there was no prospect of retaliation for disobedience (Fromm, 1941, 1961). The god-like figure of Stalin in school textbooks is still before my eyes. When I was 6 (it was in 1954), I remember discussing with other children the issue of whether Stalin had to go to the toilet, and most of us were of the opinion that he did not. In the democratic electoral process today, "elections are won and lost not primarily on 'the issues' but on the values and emotions of the electorate, including the 'gut feelings'" (Westen, 2007, p. 423). Furthering his "emotional-based" account of the political persuasion technique, Westen writes, "Campaigns ... are won by candidates who can convince voters, through their words, intonation, body language and actions that they share their values, that they understand people like them, and that they can inspire the nation or save it from danger" (p. 430).

An example of emotion-based political persuasion can be found in recent Russian history. According to Russian sociologist Kara-Murza (2007, p. 4):

> The campaign of manipulation with mass consciousness carried out in the USSR was exceptionally effective. Thus, just for two years (from 1989 to 1991) the ideologists of a free market economy have managed to sell the workers the idea that privatization of plants and factories and the inevitable unemployment that accompanies this process are in their own interests. This was an outstanding achievement of manipulative technology, given that for these two years the workers received no experience whatsoever that could persuade them in the benefits of privatization and unemployment, and were not given a single logical proof or a commonsense reason for this. All was achieved by suggestion.

Of course, some would argue that reducing the Russian revolution of 1989–1991 to suggestion is an oversimplification; in reality, the collapse of the Soviet Union happened due to the ineffectiveness of the socialist economy and various chronic shortages of goods and services. Nevertheless, for many years since it has become clear to the people of Russia that the average standard of living for most of the population in 1989–1991 plummeted and the mortality rate increased. The fact that there has been no single major revolt against the "velvet revolution" (compare this situation with the massive civil war that the revolution of 1917 in Russia had launched) testifies that the "suggestion explanation" of this revolution is at least partially true. In addition, research has shown that when a society is in crisis, which is the case with modern Russia, magical beliefs increase (Subbotsky & Trommsdorff, 1991). If we accept the idea that magical and ordinary types of suggestion are based on the same psychological mechanism (participation) and target people's PERSIM objects, then suggestive persuasion techniques used in political rhetoric today could be viewed as historically evolving from magical practices.

One more example of participation-based techniques today is psychotherapy. The founder of modern psychotherapy began his career as a hypnotherapist, but then broke away from hypnosis because it reminded him of magical conjuring (Freud, 1935, p. 391). However, Freud later had to acknowledge that psychoanalysis had abandoned hypnosis only to start using suggestion again, this time in the shape of transference (ibid, p. 388).[6] At about the same time, Coriat (1923) argued that psychotherapeutic techniques were based on magical thinking, using suggestion as a form of medical magic. Following the same logic, a modern author links explanations used in psychoanalysis to "beliefs related to witchcraft" (Wolpert, 2006, p.181). Psychologically, these techniques rely on the individuals' tendency to involuntarily accept messages that they rationally might find unacceptable.[7] The psychological mechanism of participation can account for the empirical fact that in many cases these persuasion techniques work: in high-cost conditions, suggesting certain ideas to people with regard to their PERSIM objects is enough to make many people uncritical, and contrary to rational evidence embrace these ideas and act accordingly (see Singer et al., 1986).

Perhaps the most striking example of participation-based suggestion comes from the famous study on "obedience to authority" (Milgram, 1992). In this study, participants were aware that what they were asked to do (giving an anonymous "learner" electric shocks of increasing intensity) was wrong and against their conscious intention, and that defying the experimenter's demand to go on would not endanger their lives or well-being. Yet, in the "voice feedback" condition, 62% of participants followed the experimenter's suggestion to continue the electric shocks up to the highest level of 450 volts. It was obvious that, from a certain moment of this experiment, the participants' behavior was not a consensual cooperation with the experimenter, and not obedience to an unlimited and overwhelming power of authority. Rather, it was a clear case of participation. Many participants displayed tension and a dissociation between word and action—a key feature of the participation-based pattern of behavior. Just in accord with the original definition of participation in terms of shared or blended "essence," in Milgram's experiment the participants shared (or blended with) the "essence" of the suggested message (to keep increasing the shock's intensity) even though they viewed this message as wrong and harmful to both the "learners" and their own morality. To put it in Milgram's own words, "...something akin to fields of force, diminishing in effectiveness with increasing psychological distance from their source, have a controlling effect on the subject's performance" (Milgram, 1992, p. 147).

As in the case of the "reciprocation to a concession" mechanism, the "obedience to authority" mechanism could have originally been shaped as obedience to divine magical powers—gods and spirits. In earlier times, obedience must have been unconditional, because gods' orders could not be questioned on their rightness. Over the course of history, the role of the power that expects obedience shifted from gods to secular members of society (a doctor, a psychology experimenter, a political leader) whose orders can be questioned, yet frequently they are not because the participation mechanism that underlies mind-over-mind magic is still at work. To cite Cialdini (2007, pp. 217–218) once again, in the Old Testament we read

> what might be the closest biblical representation of the Milgram's experiment—the respectful account of Abraham's willingness to plunge a dagger through the heart of his young son, because God, without any explanation, ordered it. We learn in this story that the correctness of an action was not adjudged by such considerations as apparent senselessness, harmfulness, injustice or usual moral standards, but by the mere command of a higher authority. Abraham's tormented ordeal was a test of obedience, and he—like Milgram's subjects, who perhaps learned an early lesson from him—passed.

One can assume on this ground that the gap between the "primitive" (traditional, magical, religious) type of thinking and today's logical thinking (Frazer, 1923; Lévy-Brühl, 1966, 1984; Luria, 1931, 1971, 1976) may have been exaggerated. Recent studies have shown that under certain conditions, traditional and Western participants behave in similar ways, displaying either a magical (Subbotsky & Quinteros, 2002) or a logical-analytical (Cole, 1996; Harris, 2000; Mead, 1932) mode of thought. The study reviewed earlier in this chapter showed that the similarities between traditional and Western types of thinking include the fundamental psychological mechanism of suggestion and indirect persuasion—participation.

In the previous chapters, I argued that one way through which noninstitutionalized magical beliefs (NIMBs) can survive under the pressure of science and religion in the modern world is to go into the domain of the subconscious. The study reviewed in this chapter suggests another way for NIMBs to survive: *communicative magic survives through dropping its "old skin" (association with the magical power of gods and ancestral spirits) and taking on a "new skin" (association with the powers of society, evolution, and natural selection). Stripped of its original sacred context and renamed as suggestibility, compliance, and obedience, modern people's vulnerability toward communicative magic survives in societies that otherwise strictly adhere to science and rational logic.* Viewed in this light, suggestion is literally the magic of today.

10

Magical Beliefs and Psychological Defense

As I will argue in Chapter 11, magical thinking and behavior perform many positive functions. One function can be easily misused, however, and this is *bonding* through participation. On the one hand, this function of magical thinking benefits society and individuals, giving a sense of unity. In most tribal mythologies, people are believed to originate from a common (usually animal) ancestor, a totem (Frazer, 1923; Lévy-Brühl, 1966), and in modern religious traditions, such as Judaism, Christianity, and Islam, believers are united by their sacred relation to God. On the other hand, as argued in the previous chapter, participation can also be used for manipulation of people's minds in the interest not of the people themselves but of other powerful individuals and companies, the object of which is to obtain psychological, political, or economic profit. Commercial advertising, political rhetoric, intrusive psychotherapies, controversial religious cults, and fake magical healers exploit mechanisms of magical thinking in order to solicit suggestibility, compliance, and obedience in individuals to serve their own goals. Those goals are not always beneficial or even safe for the individuals who are being manipulated. It is not surprising, therefore, that a psychological defense mechanism should exist that protects people against exploitative suggestion techniques. And indeed, research has shown that although suggestive messages in politics and economics are an everyday occurrence in the world of mass media, they do not always work, and individual differences in people's sensitivities to suggestion and persuasion are great (Kisch & Braffman, 2001).

Dealing with psychological defenses is typical in psychotherapy (Eriksen, Nordby, Olff, & Ursin, 2000; Punamäki, Kanninen, Qouta, & El-Sarraj, 2002). Freud (1976) was one of the first to introduce the concept of the psychological defense mechanism. He argued that overcoming patients' resistance is key to successful psychoanalytic treatment. According to Freud, the cause of resistance to psychoanalytic interpretation of a patient's problem rests in the patient's subconscious and suppressed fears and desires. "A violent opposition must have started against the entry into consciousness of the questionable mental process, and for that reason it remained unconscious.... This same opposition, during psychoanalytic treatment, sets itself up once more against our effort to transform what is unconscious into what is conscious. This is what we perceive as resistance" (Freud, 1976, p. 335). Because of this subconscious resistance, patients emotionally reject the psychoanalytic interpretation of their symptoms, even if accepting this interpretation superficially, and this makes the treatment powerless.

Although the mental processes that Freud referred to were desires of a predominantly sexual nature, his model can be used to understand certain aspects of our modern attitude toward magical reality. *As hypothesized in Chapter 1, as with certain aspects of human sexuality, in the Western cultural tradition noninstitutionalized beliefs in magic are repressed and ousted into the domain of the subconscious.*

ALLIANCE AGAINST MAGIC: SCIENCE AND RELIGION

As I have argued before, one force that executes the repression of noninstitutionalized beliefs in magic is *science*. Studies reviewed in Chapters 2 and 3 have shown that in childhood, magical beliefs are entrenched and coexist with rational beliefs in children's verbal judgments and nonverbal behavior. Later, at school age, they gradually disappear from older children's verbal reasoning. However, under certain circumstances, these beliefs can be reactivated in older children and adults' reasoning and nonverbal behavior (Chapters 5 through 8). This supports the notion that magical beliefs share the fate of suppressed sexual desires. In older children and adults, they lurk in the area of the subconscious.

One can infer on this ground that when, in a psychological experiment, participants are shown phenomena that assert magical beliefs, these phenomena should elicit *resistance*. As with resistance to psychoanalytic interpretation of the causes of neurotic symptoms described by Freud, resistance to *magic is also a subconscious process.* The same force powers this resistance that earlier confined magical beliefs to the subconscious: the culturally adopted belief in the all-embracing power of physical causality. By exercising this subconscious resistance, people protect their solidarity with official scientific ideology. In this chapter, I refer to this mechanism as "psychological defense against magical intervention" (PDAMI). The defense that is powered by the belief in science is essentially of a cognitive nature: it aims to eliminate cognitive dissonance between contrasting causal beliefs (physical versus magical) that arise when a person is confronted with magical events or other unexplained and "paranormal" events, such as extrasensory perception. This *cognitive PDAMI* can be viewed as a special case of people's general strategy of reinterpreting anomalous events in order to make them fit with the existing cognitive framework (Chinn & Brewer, 1993).

Another force that confines magical beliefs to the domain of the subconscious is modern *religion*. In the Judeo-Christian tradition, magic is associated with dark forces and paganism. This attitude toward magic can hardly be illustrated better than by literary masterpieces such as Goethe's drama *Faust* and Thomas Mann's novel *Doctor Faustus*. With the devil's help, one can achieve the heights in art and science, yet one must pay for this with his or her immortal soul. In psychological research, it has been reported that some fundamentalist Christian parents exhibit negative attitudes about their children having imaginary companions (a form of imagination akin to magical thinking) because in their view imaginary companions are associated with the devil (Taylor & Carlson, 2000). Similarly, Clark (1995) reported that some fundamentalist Christian parents felt uneasy about their children's belief in Santa Claus, and one even pointed out that Santa was Satan with the letters changed. Some fundamentalists even see a danger in public elementary schools, because in their view the curriculum in such schools exposes children to dangerous ideas about witchcraft and the occult (Howse, 1993). Directly (through religious education) or indirectly (through fiction, movies, children's books, and other media), religion creates the fear of magic in many, even nonreligious, individuals. When in a psychological experiment a person is offered magical help, he or she can feel resistance toward the idea of accepting this help. Even if accepted, this help may elicit a subconscious fear that there might be a price to pay for magical services, and this may activate the PDAMI mechanism. Unlike the defense powered by science, which is essentially cognitive, the defense powered by religion is emotional. Cognitive dissonance that results from the confrontation between magic and science is uncomfortable but not dangerous. In contrast, emotional dissonance (between the desire to benefit and the fear to have to pay for this) that emerges if a person accepts magical help may produce the feeling of danger. I will refer to the defense mechanism that deals with this kind of dissonance as *emotional PDAMI.*

NOW IT'S THERE, NOW IT ISN'T: COGNITIVE DEFENSE AGAINST MAGICAL INTERVENTION

In order to examine the cognitive PDAMI hypothesis, study participants were presented with an effect that looked like a case of nonpermanence magic (see Chapter 1). They were familiarized with an apparently empty wooden box (as described in Chapter 2) and two objects: a postage stamp and a scrap of paper (Subbotsky, 1996). First, participants were asked to do a distracter task—to bring the experimenter a toy car from the other corner of the room—and then encouraged to place the postage stamp and the piece of paper into the box and close the lid. In about 5 seconds, participants were asked to open the box and remove the objects. Upon opening the box, they discovered that the postage stamp was still there, but the scrap of paper had disappeared (in another condition of this experiment, the scrap of paper was not available before, and appeared in the box "out of thin air"). They were then encouraged to examine the box as thoroughly as they could. After the examination had failed to reveal any mechanism behind the effect, participants were asked to report the order of the two events: their bringing the toy car from the corner of the room (the distracter event) and their placing the objects into the box. The aim of the experiment was to find out if participants would remember the order of the events incorrectly, by placing the distracter event in between the hiding of the objects in the box and the finding that one of the objects had vanished. By changing the order of the events in their memory, participants would be able to ignore the magical effect and reinterpret it as an ordinary effect (while the participant looked away in order to bring the toy, the experimenter removed the object from the box).

And indeed, in the "disappearance" condition, 75% of participants wrongly recollected the order of events, against 15% in the control condition in which no magical effect had happened (both objects that participants had placed in the box remained in the box) (see Figure 10.1). This, however, did not occur in the "appearance" condition, in which it was still possible to explain the magical effect as an ordinary one (by the fact that the extra object that appeared had been hidden in the box and the participants did not notice it on their first examination of the box).

The distortion of the order of events effect was replicated cross-culturally (Germany versus England), and it took place even if the participant was not actually performing the task but was only watching another participant doing it (see Figure 10.2).

Interestingly, the distortion of memory effect was not observed in 6-year-old children; in these children, 80% correctly remembered the order of events both in the disappearance and control conditions (Figure 10.3). This result could be expected on the base of Vygotsky's (1982) theory, according to

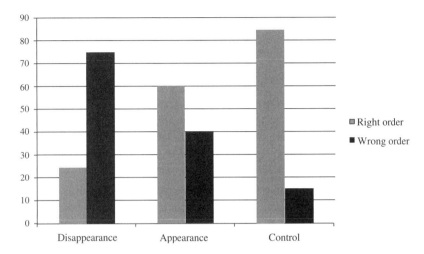

FIGURE 10.1. Percent of participants who recollected the right and wrong order of events as a function of condition.

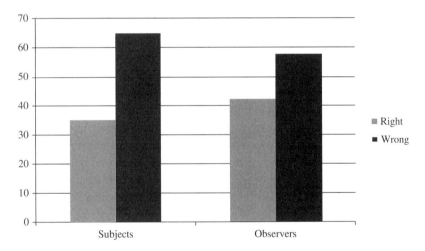

FIGURE 10.2. Percent of participants who recollected the right and wrong order of events as a function of a position in the experiment (subjects versus observers).

which the "power relations" between psychological functions, such as memory and thinking, change during development: whereas at early stages of development (early and preschool years) memory dominates over thinking and is essentially independent of thinking, in school years this relationship changes and thinking begins to dominate over memory. As Vygotsky puts it "for the child of an early age to think means to remember, while for an adolescent to remember means to think" (ibid, p.394). And indeed, as

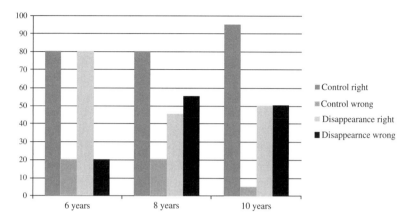

FIGURE 10.3. Percent of children who produced right and wrong recollections as a function of age and condition (disappearance versus control).

Figure 10.3 shows, in 8- and 10-year-old children, in the disappearance condition only about 50% of recollections were correct. This suggests that in children of these age groups, the PDAMI mechanism is already at work, even though it is not yet strong enough to move the number of wrong recollections significantly above chance, as happened in adults (Subbotsky, Chesnokova, & Greenfield, 2002). This explanation gets support from the study reviewed in Chapter 3. This study showed that in 6-year-olds, magical and physical causality coexist in balance, with neither of these alternative causal beliefs being entrenched. In contrast, in 9-year-olds, verbal belief in the universal power of physical causality becomes entrenched, whereas the belief in magic is no longer entrenched. This supports the notion that cognitive PDAMI is created by the pressure of scientific ideology. PDAMI is absent in 6-year-olds, where this pressure just about brings the magic/science rivalry into balance, and it appears in 8- and 10-year-olds, where the pressure of science education has already entrenched the belief in the universal power of physical causality. In adults, where this pressure achieves its peak, cognitive PDAMI is fully activated and changes participants' memories in order to make them fit the science framework.[1] The assumption that cognitive PDAMI works subconsciously gains credit from the fact that *the majority of adult participants who changed the order of events were surprised that they had done so, and refused to accept the real order when it was revealed to them.*

Cognitive PDAMI is, however, constrained by time. In another experiment of the aforementioned study (Subbotsky, 1996), the time between the magical effect and the distracter task was increased from 5 seconds to 30 seconds. After accepting the toy car from participants and placing it on the floor, the experimenter kept filling up a protocol for 25 seconds, and only after this did

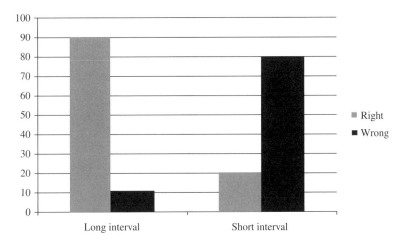

FIGURE 10.4. Percent of participants who produced right and wrong recollections of the events' order as a function of the interval (long versus short) between the distracter event (fetching a toy car) and hiding the objects in the box.

he ask the participants to put their objects into the box and close the lid (another 5 seconds). The increased interval proved enough to let the order of events consolidate in the participants' memory, and this eliminated the PDAMI effect (see Figure 10.4)

SEEING BAD DREAMS: MAGICAL INFLUENCE AND EMOTIONAL DEFENSE

The effect of emotional PDAMI has been examined in another study (Subbotsky, 2009a). In contrast to the aforementioned study in which magical effects happened to physical objects (pieces of paper) and did not have any relation to participants' personalities, in this study, participants had to handle magical effects that aimed to affect their subjective experiences, such as their practical skills, feeling of satisfaction with their lives, and dreams (communicative magic). Although these subjective experiences are not personally significant imagined (PERSIM) objects, they nevertheless are part of the participants' personality. When participants agree to allow magic to affect such experiences, they become personally and emotionally involved with magic. Such involvement with communicative magic may activate the emotional PDAMI mechanism.

As argued in previous chapters, there is evidence that mind-over-mind magic works in modern societies. As noted earlier, preschool children who were apparently "visited" by a novel fantastic entity, the Candy Witch, exhibited stronger beliefs in this entity's reality than did those who were not (Woolley, Boerger, & Markman, 2004). Undergraduates have also been shown to believe that fantastical objects could be magically transformed into other fantastical objects and that their PERSIM objects could be affected by magical and ordinary suggestive influences (Subbotsky, 2005, 2007). One more example of the mind-over-mind magic comes from research on religious thinking. In certain circumstances, individuals are likely to believe that their prayer can affect other people psychologically (Barrett, 2001). People who offer or seek magical healing are not a rarity in modern societies (Jahoda, 1969; Luhrman, 1989).

The issue that remains to be explored is whether participants who seek and accept magical help can indeed benefit from such interventions. It has been shown previously that undergraduates unanimously declined the offer of magical intervention when it was intended to produce undesirable effects. However, approximately 50% of undergraduates were ready to accept a positive magical intervention that aimed to improve their lives (see Chapters 8 and 9). In the aforementioned studies, magical intervention was presented as a hypothetical opportunity. *The question that remains unanswered is whether individuals would be prepared to accept the offer of positive magical intervention if this offer were real and not imaginary.*

One further issue is how those participants who accepted the offer of magical intervention would react if such magical intervention were indeed executed. Given that in most modern adults magical beliefs are confined to the subconscious, it is possible to predict that *a conscious acceptance of the offer of magical help will be accompanied with subconscious resistance to such help—the emotional PDAMI.* Such prediction becomes even more likely as the research discussed earlier shows that adult participants were generally anxious and fearful of suggestive magic, especially if this magic promised outcomes that participants viewed as undesirable (Subbotsky, 2001, 2005, 2007; Subbotsky & Quinteros, 2002).

In order to test the emotional PDAMI hypotheses, in Experiment 1 of this study, participants (graduate and undergraduate students) were invited to participate in the experiment on magical intervention that aimed to help them achieve their desired goals. First, participants were asked to select a practical task that they would like to improve on (writing essays, computer skills, speaking foreign languages, giving up bad habits such as smoking or nail biting, and so forth).

Next, the experimenter suggested that he could put a magic spell on the participant that might make the participant, in 2 weeks' time, experience an improvement in his or her chosen goal. Participants were then informed that they were free to decline the offer with no consequences to themselves or to the experiment. If participants agreed to accept the offer, they were invited to join the experimenter in placing their hands on the "magical object" (a nicely carved piece of wood with a distinctive pattern on it), and the experimenter, looking intently into the participant's eyes, pronounced out loud a series of nonwords that sounded like a magic spell.

In the control no-suggestion condition, following the questioning of participants concerning their practical goals and selecting a goal they would like to improve on, they were thanked and told, "It's nice to have goals." In addition, in two pretest interviews, participants were screened for their understanding of the difference between genuine and fake magic (as described in Chapter 5) and on their general levels of verbal magical beliefs.

In both conditions, participants were asked to contact the experimenter via e-mail 2 weeks after the initial interviews in order to assess their progress in achieving the chosen goals. Their responses were coded from 0 (no improvement) to 3 (improved a lot).

On the grounds discussed previously, we predicted that the participants would show a pattern of behavior based on PDAMI. Consciously, they would be skeptical toward the idea of the magic spell improving their skills, yet curious to experiment with magic, viewing it to be "a no-lose game" (see Chapters 7, 8, and 9). Subconsciously, they would believe that the magic spell could indeed help them improve on their selected goals and be fearful of indebting themselves to the unknown magical force. Although in the experiment the offer of magical help was presented as an altruistic exercise, participants might still be suspicious that the magician had some motive in the back of his mind that could be potentially undesirable to participants. *In order to protect themselves against this undesirable perspective, participants would have to invalidate the effect of the magical suggestion by systematically underestimating their achievements in the magical suggestion condition compared to those in the control condition in which no suggestion was made.*

The results supported the prediction. When offered a choice to withdraw from the experiment at no cost to them, 88% of participants opted to stay and said they were curious to see if the improvement would really happen. Yet in 2 weeks time, in the magical suggestion condition, a significantly larger number of participants reported having no progress at all than in the control condition, in which participants reported humble improvements that happened naturally.

One cannot explain this effect by the participants' trying to meet the expectations of the experimenter (the hope that they would improve on their goals). The "meeting expectations" explanation could explain overestimation of progress, but not underestimation. It is also not possible to account for this effect using differences in participants' magical beliefs, as participants' magical belief scores were approximately the same in both conditions. One more explanation for this effect is that participants were explicitly skeptical toward the idea that magical intervention could change their practical skills and therefore simply ignored the intervention. Although this possibility cannot be completely overruled, it is unlikely, because if it were true, the participants would have reported some naturally occurring improvement rather then denying any progress at all. Another possible strategy for participants who were skeptical toward magic would be systematically and consciously underestimating their improvement to demonstrate to the experimenter that the intervention did not work. But if this were the case, why would these participants accept the offer of magical intervention in the first place? Would it not be easier to demonstrate their skepticism by simply rejecting the offer of the magic spell?

These considerations gave credit to the original assumption that in the magical suggestion condition, participants would fear that there might be a price to pay for the magical help. By devaluing the effect of the magical intervention, participants made the imaginary "payment" redundant.

However, an explanation of the detrimental effect of magical intervention alternative to the one based on PDAMI is still possible. Despite explicitly denying their magical beliefs, subconsciously, participants believed that the magic spell would help them to achieve their chosen goals. Instead of producing fear of the magical intervention, the implicit belief in magic may have boosted the participants' expectations of their progress beyond a reasonable limit. As soon as the nature of subjective experience targeted in this experiment (improvement on practical skills) allowed participants to monitor whether the improvement had actually taken place in the following 2 weeks, the progress should have been less than expected with the assistance of magic. For instance, if the desired effect was to quit smoking, then in 2 weeks' time, participants would have hoped to have stopped completely, but in reality they may still smoke occasionally. When the miracle did not happen, participants were disappointed and, instead of appreciating the slight improvement that had occurred due to their own efforts, they reported no improvement at all.

In order to examine the alternative explanation, a subjective experience should be employed that does not allow a straight comparison between the expected and achieved effects. If the "inflated expectations and disappointment" explanation were correct (with other conditions being equal), participants would not exhibit the detrimental effect of magical suggestion on this kind of subjective experience. If, however, the PDAMI explanation were correct, the detrimental effect of magical intervention would be replicated with regard to the "feedback-free" subjective experience.

Accordingly, in Experiment 2 of this study, participants were asked to assess general satisfaction with their lives, on a scale between 0 (very dissatisfied) and 10 (very satisfied), with 5 meaning that they were neither satisfied nor dissatisfied. They were then offered a magic spell that aimed to increase their satisfaction in 2 weeks' time. Participants' satisfaction with their lives was selected because this type of subjective experience is relatively "feedback free" and does not necessarily reflect objective reality. For example, a person could feel significantly more or less satisfied with his or her life today than he or she felt yesterday simply because of a change in weather, mood, health, and other situational factors. This makes participants' estimates of satisfaction with their lives a type of subjective reality that is relatively independent of participants' objective achievements.

In this experiment, a large group of participants declined the offer of magical help, yet were still asked to report changes in 2 weeks' time.[2] The participants' estimates are shown in Figure 10.5.

As expected on the basis of the PDAMI hypothesis, in the magical suggestion condition, participants reported a significant deterioration in their satisfaction with their lives, and in the control no-suggestion condition the level of satisfaction did not change. Interestingly, participants who declined the offer of magical help reported a significant improvement in the feeling of satisfaction with their lives, and this is also in concordance with the PDAMI hypothesis: participants felt relief from the potential danger of being involved with the magical force, and this increased their feeling of satisfaction with their lives.

Finally, Experiment 3 explored the notion that the emotional PDAMI mechanism involved in Experiments 1 and 2 worked subconsciously.

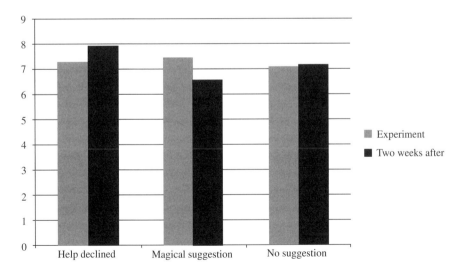

FIGURE 10.5. Mean scores that assessed participants' general satisfaction with their lives as a function of condition (help declined, magical suggestion, and no suggestion) and time (in the experiment and 2 weeks after).

Indeed, in Experiments 1 and 2 participants' conscious tampering with their assessments was still possible. In order to prove that participants' resistance to magical intervention was not an intended conscious action, a reality should be targeted that is unlikely to be intentionally "adjusted." Dreams are this kind of reality. On this ground, in Experiment 3, magical assistance aimed to help participants see their chosen dream.

Studies of dream content have shown that dreams can be influenced implicitly. Wearing red goggles just before sleep changed participants' subsequent dreams, filling them with red-tinted images (Roffwarg, Herman, Bowe-Anders, & Tauber, 1978). Explicit self-suggestion can also affect dreams. A conscious wish to change a personally relevant trait in a desired direction used as a presleep stimulus influenced dream content so that this quality appeared in dream characters (Cartwright, 1974). The effects that were demonstrated in participants' accounts of their dreams were achieved without the participants' awareness of these effects, as the participants had not been primed about the link between dream content and the presleep stimuli. In these experiments, as in Experiment 3 of this study, participants did not know (and were unlikely to guess) what dreams they were expected to see and, therefore, were unable to consciously "adjust" their dream reports.

If the detrimental effects of the magical interventions in Experiments 1 and 2 were a result of participants' conscious "adjustment" of their assessments to discount the effect of magical intervention, then in Experiment 3, this effect would show in participants' withholding their memories of having seen their target dreams in the magical suggestion condition, but not in the no-suggestion condition. This should result in participants' reporting seeing their target dreams in the magical suggestion condition significantly less frequently than in the no-suggestion condition.

However, if the detrimental effect was a result of the subconscious work of the mind, then the manifestations of this effect in this experiment could be twofold. First, this effect could reveal itself in the repression of memories concerning the target dreams seen in the magical suggestion condition. This would result in the same effect as the conscious manipulation of dream reports (in the magical suggestion condition, participants would report their target dreams significantly less frequently than in the no-suggestion condition, thus demonstrating that the magical help had no effect).

On the other hand, the subconsciously operating detrimental effect could also result in participants seeing or reporting undesirable bad dreams in the magical suggestion condition significantly more frequently than in the no-suggestion condition. *If participants subconsciously fear that magical intervention might indeed make them see their target dreams, and as a result want the intervention to fail, this may result in dreams that are at the opposite end of the scale from the target dreams—unwanted scary dreams.* Importantly, the latter effect, if it occurred, would be beyond participants' conscious control. Indeed, while withholding reports of seeing the target dreams in order to devalue a positive effect of magical intervention is a possible strategy, it is unlikely that participants would deliberately invent bad dreams to devalue the effect of white magic, for two reasons: (*1*) inventing bad dreams would mean deliberately telling lies, which most participants would not want to do, and (*2*) if participants consciously wanted to devalue the effect of magical suggestion, they had a simpler and more economical way to do so—by simply not reporting their target dreams in the magical suggestion condition, or reporting having seen no dreams at all.

First, participants were questioned about whether they ever dreamt and what dream they would like to have that night. In the magical suggestion condition, they were then offered a magic spell as in Experiment 2. This spell aimed to assist them in dreaming their chosen dream in the following 3 nights. Participants were given a standard printed form and asked to write their dreams on this form, which they were supposed to mail back to the experimenter. On this form, they were asked to report any dreams they had experienced during this period. In the no-suggestion condition, after participants chose the dreams they wanted to see, they were simply asked to report their dreams as in the magical suggestion condition.

The content of the dreams was coded into the following three categories: target dreams, scary dreams, and ordinary dreams. Target dreams were dreams that participants were set up for experiencing on the nights that followed the experiment. For example, if a participant wanted to see herself in the role of an Egyptian queen, then the target dream had to be the participant seeing herself in Egypt and being a queen. A dream was classified as a scary dream if a dreamer experienced personal danger or had a negative life-changing experience (such as having cancer, being pursued by predators, or being kicked out of school). Ordinary dreams were dreams that could be quite odd yet they reflected everyday life, family, or university events (a woman covering the carpet with cream and mud, two young boys misbehaving, a small town with a canal).

Two independent judges who were unaware of the purpose of this experiment and blind to each participant's condition (magical versus not) coded the responses. In addition, four more independent judges (two psychology graduates and two nonpsychologists) who were blind to the purpose of this study assessed the nontarget dreams on a scale from "very bad" (0) to "very nice" (6). Dreams were presented in random order.

It was expected that, if the detrimental effect of magical intervention were a result of participants' conscious tampering with their reports, in this experiment participants would report seeing their desired dreams in the magical suggestion condition less frequently than in the control condition. However, if the detrimental effect of magical intervention was the result of the PDAMI mechanism that works subconsciously, then in this experiment this mechanism would produce dreams that are at the opposite end of the scale from the desired dreams—unwanted scary dreams. Importantly, the latter effect, if it occurred, would be beyond participants' conscious control. The results (see Figure 10.6) favored the PDAMI explanation: in the magical suggestion condition, partici- pants reported seeing scary dreams significantly more frequently than in the no-suggestion condition. In addition, in the magical suggestion condition, nontarget dreams scored as significantly less pleasant than in the control condition. Interestingly, the frequency of the target dreams in the magical suggestion condition was about three times higher than that in the control condition, yet it failed to reach a significant level.

Altogether, the data showed that adult participants resisted the possibility of a positive magical intervention affecting their subjective experiences. This resistance took place regardless of the type of subjective experience targeted by magical intervention—consciously controlled (practical skills or general satisfaction with one's life) or not controlled (participants' dreams). The resistance showed that, despite the participants' declarations that they were nonbelievers in magic, magical suggestion affected their feelings and actions by switching on the PDAMI mechanism.

Indeed, if participants exclusively acted on the basis of their declared skepticism toward magic, they would simply remain indifferent to magical intervention. Instead, participants reported deterioration in their subjective

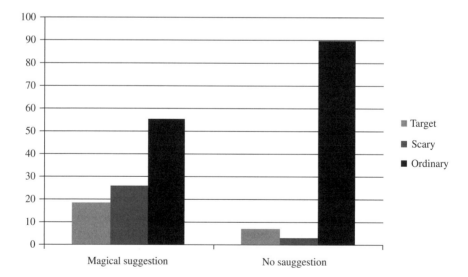

FIGURE 10.6. Percentage of dreams as a function of condition (magical suggestion versus no suggestion) and the dream type (target, scary, and ordinary).

experiences or having had subjective experiences that possessed qualities opposite to those the magical intervention was supposed to provide. This implies that participants considered the possibility of magical intervention affecting their subjective experiences as a threat—the kind of threat that required active suppression of changes, even those that happened naturally and independently of the magical help. Given that verbal tests on magical beliefs produced generally low scores, most participants were explicit non-believers in magic. Their behavior, however, suggested that explicit skepticism toward magic was paired with the subconscious belief that magical intervention could change their subjective experiences, and this activated the emotional PDAMI mechanism.

Interestingly, while in the studies reviewed in Chapters 5 through 9 adults' resistance to magical intervention was only evident in their reactions to the possibility of this intervention producing undesirable effects, in this study the resistance was revealed with regard to a positively aimed magical intervention. Indeed, a surprisingly large number of participants (62% to 88%, in various experiments) opted to accept the offer of magical intervention that aimed to assist them in attaining their chosen goals. This shows that consciously, participants were inclined to engage with white magic. Yet, most participants acted in a way that suggested the subconscious rejection of the magical help. While participants' rejection of magical intervention that promised outcomes undesirable to them was not surprising, their defensive reactions to positive magical intervention were more unexpected. These reactions show that *even if the outcome of magical intervention is desirable and participants consciously hope to benefit from such intervention, unconsciously they reject magical intervention by devaluating the results of such intervention.*

The results of Experiment 3 further support the assumption that the emotional PDAMI mechanism works subconsciously. Explicitly, participants merely reported dreams that they saw, yet the type of dreams they frequently saw in the magical suggestion condition were contrary to the one that the magical intervention was intended to make them see. Instead of seeing the suggested nice dreams, participants saw bad dreams. This result also suggests that in Experiments 1 and 2, participants' reports concerning their improvement were subjectively accurate as well. However, as in Experiment 3, these reports devalued the effects of magical intervention.

While the detrimental effect of positive magical intervention on participants' subjective experiences may be interpreted as the work of PDAMI, the proportion of participants who accepted the offer of magical intervention across various experiments depended on the magnitude of the benefit offered by magical intervention. When the benefit was large (changing participants' future lives for the better, making them "rich and happy") in the earlier hypothetical experiment (Subbotsky, 2005) and in the hypothetical situations of Experiments 1 and 2 of this study, only about 50% of participants were willing to accept the offer. When the benefit was small (helping participants to improve on certain skills or to see good dreams in the real-life situations of Experiments 1 and 3 of this study), the number of participants who accepted the offer was significantly above 50%. In other words, when the potential cost decreases, the number of those who accept the offer of positively aimed magical intervention increases. This result is in accord with results of the earlier reviewed study on people's curiosity toward magic, which showed that curiosity increases when the cost of exploration decreases (Chapter 7).

As the study reviewed earlier in this chapter showed, cognitive PDAMI was not found in 6-year-olds, and it gradually builds up in older children and adults. It will be important in further research to examine whether the emotional PDAMI mechanism follows the same developmental pattern. It may also be the case that in cultures that are more tolerant to magic, participants will be more likely to react to positive magical intervention in a more inviting way. In Western countries, the emotional PDAMI mechanism can serve as a psychological shield against misuses of magical intervention or similar types of suggestive influence (such as controversial religious practices, fake magical healers and fortune tellers, unconventional medicine, and manipulative psychotherapies). In other words, *the emotional PDAMI mechanism is a counterweight to the participation-based communicative magic.*

A challenging task would be to investigate under what conditions the emotional PDAMI mechanism can be *deactivated.* Such deactivation or partial relaxation of psychological defense is necessary for participation to work. One striking example of inactivity of the PDAMI mechanism is the fate of the members of the People's Temple—a cult organization that began in the United States and moved to the jungle in Guyana, South America. Around a thousand members obeyed the order of their spiritual leader Jim Jones and willfully poisoned themselves to death, with only a few escaping. Among other social and psychological factors that made this collective suicide possible, Cialdini (2007) names *the feeling of uncertainty* that resulted from moving into a hostile and unknown environment. The fact that uncertainty can deactivate PDAMI also follows from studies showing an increased tolerance of magical beliefs in situations of stress and danger (Keinan, 1994). Similarly, in the studies reviewed in Chapters 8 and 9, adult participants became more likely to explicitly acknowledge that magic is real when their PERSIM objects were put at risk.

Another condition that might work toward the relaxation of PDAMI is a *conscious belief in magic.* In this regard, it would be interesting to study the work of PDAMI in certain clinical populations, such as those with schizophrenia. Given that participants in these populations have generally been found to be stronger believers in magic than either control participants or patients with other psychiatric disorders (George & Neufeld, 1987), it might be expected that these participants' protective mechanisms would be weakened or deactivated. This would make these participants more receptive to positive magical intervention than were participants in the aforementioned study, who were explicit nonbelievers in magic.

To summarize, when faced with magical events, adult participants tend to show defensive strategies—PDAMI. In the case of cognitive defense, the driving force is participants' desire to stay in line with the official scientific ideology. In contrast, the emotional defense is powered by subconscious fear, created by religious education, that magic, even if well intended, harbors hidden dangers. As PDAMI works subconsciously, participants are not aware of it. Altogether, the data show that the attitude toward magic in modern educated participants is complex and ambivalent. Many of them are curious enough to experiment with magic, and yet anxious about the possibility that this experimentation could involve them with forces that are unpredictable and potentially dangerous.

Magical Thinking and the Mind

In the previous chapters, I reviewed various aspects of magical thinking and magical behavior. It is time now to take a broader look at what place magical thinking occupies in the whole of an individual's mind, particularly in relation to scientific and religious thinking. This, however, necessitates some clarification of what the human mind is.

As I have posited in the past (Subbotsky, 1993), two perspectives on the human mind exist in psychology: the explanatory and the phenomenological. The explanatory perspective defines the mind through more specific concepts, such as "collective representations"—socially and historically determined views about the world (Frazer, 1923; Lévy-Brühl, 1966; Tambiah, 1990). Others upgrade this view by distinguishing between areas in the mind that are socially determined (such as scientific theories) and those that are relatively independent from social and cultural factors (such as intuitive "folk" theories and innate "modules") (Boyer, 1994; Carey, 1999; Fodor, 1988; Gopnik & Wellman, 1992; Keil, 1989; Leslie, 1986; Sperber, 1997).

Another way of defining the human mind is to present it either as a complex computational system capable of receiving, storing, and transforming information (Jackendoff, 1987) or as a product of functioning neural networks in the brain: "The consensus today among neuroscientists and philosophers is that mind is an emergent property of brain function. That is, what we refer to as the mind is a natural consequence of complex and higher neural processing" (Dowling, 1998, p.4). Advancing the information-processing approach, Dennett rejected the Cartesian theater model, which states that the human mind has a central meaner, or "I"; he replaced this idea with the multiple drafts model, in which the mind consists of multiple channels working in parallel that are promoted "by the activity of a virtual machine in the brain" (Dennett, 1991, p. 254).

Yet the explanatory-analytical model is only one of the possible ways of viewing the individual mind. Another way is to approach the mind as a phenomenon. Indeed, in contrast to such concepts as society, history, brain, and other objects of science, the mind is presented to the individual directly in self-reflection. Taken in this phenomenalistic-descriptive perspective, the individual mind loses its static and conceptual form, but is presented in all its complexity and dynamism as a "live entity." According to Husserl, after the whole reality of the mind is reduced to the sheer "cogitatum," we still have much of what we had before: we experience (perceive) things and processes; we give meanings to them; we judge, evaluate, and decide; we set ends and willing means; and we imagine and fantasize (Husserl, 1960). This living mind allows one to approach the world with a view that is less biased by historical traditions or dominant paradigms. As with the explanatory-analytical perspective, the phenomenalistic-descriptive perspective is limited and insufficient in itself; yet the latter may illuminate the aspects within the individual mind that are not sufficiently covered by the former.

René Descartes (1988) most clearly outlined the phenomenalistic-descriptive view of the mind. William James (1980, Ch. XXI) also presented the mind as a flow of consciousness, which is accessible to an individual through self-reflection. He described the structural elements of the mind as including different realities, contrasting the reality of ordinary objects to the reality of fantasies and dreams. Still, James left open the question of how the mind relates to other psychological functions such as thinking, perception, and memory. One might wonder whether the mind is a mere sum of these functions, or if instead it is a separate entity that exists independently and alongside other psychological processes. The view of the mind as a sum of psychological functions prevails in contemporary psychology: "Nowadays...every general psychology text has chapters or larger divisions on specific topics, for example, perception, emotion, learning and thought. These, by and large, are a reflection of the currently held view of the structure of the mind" (Plotkin, 1998, p. 122).

Challenging this view of the mind as a sum of psychological functions, I have attempted to show that the mind of an individual, though tightly linked to other psychological functions, nevertheless is a separate entity with a *structure* and a *function* of its own (Subbotsky, 1992). I have also argued that constituent components of the mind's structure are not psychological functions, like intelligence, perception, or memory, but *domains of reality*, which include psychological functions as their subordinate elements.

I have also presented an argument against the view that the development of the individual mind occurs as the immature mind of an infant is progressively replaced by the rational mind of an adult (Piaget, 1971). In contrast to this, I have argued that (*1*) rational and irrational types of realities coexist in the individual mind at all times during development, and (*2*) development occurs as a growing differentiation and specialization of alternative realities within the individual mind. I will briefly repeat this argument here and then proceed to analyzing the role that magical thinking plays in the general economy of the mind.

TWO REALITIES: THE STRUCTURE OF THE MIND

Various phenomenological analyses, such as those of Descartes or James, share the idea that the mind consists of separate and different domains or realities. The most impressive of these domains is the domain of *ordinary reality*.[1] We enter this domain with the sound of the alarm clock. The reality we experienced before waking was a different kind of reality—a weird and unstable reality of dreams. In the reality of dreams, time can run backward, people can go through solid walls, and animals can talk. Returning to the domain of ordinary reality, we indeed find ourselves in a flow of time that carries us from our past into our future. Yet even here, in the waking state, we often fall into another world that is different from the world of ordinary reality: this world is a creation of fantasy, imaginary pretend play, fairy tales, and art.

Taken in the most global terms, *magical reality* (the reality that emerges in dreams, fairy tales, fantasy, and art) differs from ordinary reality in some important characteristics. First, within magical reality, laws that govern the physical world of ordinary reality can be violated. These laws include the irreversibility of time, the permanence of physical objects, the impermeability of solid objects for other solid objects (a fundamental requirement for the existence of physical space), and physical causality. Second, within magical reality, the lines between animate and inanimate objects or natural and social worlds become blurred. In this reality, inanimate objects acquire the capacity for thinking and feeling and animals can speak human languages. Finally, within magical reality, the inseparable bond between mind and body no longer exists and ghosts and spirits—refugees of ordinary reality—acquire the right of abode.

Dividing the whole reality of the mind into ordinary and magical domains is not an arbitrary assumption. What I would like to emphasize is that the mind necessarily contains these domains. *Ordinary and magical realities are conceptual opposites that condition each other.* Whenever we think of physical causality, we inevitably think about the possibility of its violation, and this is magical causality. Similarly, thinking of physical space, time and object permanence has its necessary extension in thinking of magical space, time, and nonpermanent objects. *Just as the human brain is not a single sphere but consists of two hemispheres, the mind consists of ordinary and magical realities.*

In today's science-biased view, magical (religious) reality derives from ordinary reality. According to this view, magical/religious reality evolved from ordinary reality through the mechanisms of biological and social adaptation and selection (Bering, 2006b; Boyer & Bergstrom, 2008). This view would imply that, at a certain time in human history, and in child development, magical reality was absent and ordinary reality reigned unrestricted. Taking this view creates some problems for explaining the phenomenon of magical reality and its genesis.

One of these emerging problems, for instance, is the issue of why we should feel real emotions while engaged in the world of fiction. If we accept a science-biased standpoint that imaginary (magical) reality is derived from ordinary reality in the course of individual and evolutionary development, then a special cognitive mechanism in the brain (such as the "appraisal mechanism") has to be postulated to exist in order to explain this phenomenon (Harris, 2000). Another problem is why "all versions of religion are based on very similar tacit assumptions" (Boyer, 2008, p. 1039). The science-biased approach would have to explain similarities in religious and magical experiences across the world by locating them within a set of certain universal "core" human abilities. These abilities include "natural" cognitive mechanisms and predispositions, such as animism, the phenomenon of imaginary companions, theory of mind, the tendency toward ritualized behavior, children's early intuitions of moral behavior, and other mechanisms of memory, perception, and thinking.

The assumption of multiple realities eliminates these problems. On this assumption, the magical reality of the mind is as "natural" to the mind as ordinary reality, and coexists with ordinary reality at all times of cultural and individual development. It is therefore natural to feel real emotions when engaged in magical thinking or behavior, and it is also natural for magical and religious thinking to be based on similar mechanisms and assumptions across cultures, not because genes are "the same," but because the reality is the same.

Other problems discussed in research would, however, remain important, such as the problem of "how impenetrable is the barrier between the different mental spheres: the sphere of mundane reality where ordinary causal principles hold sway, and the world of fantasy and metaphysics, where the impossible can

TABLE 11–1. Types of Activity of the Mind

LEVELS OF ACTIVITY	DOMAINS OF REALITY	
	ORDINARY REALITY	MAGICAL REALITY
Involved	Action	Hallucination
		Night dream
Uninvolved	Planning	Magical fantasy

happen" (Harris, 2000, p. 173). The assumption of multiple realities would also create new problems for developmental analysis, such as what the architecture and functions of magical reality are, and how the ontological hierarchy emerges between the realities in the course of development.

Orthogonal to the division between ordinary and magical realities is the distinction between two different levels of the individual mind's activity. At the *involved level,* our mind functions when it deals with objects of vital value, such as passing an important examination. This means that the well-being of our mind, and even its very existence, may depend on the results of this activity. At this level, an action of our mind is usually irreversible and we are aware of both great responsibility and strong motivation for success. In contrast to this, at the *uninvolved level,* our mind deals with objects that are not directly linked to our basic needs. Although our motivation of actions on this level can be rather strong (for instance, when reading an exciting novel or watching a movie), the results of these actions can never be of vital value and, in most cases, are reversible. In social psychology, the division between uninvolved and involved levels of functioning is reflected in the distinction between attitudes and behavior (Thomas, 1971).

The crossing between domains of realities and levels of the mind's activity is presented schematically in Table 11.1.

FUNCTIONS OF MAGICAL REALITY

As soon as the main domain of reality is made synonymous with life itself, it has no function. In the modern Western tradition, this is the domain of ordinary reality.[2] The only aim of the individual within ordinary reality is living, creating, and pursuing goals, and thus increasing the order and harmony of his or her mind. In contrast, being a subordinate reality, magical reality acquires its functions in relation to the main domain of reality— ordinary reality.

The first and most frequently discussed function of the magical reality is the *realization of unrealized wishes*. Thus, according to Freud (1976), a significant part of the individual's vital needs cannot find legitimate gratification within ordinary reality due to its rigid structure and multiple taboos. Since magical reality is free from these limitations, unrealized wishes find their outlet there. In our dreams, we can see and speak to our dear ones who have passed away, fly, or be young again.

A special sensitivity of magical reality to the individual's suppressed needs also creates the second function, *expressive function*. This function was first appreciated in psychoanalysis through interpretation of dreams and neurotic fantasies, and later laid the foundation for projective techniques, such as free association, inkblot tests, the Thematic Apperception Test, and others (Flanagan, 1995; Freud, 1995).

The third *creative function* of magical reality is based on the notion that magical reality allows unusual counterfactual and counterintuitive combinations of structures and events that cannot happen within ordinary reality due to its rigid constitution. Usually this function is known as the role of fantasy and is important in all sorts of creative activities, from arts to sciences (Borel, 1934; Freud, 1995; Thalbourne & Delin, 1994). This function can explain why watching a magical movie facilitates creative divergent thinking in children (see Chapter 4).

Magical thinking can help us better understand physical objects, animals, and other people by projecting into them our own thoughts and feelings. This *animistic function* of magical thinking has long been appreciated in psychology, under the name of animism and anthropomorphism (Bullock, 1985; Lévy-Brühl, 1984; Piaget, 1971; Subbotsky, 2000a). Not only is our everyday language full of animistic constructions (the sun is *rising*, the rain is *coming*), but many scientific terms (gravitational *attraction, charmed* particles in physics) are animistic as well. Even in their reasoning about the dead, children and adults cannot avoid concepts and expressions that attribute to dead people mental states pertinent to the living (Bering, 2006a,b). This function of magical thinking has played an important role in maintaining ecological balance between the pressure of human activity and natural ecosystems. Early hunters did not consider themselves to be superior to the animals they hunted. For this reason, they avoided overhunting and performed special rituals in order to pacify the spirits of the prey and thus prevent their retaliation (Frazer, 1923). This animistic attitude helped to maintain balance between people and their natural environments. In contrast, demystification of nature by monotheistic religions and science converted nature into a resource and gradually brought relations between human activities and their natural habitat to the edge of an imbalance that today threatens the very existence of life on Earth (Danilov-Danilian, Losev, & Reif, 2005).

One more function of magical reality is the *bonding function*. Historically, shared magical beliefs and mythologies united individual members of a community, making them feel as though they were parts of a single social whole. These same beliefs and mythologies could sanction various societal institutions, such as morality and political power. Although in modern industrial societies this function is largely ignored or reinterpreted in secular terms (morality is viewed as a set of conventional rules that benefit the society), in other cultural traditions (like Islam), it is still in action. In addition, as argued in Chapter 9, some implicit rules of human communication (such as "reciprocation to a concession") may have historically originated as having been sanctioned by magical agents with the purpose of encouraging interaction and cooperation between individuals.

One can also distinguish a *meaning-creating* function. In those who believe in magic, God, and an afterlife, these beliefs affect the meaning of their lives by putting life in a long-term perspective. The phenomenon of near-death experiences (Lundahl, 1993; Moody, 1976) can be related to this function. The meaning created by magical thinking and magical (religious) beliefs can help people to cope with metaphysical problems such as lack of good fortune or fear of death, which are impossible (for most people) to cope with through scientific knowledge or logical reasoning alone.

The *heuristic* function of magical thinking was first asserted by Shweder (1977), who viewed the law of similarity as the representativeness heuristic— the built-in labor-saving device of the mind. Nemeroff and Rozin (2000) agree that the law of contagion and the law of similarity serve the role of heuristics in the domain of disgust and fear of contagion where these laws are "substitutes for actual causal analysis" (p. 21). As I argued in Chapter 9, the heuristic function of magical thinking can go beyond cognitive processes and into the domain of human communication. The law of participation—the underlying mechanism of magical thinking—provides humans with special and usually subconscious "modules" of communication (such as "reciprocation to a concession" or "obedience to authority") that are widely used for influence and control over individuals' minds in politics, economics, religion, and psychotherapy.

An *auto-therapeutic* function can also be distinguished. Nemeroff and Rozin (2000) named this function "sense of prediction and control." When people's personally significant imagined (PERSIM) objects are at stake, attending to magical gestures and rituals may overcome frustration and bring the person back into emotional balance, through simply asserting that all that is possible has been done in order to protect PERSIM objects from harm. Most superstitious behaviors are based on this function of magical reality. Art therapy and some other therapeutic approaches exploit this function of magical thinking (Cohen, 1981; Kaufman, 1990). The vulnerability of many people today to fake magical healers and charlatans or to obsessive-compulsive disorder (OCD) is due to this function of magical thinking.

Finally, in the domain of magical reality, a human individual can experience a state of ecstasy—a supreme harmony with the universe, a feeling of personal fulfillment and perfection (the *resurrecting function*). Some theorists collapse this function with the meaning creation function and name the outcome "experience of connection, participation, and meaning" (Nemeroff & Rozin, 2000; Tambiah, 1990). This kind of state is hardly achievable within ordinary reality due to its rigid and restrictive nature. Thus, it is in the state of imaginary pretend play that a child can achieve the feeling of having absolute power and control over things, and it is in our dreams and fantasies that we can experience our ultimate value and worthiness of being (see Freud, 1995). By immersing oneself in the domain of magical reality (through fantasy, dream, or play), a person liberates himself or herself from the claws of spatial-temporal and causal-physical limitations of everyday life. Breaking away from the repetitive rhythm of ordinary reality and entering magical reality, the individual periodically restores the feeling of his or her unconditional value, which gives the him or her the strength needed for coping with the mundane periodicity of everyday life.[3]

This function of magical reality explains the power and influence of entertainment industries as well as hallucinogenic substances. For instance, intake of certain substances, such as mescaline (peyote) and LSD, induces altered states of consciousness, which are comparable with magical reality. Use of such substances was typical in the religious rituals of certain Native American cultures, and in Western cultures the use of psychedelic drugs formed a special counterculture of the 1960s. Laboratory experiments with psychedelic substances have shown that some time after intake a person can feel that some fundamental changes occur in his or her subjective reality: the person's identity can change (one participant saw himself in the mirror being converted into a mighty tiger), and space and time can seem to shrink or expand to infinity (Aaronson & Osmond, 1971; Stafford, 2003). The experiments also showed that the experience participants reported had many common features with the experience commonly known as mystical: the subject has the feeling that the usual separation between himself or herself and an external object (inanimate or animate) disappears (sense of unity), there appears the feeling that all things possess divine properties and beauty (the sense of sacredness), and the converted reality becomes so vividly real that it incommensurably surpasses the reality of everyday life (the sense of objectivity and reality). Clearly, most of the features of "psychedelic reality" (violations of physical causality, physical time, and space) are the same as those described as features of magical reality (Chapter 1). The fact that participants have a feeling of positive mood, joy, and blessedness adds to the point that the state of psychedelic reality can be viewed as highly desirable. Not surprisingly, psychedelic drugs have found an application in medicine and are extensively used for healing purposes (Aaronson & Osmond, 1971).

The questions arise, What makes ordinary reality a supreme and dominant reality in the Western cultural tradition? What gives it the status of the "true reality"? Under what conditions can this subordination be disturbed and ordinary reality made to yield its privileged status to magical reality? To answer these questions, one needs to look more closely into the structure of realities of the mind.

ORDINARY REALITY: THE REALM OF SCIENCE

An important assumption that underlies ordinary reality is that within this reality, all things can be reduced to a limited number of prototypes. Individuals have access to these prototypes, and they can use them as mediators between themselves and real objects and events. This assumption acquired its classical image in Plato's teaching. Essentially, Plato's "ideas" are prototypes and mental constructions for empirical objects. Although the "idea" comes to us as a result of comparison (ratio) between empirical objects, it is not the sum of general features extracted from a certain group of empirical objects; rather, it is the sum of knowledge and skills that allows one to recognize, produce, and use empirical objects of an appropriate kind (Plato, 1968). Mental entities of this kind will be referred to in this chapter as "rational constructions" (from *ratio*, "relation").

In the Western cultural tradition today, science is the chief producer of rational constructions, or theories. Rational constructions exist for all properties of physical objects, such as dimension (metric length, width, and volume), weight (the concept of gravity), form (the concept of geometrical shape), and color (the wave theory of color). There are rational constructions for space (absolute physical space), time (physical time), and causality (physical causality). History and society are understood via rational constructions as well. Theories such as humanity progressing from capitalism to communism or the superiority of the Aryan race, have claimed millions of human lives in an effort to promote themselves as reflecting truth about reality, and yet they have proven to be wrong. Even God is presented as a rational construction that helps us to understand the universe (Kant, 1929; Swinburne, 1979). Some rational constructions, such as atoms, geometrical figures, and numbers, are thousands of years old. Others, such as new theories in quantum physics, are of recent origin. And still others are yet to come. Rational constructions aim to present the diversity of perceptual objects in a more economic and condensed way. The external world thus becomes doubled: every object and process of the world is given to the mind of an individual as a perceptual image (phenomenon) and a rational construction (see Figure 11.1). Clearly, the relationships between phenomena and rational constructions are of the correlation, and not of the causal, type.

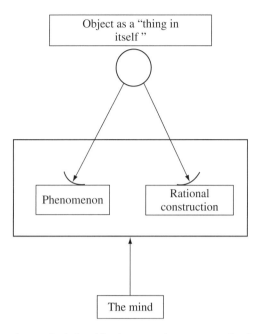

FIGURE 11.1. The scheme of relationships between phenomena and rational constructions.

Among other things, this means that an insurmountable causal gap exists between phenomena and rational constructions, and this gap is vital for maintaining the structure of ordinary reality. It also means that any attempt to bridge this gap would undermine the very foundation on which ordinary reality is built. Ignoring this fact can create problems that are theoretically unsolvable. One classic example of this is an attempt to reduce mental phenomena to brain processes. Since Descartes, there has been a long debate on this problem, with theorists divided into two main camps: the skeptics who deny that such reduction is possible, and their opponents who think that it is (see Burns, 1991; Hardcastle, 1993; Krellenstein, 1995).

The skeptics' argument is a theoretical one, and, by and large, it follows the original argument of Descartes about the primacy of perceptual experiences (see McGinn, 1989; Mills, 1998; Swinburne, 1979). Indeed, phenomenal experiences, such as seeing color or tasting food, existed independently of our knowledge about the accompanying brain processes, and they existed long before any ideas about the structure of the brain or neural networks had been formulated. The opponents' argument is mainly empirical, and it draws on the fact that the functioning of some systems in the brain is regularly accompanied by (correlated with) some subjective experiences in the mind (Damasio, 1994; Grobstein, 1990; Stuss & Benson, 1986). But this, too, is compatible with the views of Descartes, who stressed that the mind and the brain are connected, and even identified the seat of consciousness in the pineal gland (as it appears, wrongly, but not without a good reason, see Penfield, 1975).

Paradoxically, with all the advances of neuroscience in particular areas, what we now know about the brain–mind connection does not exceed considerably what Descartes himself knew. All we know is that certain processes in the brain are related (correlated) with certain phenomena in the mind, and evidence is increasing that most of these correlations are of a rather loose and flexible type (Aguirre & D'Esposito, 1997; Delacour, 1995; Donald, 1995; Farah, 1994; Luria, 1980). In its classical form, a causal explanation means that there is nothing in the effect that had not been previously present in the cause (see Kant, 1929). This means that an effect is completely predictable from its cause. If we know the cause, we know the effect. A correlational link is different in principle from a causal one: since correlated processes are caused by a third factor, each of these processes can contain elements that are not predictable from the other.

The apparent lack of progress in solving the brain–mind problem suggests that the problem has been approached in the wrong way. It has been framed as a problem of finding a causal bridge between the subjective experiences in the mind and the processes in the brain, and, *if solved, it would undermine a vast body of educational, juridical, religious, and political practices based on the belief in an individual's free will and personal responsibility.* Certainly, when a problem is put in this way, it does not want to be solved. Indeed, my brain can exist for me in two ways: the way I see it, and the way I know about it. My brain as I see it is a part of my mind, and, though it is a privileged part, it cannot causally explain the whole mind. My brain as I know it is a biological computer of enormous complexity, and as such, it is a rational construction. This again makes it impossible to causally derive the subjective events in my mind from the processes in my brain.

This gap does not mean that the mind can exist without the brain. On the contrary, the inseparable bond between mind and brain is one of the fundamental assumptions on which ordinary reality is built. The subjective experience in my mind can only be activated if my brain is working, and this experience suffers when the brain is damaged. Influential authors (Damasio, 1994; LeDoux, 1996; Luria, 1980) have convincingly argued for the dependency of the mind on somatic neural processes. The brain–mind gap nevertheless remains, allowing such notions as free will, freedom of choice, and moral responsibility to stand. *All this gap entails is the correlational nature of the relations between brain and mind processes, with the element of unpredictability in these relations being unavoidable.* Yet, this element of unpredictability can be reduced, and in no way can the brain–mind gap impede the further progress of neuroscience in establishing correlations between the brain systems and mental phenomena and producing various hypothetical models of why these correlations are there.

Accordingly, the ordinary reality of the mind is a doubled, perhaps even tripled, kind of reality: it includes the phenomena (sensory and perceptual images of objects and events), the rational constructions of the first order (theories, schemes, and models of all sorts created for objects and events of the external world), and the rational constructions of the second order (theories about the work of the mind and the brain existing in psychology and physiology). At that, phenomena are entities of a more primary order then are rational constructions as soon as the latter appear as a product of handling the former in a certain special way (comparisons, measurements, analysis). As sciences advanced, the rational constructions increased in number and complexity. That obscured the primary status of phenomenalistic experience and created the illusion that this experience can be causally derived from rational constructions. As a result, because of the more stable and consistent structure of rational constructions, in the contemporary Western tradition they are believed to have the higher degree of reality (truthfulness) then phenomena have. This belief laid a foundation for contemporary science and rationality (Heidegger, 1959).

Ordinary reality can further be divided into physical and social subdomains. Although these subdomains share some features (both are governed by the laws of physical space, time, and causality, as far as physical bodies are concerned), there are substantial differences between them. Social bodies have minds, whereas physical bodies do not. Consequently, various types of symbolic communication—through language, moral, and social rules—are possible between subjects of social reality, but not between the objects of physical reality. Like physical ordinary reality, social ordinary reality is constrained by certain assumptions. One is the already mentioned inseparable bond between mind and brain (there can be no mind without a brain). Another is that individual minds are private and have no direct access to each other. The individual mind's privacy is crucial for maintaining the structure of ordinary reality because the concepts of independent judgment and objectivity are based on it.

As can be seen, one cannot reduce the domain of ordinary reality to a certain plane of representing reality in the mind: perceptual (external physical reality), imagery (imaginary reality), or symbolic (reality represented through thoughts, words, and symbols); rather, it can be projected on each of these planes. Nor can ordinary reality be identified with the natural world or physical causation. Thus, processes such as logical thinking and symbolic communication are parts of ordinary reality, yet they are not parts of the natural world and can not be reduced to physical causality.

Finally, on a historical scale, the Western cultural version of ordinary reality was created relatively recently. In the time before science, and in traditional cultures today, people create their rational constructions and theories about ordinary reality in different ways, yet ordinary (profane, mundane) reality was (is) there (Boyer & Walker, 2000; Lévy-Brühl, 1966; Frazer, 1923; Tambiah, 1990).

MAGICAL REALITY: THE REALM OF MAGIC AND RELIGION

Freud and Jung emphasized the kinship between neurotic fantasies, night dreams, and fine arts, and some areas of contemporary art (such as surrealism) deliberately exploit dreams, fantasies, and hallucinations. All these states of mind share the feature that they can exist outside of formal logic or other constraints of ordinary reality. And yet dreams, fantasies, and art are not magical reality per se—they are a medium, a substrate upon which magical reality can operate. A piece of art or a dream could be entirely within ordinary reality. Engineering sometimes requires a powerful imagination, yet the laws of ordinary reality strictly govern these images. However, when even a single element in the picture transcends the limits of ordinary reality, the whole piece becomes a representation of magical reality. For example, in Sandro Botticelli's masterpiece "The Birth of Venus," we see two beautiful but otherwise ordinary women, the sea, the sky, the beach, and trees. The only elements that make the painting magical are the two figures suspended in the air in the upper left corner, but they are enough to make one understand that the scene represents the magical world of Roman mythology and not the ordinary world of two Renaissance beauties enjoying themselves on a beach.

Within magical reality, the constraints that are imposed on structures within ordinary reality disappear, and nonpermanent physical objects (such as UFOs), reversible complex processes (such as dead people coming to life), and magical causality (such as affecting weather or crops by a magic spell) emerge. Nevertheless, within magical reality, magical elements are always set against a background of ordinary reality. The inherent feature of magical reality is its marginality, the compromising composition of ordinary and supernatural structures and events. We weave magical reality from the elements of ordinary reality, and "...the one who sees a person with wings in his dream would not be able to see this without having seen previously a person and something which has wings" (Sextus Empiricus, 1976, pp. 160–161).

By definition, magical reality is an alter ego of ordinary reality. Just as ordinary reality includes intuitive and scientific knowledge about physical, biological, and psychological properties of things, magical reality contains magical physics (such as the expectation that gods, spirits, and wizards can go though walls, create things by just thinking about them, or move in space instantaneously), magical biology (such as the idea that gods can feed on the emanations of sacrificed food or live forever), and magical psychology (such as the expectation that gods can see into people's minds or through opaque obstacles, know everything, or perceive everything at once) (Boyer & Walker, 2000). In the magical social reality, the constraints of ordinary social reality are no longer unbreakable. Gods, spirits, and witches can read people's minds, and minds can exist without bodies (ghosts, souls that survive the physical death of their owners).

Since magic and religion originated from a common root, it is not surprising that magical reality is also the realm of religion. Although in the modern Western tradition religion is divorced from magic, magical and religious thinking have common features. In essence, *religion is a culturally adopted and highly sophisticated practice based on the fundamental capacity of the human mind for magical thinking and magical beliefs.* Perfected for millennia, this practice became a worldwide institution that is highly capable of dealing with metaphysical problems such as the meaning of life, the fear of death, and the desire to be in control of one's destiny (Gellner, 1989). As an institution, religion has separated itself from everyday magic, which religion now associates with evil supernatural forces. But the "umbilical cord" that links religious thinking to magical thinking—magical causality—is undeniably there.

In both the Old and New Testaments, God often reveals himself through miracles that violate known physical principle. This common core feature between magic and religion has long been noted in anthropological studies (Malinowski, 1935; Tambiah, 1990). Anthropologists Boyer and Walker (2000) claimed that there exist common religious ontologies throughout the world; they include such concepts as agents with counterintuitive physical, biological, and psychological properties (such as spirits that can go through physical obstacles, gods that procreate in nonstandard ways, zombies that are alive but unintentional creatures), animals with counterintuitive biological properties (able to metamorphose across species), and artifacts with intentional properties (statues that can listen). But the same ontologies lay in the foundation of magical thinking. In fact, these authors acknowledge that magical thinking " ... is part and parcel of specific religious belief systems" (Boyer & Walker, 2000, p. 148).

Another point of view is that magic and religion, along with sharing views on supernatural causality, also complement each other in a more pragmatic sense. Magical practices are attractive because they promise immediate and easily achievable results, but they are also easy to falsify. In contrast, religion offers a person rewards in a distant future, sometimes even after death, but the claims of religion are difficult to reject on the basis of empirical evidence. As a result, "most enduring complexes of belief and action would be those that have achieved an ideal balance between magic and religion" (Pyysiäinen, 2004, p. 108). This is not to say that religion is indistinguishable from magic. For centuries, religion perfected its representation of supernatural entities

(God, angels), its cosmological representations (creation of the universe), its code of morality, and other features that made religion a more advanced and sophisticated part of magical reality than are noninstitutionalized magical beliefs.

In sum, the structure of the individual mind can be presented as in Table 11.2.

One might think that this structure represents the mind as it is conceived in the modern Western tradition only, and is inapplicable to the mind of a person living in a time before science or in a modern traditional society that relies on myth rather than on science. However, even in traditional cultures, people rely on "intuitive theories" about physics, biology, and psychology—theories that are violated by the magical characters of their religions. Coexistence of intuitive rational beliefs in mundane circumstances and magical beliefs in the context of sacred religious ceremonies in traditional cultures has long been noted (Frazer, 1923; Lévy-Brühl, 1966; Tambiah, 1990). Thus, in a relatively recent work, Walker (1992) reported that the Yoruba of southwestern Nigeria refused to acknowledge that in an everyday context a cat could turn into a dog, yet in the context of a ritual involving sacrificing a dog, they insisted that a cat disguised as a dog was really a dog. This suggests that the division between ordinary (mundane) and magical reality is a cross-

TABLE 11–2. The Structure of the Individual Mind

SUBDOMAINS	DOMAINS OF REALITY	
	ORDINARY	MAGICAL
Physical	Permanent Inanimate objects	Nonpermanent Inanimate objects
	Physical causality, space, and time,	Magical causality (affecting nature by spells)
		Magical space (physical objects moving through walls)
		Magical time (time travel, dead people coming to life)
Social	Ordinary Animate entities (people and animals)	Magical Animate entities (gods and spirits)
	Scientific biology and psychology	Magical biology (gods and spirits that feed on smells and live forever, ghosts and souls that exist without physical bodies)
	Inseparable bond between mind and brain	Magical psychology (gods and spirits that know everything, can see in people's minds, and attend to all tasks at one time)
	Privacy of individual minds	

cultural phenomenon, and that it existed in Western cultures in a time before empirical science.

But if the individual's mind contains two alternative realities, then these realities have to be put in a hierarchical order, with one being a primary reality and the other a subordinate one. This hierarchical order is necessary because a person cannot maintain consistency in his or her life while relying on both physical and magical causality, or physical and magical space and time simultaneously; if these alternative modes of reality were mixed, the world would lose order and predictability for that individual. The onset of such hierarchical order would make primary reality "a figure" and the subordinate reality "a ground." Questions then arise: (*1*) What psychological process creates the hierarchical order between these alternative realities? (*2*) Is the hierarchical order between realities maintained at both levels of the mind's functioning (involved and uninvolved) or only at one of them? (*3*) When does this hierarchical order emerge and how does it change over the course of child development? Elsewhere I have termed the process that creates the hierarchical order between ordinary and magical realities *existentialization* (Subbotsky, 1993).

EXISTENTIALIZATION AS THE WORK OF THE MIND

Undoubtedly, every element in the subjective field of the mind exists. Even nothingness exists, as long as we think about it (Aristotle, 1976). Yet the degree to which elements of the mind are "real" varies. We perceive some of these elements as true, others as problematic, and still others as wholly false (James, 1980). It follows from this that the mind must perform a special function—grading its elements on a scale of "reality/nonreality." This function of the mind will be referred to as *existentialization*.

Existentialization is the process of reducing an element of reality in such a way that this element's existence (authenticity) becomes self-evident, in other words, as evident as the subject's own existence (Descartes, 1988). If we are able to do this, then we recognize that piece of reality as a true one. If we fail, then we qualify the object as problematic or false, "nonexistent" within ordinary reality. *Existentialization precedes thinking and is an intuitive, experience-based decision-making process.* The fact that even preschool children, under certain conditions, can draw correct logical conclusions from false (counterfactual) premises (Dias & Harris, 1988) illustrates the independence of existentialization (deciding whether premises are true or false) from thinking (making logical inferences from these premises). So, how does existentialization work?

In ordinary reality, any element (an object or an event) can appear in the mind in three different forms: as a phenomenon (the tree that I am seeing), a mental image (the tree that I am imagining if I close my eyes), and a rational construction (my intuitive and scientific knowledge about what a tree is). Starting from this, I can present the concept of existentialization as in Figure 11.2. The relations 1, 2, and 3 signify that each of the three forms of representation are available to the mind, without qualifying them as true or false. This means that the existential status of each of these representations is unclear. It can represent something of the external reality, but it can also represent a sheer product of the mind. In other words, the ontological status of each of these representations is problematic.

To qualify these representations as true or false, the mind needs to compare (match) them to each other (shown in Figure 11.2 as relations 4, 5, and 6). If the result of this comparison indicates that they match (they represent one and the same object or event of the external reality), then this object or event is given the higher status of an actual (true) thing. In everyday language, we would simply say that the object or the event really exists. If the result of the comparison brings only partial success (for example, if it shows that an object or an event is presented only as a mental image and a rational construction, but not a perceptual image), then we attribute a lower (problematic) existential status to this object or event. For instance, my car left in a parking lot still exists for me as a mental image in memory and as a rational construction (documents of possession, driver's license, and the concept of a car), yet its existence is problematic because I have no definite proof that it has not been stolen and destroyed. Obviously, most of the elements of the mind have this kind of existential status. Examples of entities with the diminished existential statuses include the memory of a person who died or the knowledge of a species that has become extinct. Lastly, the weakest existential status of "falsity" is attributed to entities that contain a direct contradiction between their representational elements, such as errors of perception or judgment. Thus, phenomena such as the inequality of line lengths in the Müller-Lyer

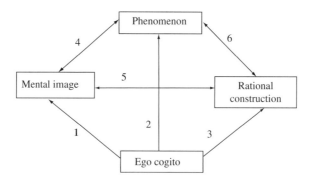

FIGURE 11.2. The scheme of the relations of existentialization.

TABLE 11–3. The Ontological Hierarchy of the Elements in the Mind as a Function of the Presence and Correspondence of the Forms of Representation—Phenomenon, Mental Image, and Rational Construction

EXISTENTIAL STATUS	PRESENCE IN THE MIND	CORRESPONDENCE WITH EACH OTHER
Full (strong)	All present	Correspond
Deficient (medium)	Some absent	Correspond
False (weak)	All or some present	Do not correspond

illusion or the Sun rotating around the Earth are viewed to be false because measurements and scientific theories contradict these phenomena.

In sum, the hierarchy between the ontological statuses of elements of the mind can be represented as in Table 11.3.

Although a healthy individual is usually unaware of the process of existentialization, this process is vital for maintaining a normal picture of the world. This process is basic, and it can resist even conditions that interrupt the normal functioning of the brain. Penfield's brain-operated patients exhibited two streams of consciousness—one authentic but artificially evoked by electric stimulation of the cortex, and another driven by output from the environment—running in parallel during their operations. But the patients were fully aware which of the streams was real and which was apparent (Penfield, 1975).

Applied to the division between ordinary and magical realities, existentialization puts these realities into a hierarchical order. For example, gods and ghosts can be imagined (mental representation) and intuitively understood depending on what features gods and ghosts are attributed in a particular culture (rational construction), yet people do not quite see them within ordinary reality. These images, therefore, are attributed a weaker existential status than, for example, objects and people that we can see around us. This does not mean that ideas of magical reality are necessarily false. Rather, they become false only if they trespass into the realm of ordinary reality (for example, if someone in a waking state hallucinates actually seeing gods or ghosts).

The importance of existentialization becomes especially evident when this process is disturbed. A typical case of disturbed existentialization is madness. Although it is not unusual for a healthy person to conjure up strange ideas and frightening images, the person usually has no difficulty keeping these ideas and images under control by ascribing them an appropriate existential status and placing them in the appropriate domain of reality. In madness, however, the lines between realities become blurred and ideas that normally lurk in the realm of magical reality (ghosts, spirits, gods) can permeate the domain of ordinary reality. Another way for magical characters to acquire the full existential status is faith. For a believer in magic or religion, gods and spirits are real, despite the fact that one cannot actually see them. Whereas in the state of mental illness the hierarchy between ordinary and magical realities disintegrates, in the state of faith, this hierarchy is forced by the effort of faith.

SEPARATING THE MAGICAL FROM THE ORDINARY: THE DEVELOPMENTAL PERSPECTIVE

So, when exactly do children start to become aware of the distinction between ordinary and magical realities? Research has shown that primary intuitions of the differences between magical and ordinary events can be found in young infants. Bower (1971) reported that 4-month-old infants express surprise if they unsuccessfully tried to grasp an illusory cube possessing visual clues of solidity. A similar sensitivity of 3½-month-olds to the impermeability of solid objects for other solid objects was shown by Baillargeon (1987). At the age of 5 months, infants are capable of distinguishing ordinary causal visual displays from displays in which ordinary causality is violated (Leslie, 1982).

In later ages, children develop linguistic awareness of the difference between ordinary and magical realities. Some investigators studied this awareness by assessing children's growing capacity to verbally discriminate between (*1*) real and fantastic entities (Morrison & Gardner, 1978; Prawat, Anderson, & Hapkiewicz, 1983) and (*2*) phenomenal and imagined objects (Johnson & Wellman 1980; Wellman & Estes, 1986). Taylor and Howell (1973) reported that 3-year-olds found it difficult to distinguish between real and fantastical pictures of animals. Morrison and Gardner (1978) asked 4- to 12-year-old children to classify drawings of objects representing either real or fantastical prototypes. The capacity to distinguish between real and fantastical objects gradually increased with age, but only at the age of 11 did children become capable of justifying the difference by applying criteria like "borrowed from a fairy tale" or "invented." Prawat and colleagues (1983) investigated the idea that cognitive classification of objects as real or unreal depends on children's emotional attitude toward them, with the unreal type including those objects that children perceive as most fearsome. Data from this experiment failed to support the authors' assumption. Just as with adults, children aged 4, 7, and 10 years attributed "real" or "unreal" statuses to "monsters" featured in the pictures irrespective of the degree to which these monsters were regarded by them as fearsome or harmless. Instead, preschoolers used the same criteria as schoolchildren and adults when determining the reality status of the character, and the main criterion they used was the similarity of the character to objects they came across in real life. Sharon and Woolley (2004) added a new twist to the studies of the discrimination between ordinary and extraordinary characters by employing a new measure for this discrimination—a property attribution task. The authors hypothesized that children who were unable to categorize entities into real and fantastical groups might still recognize differences between real and fantastical characters in terms of their ordinary (for example, "Can X have a pet?") and magical ("Can X know what we are thinking?") properties. Indeed, 4- and 5-year-olds were able to differentiate between properties of real (child or clown) and magical (Santa, fairy, or Superman) entities as good as adults, although the children's capacity to correctly categorize the magical entities was greatly inferior to that of adults.

Preschool children's capacity to both distinguish conceptually between ordinary and magical characters and understand that magical characters "do not really exist" contradicts the fact that the same children may treat the magical characters as real ones. This contradiction becomes particularly obvious in children's fears of imagined magical characters. Staley and O'Donnell (1984) showed that imagination-based night fears comprise a significant portion of the list of children's fears. A distinctive feature of the imaginary monsters is that the child's fear of them does not disappear with the knowledge that they are unreal (Jersild, 1943; Jersild & Holmes, 1935). Posing this as a problem, Harris, Brown, Marriot, Whittal, and Harmer (1991) investigated the way preschool children treated imagined magical characters like ghosts and witches. Despite the fact that in their verbal judgments children did not attribute as strong a degree of reality to these characters as they did to ordinary imagined objects (such as an imagined pencil), some children's behavior indicated that they treated ghosts and witches as fearsome. Although the children knew that monsters did not exist, they emotionally projected the imaginary characters into the real world (in the room or in a box). These findings support the results of earlier studies, in which preschool children verbally denied that toys could magically come to life or magic spells could change physical objects, but then behaved as if they believed those events were occurring (Chapter 2).

Further research (Chapter 3) has shown that, even at the level of children's verbal reasoning, preschool and primary school children have problems differentiating between magical and ordinary realities. For example, 55% of 5-year-olds proved to be unable to correctly distinguish between true magical events and a trick that imitated magical events (see Figure 3.1), and of those who could distinguish, 42% said that true magic could happen in real life (see Figure 3.2). When those 5-year-olds who were nonbelievers in magic were shown a trick that looked like an instance of true magic, all of them produced or accepted magical explanations (see Figure 3.3), and 90% of these children persisted in magical explanations even after the trick had been explained to them (see Figure 3.4).

Altogether, the research data examining children's verbal judgments and nonverbal behavioral reactions brought me to the assumption that preschool and elementary school children's ability to cognitively distinguish between magical and ordinary characters, naming the former as unreal and the latter as real, is not sufficient for children to create a stable hierarchy between magical and ordinary reality. In order to emphasize that hierarchy between ordinary and magical realities in the preschool age is not yet established, I will refer to this stage as *hierarchical uncertainty*.

The second step in the development of the hierarchy between magical and ordinary realities occurs at the school age, when children acquire scientific knowledge about physical reality. Piaget described this process of duplication of everyday reality as the development of "operational intelligence." Mastering of arithmetic and algebra, learning of major physical and scientific concepts, and developing the ideas of conservation, class inclusion, and seriation create a whole new world in the child's mind. This world—the world of rational constructions—exists as a special symbolic reality that is inaccessible to the senses. Under the pressure of a science-dominated cultural tradition, children begin to view ordinary reality as the superior "true world," whereas the world of magical reality becomes apparent reality. This creates the subordination between ordinary and magical reality in children's judgments. As experiments reviewed in Chapter 3 have shown, not only did the majority of 6- and 9-year-olds (70% to 80%) explicitly state that true magic cannot happen in reality (see Figure 3.2), but 50% of 9-year-olds rejected magical explanations even when they were shown a causal effect looking like a case of true magic (see Figure 3.3), and those who accepted magical explanations returned to physical explanations as soon as the nature of the trick was explained (see Figure 3.4). A characteristic feature of the hierarchical order between ordinary and magical reality in older children is that in making this subordination, children do not distinguish between two classes of objects: the ontologically strong objects (perceived and imagined physical objects), which conform to the laws of physical causality, and ontologically weak objects (fantastic objects), which are free from the constraints of ordinary reality. For example, when perceived, imaginary physical, and fantastic objects were subjected to magical intervention by a magic spell or wishing, 6- and 9-year-olds treated both classes of objects as capable of resisting this intervention to an equal extent (see Figures 8.2 and 8.3). Emphasizing the general and global nature of hierarchy between ordinary and magical realities in older children, I will refer to this as *object-nonspecific hierarchy*.

The third step in the development of the hierarchy between magical and ordinary realities occurs when individuals are able to distinguish between ontologically strong objects that belong to ordinary reality (perceived and imagined physical objects) and ontologically weak objects that dwell in the magical reality (fantastic objects). This division was not observed in 6- and 9-year old children, but it was evident in adults (see Figures 8.2 and 8.3). In adults, conscious disbelief in mind-over-matter magic becomes even more evident: adults denied magical explanations of the apparently "magical" effects happening on physical objects even though these effects were replicated three times (Chapter 5). In contrast, when fantastic objects were subjected to magical intervention, adults acknowledged that this was possible (Chapter 8).

Akin to fictional reality, PERSIM objects develop—mental representation of a person's future life, the future lives of loved ones, and the future outcome of an important or risky activity. Studies reviewed in Chapters 8 and 9 have shown that, although adult participants consistently denied their belief in mind-over-matter magic, they believed that communicative magic could indeed change fantastic and PERSIM objects. When, in another study, suggestion was deprived of any association with magic, regarding their PERSIM objects participants demonstrated the same pattern of behavior as they showed in the magical suggestion condition. Furthermore, in their verbal justifications of their reactions, most participants explicitly acknowledged that magical manipulations might affect their PERSIM object. One consequence of the emergence of PERSIM objects is the widespread and persistency of superstitious behaviors (Jahoda, 1969; Luhrman, 1989; Vyse, 1997; Zusne & Jones, 1982). Another consequence is that an individual becomes receptive to magical (and religious) suggestion and control. This enables a person to cope with the increasing pressure of metaphysical problems (meaning of life, fear of death, desire to control one's destiny), but also creates the opportunity for manipulation by a second party of the person's mind in order to obtain some psychological, political, or economic profit. Invasive psychotherapies, controversial religious cults, and commercial persuasion techniques heavily exploit PERSIM objects by employing various suggestive techniques (Singer et al., 1986). In order to stress that at this stage the hierarchy between ordinary and magical realities is based on the distinctions between two classes of objects (ontologically strong in ordinary reality and ontologically weak in magical reality), I will refer to this stage as *object-specific hierarchy*.

This differentiation between ordinary and magical realities, however, is confined to the level of conscious reasoning. At the level of nonverbal behavioral reactions, the hierarchy between magical and ordinary reality remains either absent or fragile. In adults, certain patterns of behavior that operate implicitly (such as disgust and fear of contagion) conform to the laws of contagious and sympathetic magic (Rozin, Markwith, & Ross, 1990; Rozin, Millman, & Nemeroff, 1986). As the studies reviewed in Chapter 5 have shown, when the cost of disbelief in magic is made high, adults show a significant increase in their belief in the effect of the magic spell over physical objects. Interestingly, in this condition, Western participants' magical behavior was not significantly different from that of non-Western, uneducated inhabitants of remote villages in Central Mexico (Chapter 6).

To summarize, magical reality is a basic psychological phenomenon rooted in the very structure of the mind. The development of the conscious distinction between magical and ordinary realities is therefore a separate line in the mind's development as a whole. In this development, magical thinking, beliefs, and behavior are tightly intertwined with rational scientific thinking, beliefs, and behavior.

EXISTENTIALIZATION AND DEVELOPMENTAL RESEARCH

Although the main role of existentialization is distinguishing and subordinating between ordinary and magical realities, this process is also involved in ontological decision making within ordinary reality. This links the development of magical thinking with the development of ontological reasoning.

In recent decades, evidence has accumulated of a fundamental shift in children's capacity to verbally understand the ontological hierarchy of items and events. Usually, a task studying ontological awareness presents children with two related items that have unequal ontological statuses, with one having a privileged (strong) ontological status and the other having a diminished (weak) ontological status. For instance, in the false belief task, children are presented with a contrast between the *real state of events* and the *false belief about this state of events*. The task is usually viewed as a test of whether children do or do not understand that other people have representations that can be true or false. In one of the classic versions of this task, children are presented with a box of the candy "Smarties" that had pictures of Smarties on it and asked what they thought was inside (Perner, Leekam, & Wimmer, 1987). After they answered "Smarties," the box was opened to reveal a pencil instead of Smarties. The box was then closed and the children were asked what a friend, who remained outside the experimental room and could not therefore know what really was in the box, would think was in the box. Typically, 3-year-olds stated "a pencil," while older children correctly stated "Smarties." Summarizing extensive research on false belief tasks in a meta-analysis, Wellman, Cross, and Watson (2001) concluded that children's performance on these tasks improves dramatically from ages 3 to 5 years, from below-chance performance before 3½ years to above-chance performance after 4 years. This improvement is highly robust even in the face of various manipulations designed to simplify the task.

The *existentialization theory* predicts that children at a certain age will still give an incorrect answer to the "false belief question," regardless of whether or not they have an understanding of the representational nature of the mind. For instance, suppose that 3-year-old children cannot understand the representational theory of mind. Children in that case would simply have to choose between two items ("Smarties" and "pencil") in order to answer the research question, irrespective of the fact that the research question is not about just the two items, but instead, the representations of the two items. "Pencil" has a full existential status in the children's minds, as long as the children have just seen the pencil (the phenomenon), imagine the pencil (the mental image), and know what pencils are (the rational construction). In contrast, the item "Smarties" has a diminished existential status; although the children can imagine the Smarties and know what Smarties are, they did not actually see the Smarties.

Now, suppose that the children can understand that (*1*) both they (the children) and their friends have mental representations about a situation and (*2*) the friends' representations are wrong. Suppose that the children also understand that the research question is about their own representation (that the box contains a pencil) versus their friend's representation (that the box contains Smarties). The children's own representation (the box contains a pencil) ontologically has a full existential status, as long as they have just seen the pencil in the box (the phenomenon), *imagine* the pencil being in the box (a mental image), and *know* that although the box is meant for candies, it contains a pencil (the rational construction). On the other hand, their ignorant friend's *representation* (the box contains candies) contradicts the actual state of events and therefore has a weak ontological status (see Table 11.3). Again, when asked about their friends beliefs, the children would name their own belief; they would choose the ontologically strong item (the real state of affairs) and ignore the ontologically weak one (their friend's false belief). It is not until 4 or 5 years of age that children are able to give a correct answer, by naming the ontologically weak item.

Another demonstration of the same effect arises from an examination of children's developing awareness of the appearance–reality distinction. Summing up the data of the previous research, Taylor and Flavell (1984) described two types of errors that 3-year-old children make in distinguishing appearance from reality. Children make phenomenalistic errors, such as when they give the phenomenal description of the object as it is presented "here and now" in response to the question of what the object is "really and truly." Additionally, they make intellectual realism errors, such as when they describe the known identity of the object and ignore the fact that it presently looks different when they are asked to describe the object's appearance. This failure of young children to understand the distinction between appearance and reality proved to be rather robust (Taylor & Hort, 1990; Vinden, 1996). According to Flavell, children produce incorrect judgments because their metacognitive knowledge is limited. What they fail to understand is that one object can be represented in the mind in two different forms, for example, as red (original color) and black (apparent color) or as a sponge (known identity) and a rock (apparent identity). For 3-year-olds, reality has only one dimension. These children think that an object can only be represented in one way and not in two or more ways that may contradict each other (Flavell, 1993). Obviously, this view suggests that the enhancement of the appearance–reality distinction that takes place between 3 and 4 to 5 years of age is a step in the development of representational intelligence.

For this task, just as for the "false belief" task, the existentialization theory would predict that children at a certain age will make phenomenalistic or "intellectual realism" errors independently of whether they do or do not have representational intelligence. Let us skip the trivial case when children do not have representations and assume that they can understand that an object under a color filter will change from its original color. Due to the nature of their existentialization, children will still name the apparent color of the object if asked about its primary color. Indeed, the object's color is not tied to its identity; in fact, objects can be repainted without losing their identities. In the "color filter task," the color that is seen "here and now" (under the color filter) has an ontological advantage over the one that the object "really has." This advantage arises because the child can see the apparent color, imagine the color, and know that the object can have this color without any damage to its identity. On the other hand, perceptual access to the object's original color is denied, and this makes the original color ontologically deficient in comparison to the visible color (see Table 11.3). The children may indeed remember the object's primary color (black), but the visible color (red) is ontologically superior to the primary color; unlike the primary color, which is available in two modalities (mental image and a rational construction), the visible color is available in all three modalities: perceptual image, mental image, and a rational construction (knowledge about the color's name and functions). Likewise, when asked about the false appearance of an object whose identity is known to them, children may find it difficult to mention the false appearance. In the child's everyday life, there are no such concepts as a "sponge looking like a rock" or a "car looking like a clock," and the false appearance exists as a pure phenomenon that is unsupported by a matching rational construction. In contrast, the object's known identity is represented by its rational construction (knowledge of what a sponge or a car is) and mental image (memories about handling sponges or cars). It therefore has a higher existential status for children than the false appearance (see Table 11.3). Thus, when children are asked what the object looks like, they name the object's identity ("sponge"). This assumption is supported by experimental manipulations that aim to increase the existential status of the "ontologically deficient" feature. Thus, most 3-year-olds are able to provide correct responses in the tasks contrasting the original and apparent colors of an object when the object is not completely covered by the color filter (Flavell, Green, Wahl, & Flavell, 1987). Additionally, they can provide correct responses in tasks contrasting false appearance and identity when the importance of the false appearance is emphasized (Rice, Koinis, Sullivan, & Tager-Flusberg, 1997).

One more prediction of the existentialization theory is that children will display the errors of existentialization even at an age when they undeniably have a representational theory of mind. Existentialization errors were indeed observed in children's drawings. When asked to draw a cup that had its handle hidden from view, 5- and 6-year-old children drew it as if the handle were visible (Freeman & Janikoun, 1972). Children's tendency to include the defining feature in their drawings was observed even when the feature was physically absent in the object (Barrett & Light, 1976). The existentialization theory can explain these results. Like the false appearance, the visible image of the cup in which a handle is hidden from view exists solely as a phenomenon, as long as there is no notion of a "cup without a handle." In contrast, the children's concept of a cup is presented as a rational construction (knowledge about a cup that includes a handle as its defining feature) and mental image (a memory about holding cups by their handles). The concept, therefore, has a stronger ontological status in the child's mind than a distorted visible image. Bremner and Moor (1984) further reported that 5- and 6-year-olds included the hidden feature in their drawing only if they had an opportunity to view an object from different angles or to name the object before drawing it. Again, these findings support the "ontological deficit" explanation of distorting the object's visible image. Each of these manipulations emphasizes the object's rational construction, by strengthening either the object's mental image (seeing the handle before drawing) or its general concept (naming the object). On the other hand, children who see a cup with a hidden handle without these manipulations may not be certain that they observed a cup and not a similar-looking object with a different identity. This explanation gains support from the fact that children in the same experiment showed the same tendency in their drawings after they were shown an unknown abstract object "with a handle." To summarize, in these experiments, instead of drawing the object as it looks "here and now," children made a drawing of the object as it "must look" in order to achieve full existential status. In addition to providing one more illustration of the restricted existentialization in children, this experiment also shows that the shift in existentialization is not tied to a particular age. Like the shift from preoperational to operational intelligence described by Piaget, the shift in existentialization is spread over a certain period of time.

This tendency of children to center their attention on the ontologically strong item can be called the *error of ontological singularity*. This error means that children typically select the ontologically strong (or salient) item when they are given a choice of selecting one of two or more items with unequal ontological statuses. No compelling evidence shows that 3-year-olds can even understand that they are being asked about the ontologically deficient item. When children's existentialization matures, the ontological singularity is replaced by *ontological diversity*. At this age (roughly around 4 to 5 years), children become aware that questions may refer to an object's properties that have a deficient or weak ontological status (false beliefs, appearances, or pure phenomena). An awareness of ontological diversity means that although the concept of an object can be wrong, false, uncertain, disfigured, or misrepresented in many ways, these inaccuracies matter and are worthy of attention, presentation, and discussion. At this moment, children become aware of the *ontological depth* of the world around them.

There are alternative accounts for this fundamental change in child development. For example, the "theory theory" (TT) account claims that at ages younger than 3 years, children have a simple theory of mind that is based on the understanding of a character's desires and actions (Gopnik & Wellman, 1992, 1994). Near the age of 4 years, they develop a new and more advanced representational theory of mind that is based on understanding of the character's beliefs. This change of theories creates a shift in children's ontological judgments, because they now start to appreciate beliefs about reality (meta-reality). Other theorists postulate that there is a specialized innate brain mechanism that provides children with a representational system—the Theory of Mind Mechanism (ToMM) (German & Leslie, 2000). Initially, this mechanism is limited due to the insufficient development of inhibitory control needed to fully employ the ToMM, and this explains the failure of young children on the theory-of-mind tasks.

In reality, the developmental order is reversed. The shift in ontological awareness, during which children start to appreciate ontologically deficient representational elements of the mind (false beliefs), occurs first. Later, as a result of this shift, they develop a new (representational) theory of mind. In other words, the change in children's theory of mind is not a result of children's discovery of a new theory of mind, but rather a result of the "singularity to pluralism" shift in existentialization that makes the representational theory of mind possible. For instance, Gopnik and Wellman (1994) refer to the aforementioned false belief task when children see a candy box that contains pencils instead of candies and are asked what someone else would think is inside the box. As was mentioned, 3-year-olds typically answer that others "would think there are pencils." The authors rightly comment that the children "behave as if there is a simple and reliable causal link between the real state of affairs in the world and our mental states about it" (p. 266). However, asserting that this behavior is based on a "non-representational theory of beliefs" (p. 269) is an assumption, and a rather strong one. The 3-year-olds' "realistic" answer in this situation could be interpreted as a naïve theory of mind only if the children were able to provide justifications for their "theory," for instance, by explicitly stating that their friends have the capacity to see through opaque screens; there is no evidence to suggest that children are capable of providing these justifications. In fact, the most compelling evidence that they cannot provide such justifications comes from an experiment in which 3-year-old children, when asked, "When you first saw the box, before we opened it, what did you think was in the box?" reported their true beliefs (Gopnik & Astington, 1988). Even if the children attributed their friends' beliefs to "omniscience," they know from their own experience that they cannot see through nontransparent covers. As a matter of fact, only at the ages of 5 and 6 years do children become aware of the "omniscience" capacity as something special and different from ordinary perception (Barrett, Richert, & Driesenga, 2001). All this evidence suggests that 3-year-olds do not hold a wrong theory, or any *theory,* of others' and their own past beliefs. Instead, when asked a question about false beliefs, they simply choose the ontologically strong (salient) item and report the real state of affairs.

Another difficulty of the *special capacity accounts,* such as the TT or the ToMM accounts, is that they have to be adjusted to explain young children's failure on each particular task involving a contrast between items with different degrees of ontological power. This adjustment is necessary for tasks contrasting appearance with reality (Flavell, Green, & Flavell, 1986), opinion with certainty (Moor, Pure, & Furrow, 1990), drawings of perceived and known objects (Freeman & Janikoun, 1972), and "false photography" with the object that is photographed (Zaitchek, 1990). For each of these tasks, a separate naïve theory or a separate innate module must exist to explain young children's errors of judgment. This is not to say that children do not develop naïve (intuitive) theories. Ever since Piaget's classic work, children's naïve theories have been studied extensively. These theories, however, are produced by children of 4 years of age and older and were based on asking children questions about causes of events and then soliciting children's justifications for their answers (see Carey & Spelke, 1994).

To repeat, a more economical account of the aforementioned developmental changes would assume that children at a certain age develop a new and more advanced existentialization that allows them to take into consideration ontologically deficient and weak properties. At that point, they indeed become able to understand questions about alternative items with ontological contrasts, and this is visible in their correct answers. Before that point, children are blind to ontologically deficient alternatives that the questions imply and always attend to alternatives that have higher statuses in the ontological hierarchy.

Support for this view can be found in studies such as the "discrepant belief" task, in which the competing items were made ontologically similar (Wellman & Bartsch, 1988). In this task, pencils were available at two different locations (the real state of events), but the protagonist only knew about their availability in one location. When asked where the protagonist would look for pencils, 3-year-olds performed significantly better than they did on the typical false belief task. This improvement was presumably due to the fact that the protagonist's belief, as well as that of the child, was in fact true. Likewise, in the control experiment of Gopnik and Astington's (1988) study, the ontological status of the "weak" item (the one that was supposed to be in the container but was not) was increased; the children were actually shown the previous item (an apple) and the new item that replaced it (a doll). In this condition, all but a few 3-year-olds correctly answered the question about what had been in the container before the doll was put in it.

I must emphasize that the *ontological singularity to diversity* shift is independent from the process of developing a representational mind. For instance, 2-year-old children in their pretend play use representations of objects (a block of wood representing a piece of soap), and these representations successfully compete with real objects on the ontological scale (Harris & Kavanaugh, 1993). In spite of that, children younger than 4 years would systematically produce the "ontological singularity" error in their judgment about representations with unequal ontological statuses.

Adjacent to this line of studies lies an area of research on "reality monitoring"—the capacity to accurately discriminate between memories of real and imagined (or suggested) events that is vital for certain juridical practices (Ceci & Huffman, 1997; Johnson, 1988).[4] These studies have shown that memories of events that have really been perceived are richer in sensory and contextual information and more likely to initiate supportive memories than memories of imagined events (Johnson, Foley, Suengas, & Raye, 1988). Preschool children have also been reported to be vulnerable to misleading suggestions (Bruck & Ceci, 1999), and in certain conditions, children and adults claim that they actually experienced events that they only imagined or thought about (Belli, Schuman, & Jackson, 1997; Ceci, Huffman, Smith, & Loftus, 1994). These studies suggest that existentialization goes beyond perception and is involved in memory processes.

To summarize, in the course of cognitive development of the mind, children have to overcome the "ontological singularity" bias in their verbal capacity of existentialization. At school age, *a second level* of existentialization is reached that is characterized by ontological diversity in children's ontological judgments. Arguably, *a third level* in the development of existentialization—that of *ontological initiative*—is achieved when individuals start to be able to artificially inflate elements of reality with ontological power. Thus, we may be aware when being served by a polite and smiling flight attendant that the real emotion experienced by the tired flight attendant is not sympathy and pleasure; yet, at an emotional level, we prefer to ignore the knowledge and take false appearance for reality. This abnormal existentialization (the appearance becomes more real than reality) suits both sides: it saves us our nerves and the flight attendant his or her job. When we admire a piece of impressionistic painting, we tend to ignore the knowledge that objects do not really look as they do in the painting, and when enjoying a piece of cake we prefer not to remember that what really is happening is that we are receiving a special pattern of neural stimulation from our taste buds that are exposed to the molecular structure of the cake. For this reason, most educated adults are not even aware that sensations they perceive from physical objects are actually appearances and not physical realities (Subbotsky, 1997b). In fact, ignoring "reality" in favor of "useful appearances" is a known mechanism that underlies such social practices as politeness, diplomacy, and morality and helps to maintain the stability of social institutions like friendship and family. Ontological initiative is also shown in faith, when something that is unobservable (gods, sacred values) acquires ontological status comparable with (and sometimes superior to) the one that objects of perceived ordinary reality have.

Along with studies of progressive development in childhood, a considerable amount of work has been done on the regressive development of existentialization. This regressive development brings about a disturbance of the distinction between ordinary and magical realities in schizophrenic patients. As discussed earlier, schizophrenic patients have been shown to engage in magical thinking to a considerably greater extent than control subjects (Tissot & Burnard, 1980). According to Eckblad and Chapman (1983), healthy participants who answer questionnaires in a similar way to schizophrenic patients also show a stronger credulity toward magical events than do control participants. A stronger tendency to believe in magical events was found in schizophrenics compared to nonschizophrenic psychiatric patients and healthy subjects (George & Neufeld, 1987). Schizophrenic patients also tend to endow fantasy items with qualities of objectivity and existence (Aggernaes, 1994), and they show a stronger belief in the reality of paranormal events than do control individuals (Thalbourne, 1994; Thalbourne & Delin, 1994; Thalbourne & French, 1995).

As with studies of existentialization in children, researchers in studies of pathological subjects typically confuse the disturbed process of existentialization with impaired thinking. In reality, existentialization, rather than thinking, was targeted in most studies. This is evident from the fact that the popular scale used for assessing magical beliefs—the Magical Ideation scale—consists of ontological statements (such as "some people can make me aware of them just by thinking about me") that subjects evaluate as true or false (Eckblad & Chapman, 1983). The fact that schizophrenic patients who scored higher on magic-implicit ontological statements did not differ significantly from control subjects in their operational intelligence or from nonschizophrenic psychiatric patients in their IQ scores (George & Neufeld, 1987) also suggests that existentialization, rather than thinking, was assessed in the studies (Tissot & Burnard, 1980).

In conclusion, *developmental changes that have been described independently from each other within different domains of research—magical thinking, children's drawings, theory of mind, reality monitoring, the distinction between appearance and reality, ontological judgments in clinical populations—can be linked to a single psychological shift: changes in existentialization.*

Magical Thinking and Beliefs Across the Lifespan: A Summary

Initially, belief in magic was viewed as a phenomenon specific to childhood (Piaget, 1927, 1971). In subsequent research, this linear perspective on early magical beliefs was challenged. Increasingly, it has been argued that magical beliefs, while diminishing in older children's and adults' verbal judgments, can persist in their behavioral responses, particularly when discounting magical effects involves a large cost (Rosengren & Hickling, 1994, 2000; Rozin, Markwith, & Ross, 1990; Subbotsky, 1997a; Woolley, 1997). In light of the research discussed in this book, it can be argued that the development of magical beliefs conforms to a more complex model.

CHILDHOOD: THE DAWN OF MAGIC

At the age of about 4 years, children start to be aware of the contrast between ordinary and magical realities. *After that point, children's magical thinking and their magical beliefs diverge*. In the preschool period and onward, magical thinking flourishes. Children assert magical thinking through imaginative pretend play, imagination, and dreams, and the culture of adults is supportive of these beliefs. Magical folk characters (Santa, the Tooth Fairy), children's books (*Peter Pan*), and fairy tales (Little Red Riding Hood) are employed by adults in order to educate and entertain children, and the multi-national industries of toy production and entertainment encourage magical thinking in children while extracting considerable financial profit from it at the same time. As the studies reviewed in Chapter 4 have shown, magical thinking is beneficial for children's cognitive development, as it facilitates creative divergent thinking.

In adolescence, children continue to be engaged in magical thinking. Their answers to the magical thinking questionnaire are not different from those of 5- to 6-year-olds (Bolton, Dearsley, Madronal-Luque, & Baron-Cohen, 2002). While some forms of early magical thinking fade (imaginary pretend play, involvement with magical folk characters, imaginary companions with magical powers), new forms of practicing magical thinking appear, such as watching popular movies (the Harry Potter films, *Superman*, and *Spiderman*), reading fiction stories (*Alice in Wonderland*), and playing computer games. When and if religious education begins, children's magical thinking incorporates the initial concepts of God, angels, prayer, and other magical concepts and characters related to religion.

A different fate awaits children's early magical beliefs. Beginning in the preschool years, children are aware that magical events, such as mind-over-matter magic, contradict their intuitive and empirically acquired knowledge about how the natural world works. The adult culture, while encouraging children's magical thinking, rarely does so in regard to children's magical beliefs (Rosengren & Hickling, 1994). As a result, when directly asked about the possibility of magical events happening in real life, even most 4-year-olds answer in the negative (Chapter 2). When explaining various physical effects, children prefer physical, rather than magical, explanations (Huang, 1930).

Yet magical beliefs are there. When children are shown effects that go beyond known tricks and look like instances of true magic, most 4- to 6-year-olds and about half of 9-year-olds are quick to retreat to magical practices and explanations (Chapters 2 and 3). When doing this, about half of 5-year-old and most 6- and 9-year-old children are well aware that magical effects are counterintuitive and different from both nonstandard technical effects (such as moving a toy car remotely, Chapter 2) and magic-looking tricks (such as changing an item in a briefcase by using a secret compartment, Chapter 3). Not only are preschoolers' and primary school children's magical beliefs easy to recover, but these beliefs are also entrenched; even when the magic trick is explained to children, all 5-year-olds and 65% of 6-year-olds retain the beliefs that what they were shown was true magic and not a magic trick (Chapter 3). Further testimony to the presence of magical beliefs in the preschool age is that 6-year-olds, unlike older children and adults, do not exhibit a cognitive defense (psychological defense against magical intervention [PDAMI]) against magical intervention (Chapter 10).

Things change at about the age of 9 years. Under the pressure of science education and due to their own growing practical experience with physical objects and processes, most children's magical beliefs become unentrenched, whereas their belief in the universal power of physical causality becomes entrenched (Chapter 3). *This launches the process of the division between two kinds of magical beliefs.* While some early forms of magical beliefs (such as the belief in the power of a wish or a magic spell, the belief in fairies, wizards, and other supernatural beings) seem to disappear, other forms of magical beliefs "...do not disappear entirely but are reaffirmed by our culture, this time via religion" (Woolley, 2000, p. 118). Indeed, studies of children's and adolescents' understanding of prayer show a developmental continuity between beliefs in the efficacy of magical powers and the powers of prayer (Goldman, 1964; Long, Elkind, & Spilka, 1967; Woolley, 2000). This continuity also follows from the fact that the fundamental ontologies in magical and religious thinking are identical (Boyer & Walker, 2000). It is natural, for instance, for preschool children who believe that the Tooth Fairy is invisible and can do miracles to, at an older age, transfer these counterintuitive properties to God. In other words, children's early magical beliefs, which existed as an undifferentiated whole, become divided into beliefs that are unrelated to the official religious doctrine (noninstitutionalized magical beliefs [NIMBs]) and those that are related to this doctrine.

ADULTHOOD: MAGIC IN POWER AND MAGIC IN EXILE

In adulthood, magical thinking persists unobstructed and develops new forms, such as enjoying trends in art that involve magical objects and events (surrealism in painting, magical realism in fiction, advanced forms of music) or, on the negative side, artificially stimulating engagement with magical reality through using hallucinogenic drugs. Magical thinking abounds in the area of visual entertainment, in the form of magical and horror movies. It permeates our language in the form of animism. It fuels creative imagination in art and science. It is widely used in commercial advertising. And of course, early forms of magical thinking such as magical dreams retain their role in the life of the adult mind.

In contrast, magical beliefs are divided. NIMBs experience powerful resistance from the official institutions of science and religion. As argued in Chapter 1, science and religion are united in their efforts to exterminate NIMBs. Science denies magic on the grounds of both theory and empirical evidence. On the grounds of theory, science rejects magic because magic is in contradiction with science's fundamental principles, such as the principle of the laws of nature operating independently from the observer. On empirical grounds, science rejects magic because, according to most scientists, there is no compelling empirical evidence that magical effects (such as mind-over-matter magic) occur in nature. In contrast, religion rejects NIMBs on moral grounds by associating this kind of magical belief with bad powers (the devil, evil spirits, and paganism). While acknowledging the power and use of magical beliefs, religion demands a monopoly on these beliefs. At the same time, magical beliefs that are related to the religious doctrine (beliefs in God, angels, holy miracles) gain support from the powerful institutions—the church and religion.

As argued in Chapter 11, organized religion has developed sophisticated and effective techniques for dealing with people's metaphysical psychological problems, such as the fear of death, the meaning of life, and the desire to be in control of one's destiny. Like other institutions (political power and industries), religion targets an individual's personally significant imagined (PERSIM) objects, which are highly sensitive to magical suggestion. These metaphysical problems are eternal and beyond the scope of science. Because of this, religion, like its secular partner psychotherapy, is here to stay. Whereas in normal conditions institutionalized magical beliefs provide a resource for maintaining mental health and unity within a society, on their extreme side, these beliefs can power religious fanaticism and even suicidal terrorism.

Chased by science and religion, NIMBs descend into the subconscious. Most adults consistently deny such beliefs even if unexplainable magical effects are repeatedly shown to them (Chapter 5). They also develop a fear of magical intervention that results in the psychological defense mechanisms of both cognitive and emotional types—PDAMI (Chapter 10). In spite of this, under certain circumstances, NIMBs are consciously accepted. One form of admitting NIMBs into one's consciousness while not contradicting the dominant scientific paradigm at the same time is curiosity and exploration. As studies reviewed in Chapter 7 have shown, most adults, while declaring that they are nonbelievers in magic, are prepared to engage in exploration with magic to the same extent as preschool and elementary school children. Another form of "legal existence" of NIMBs is transformation and disguise: by throwing off their explicit link with magic, certain mechanisms of magical thinking survive today under the pseudonyms fear of contagion, feelings of disgust, and, in communicative magic, obedience, conformity, and suggestibility.

At first glance, in comparison with scientific thinking, magical thinking looks "nonserious." Likewise, with its humble undercover existence, NIMBs cannot compete with the glory of religion. This impression, however, is misleading. In some respects, magical thinking and NIMBs have an advantage over both science and religion. With regard to science, magical thinking and

NIMBs assert meaningful relationships between an individual and the universe, particularly in situations when a person meets with life-saving chance (such as when my son and I narrowly avoided being crushed by a car in Moscow). This creates in a person the feeling of spiritual unity with nature, which smoothes over the alienation and opposition between man and nature that science has created. Regarding religion, the point is that in the modern world, not every person is able to trust in God in a traditional way. Although science and religion are united in their fight with magic, they nevertheless compete between themselves for people's loyalty.

With the increasing power of science, religion is on the retreat, and such phenomena as secularization, agnosticism, and atheism have become much more widespread, especially among scientists. Despite that, all of us are still magical thinkers. As the studies reviewed in this book suggest, most educated Western individuals, both religious and nonreligious, harbor NIMBs, with individual differences here being only in how far one's NIMBs are buried into the depth of subconscious, and how strong one's PDAMI is. If a person's mind is completely overwhelmed by scientific rationality, magical thinking and NIMBs can provide the only outlet for the inseparable part of every individual's mind—magical reality. That is why, in the modern world, magical thinking and activities based on NIMBs may in fact be increasing, rather than declining.

With regard to magical thinking, this kind of behavior is being strengthened by contemporary mass media. Magical thinking thrives in fiction writing, movies, theater, art, and music. Science fiction had become a special and prosperous branch of literature. Virtual reality and the Internet, particularly with regard to online role-playing games, are places where imaginary magical effects abound. Magical thinking lives in the form of folk magical characters (Santa Claus, the Easter Bunny, the Tooth Fairy), Christmas stories and rhymes for children, comic books (*Superman*, *Spiderman*), video games, and other forms of entertainment. And of course, most of us still see magical images in dreams and engage in the magical play of the imagination.

With the dominance of religion in trouble, NIMBs become fuel for various types of magical practices and behaviors. A typical kind of magic-based practice is magical healing and other types of magical manipulation, such as putting on or neutralizing a curse, eliciting or terminating a love attraction, and so on. Whereas some rare individuals could indeed possess special powers, such as hypnosis and paranormal healing abilities, for the most part charlatans and fake magical healers simply take advantage of people's superstitions based on NIMBs.

Another type of magic-based behavior is superstition. Crossing one's fingers; touching wood; wearing lucky charms; performing protective rituals; believing in ghosts, miracles, chiromancy, palm reading, fortune telling, astrology, UFOs, and aliens; and other forms of superstitious behavior abound in Western and non-Western societies. While most educated rational adults deny that they are superstitious, their superstitious behavior can be activated through targeting their PERSIM objects (such as their concerns about the future state of their valued objects or the images of their future lives) by a magical intervention (Chapters 5, 6, 8, and 9). In fact, in these experimental conditions, educated adults exhibit a similar level of superstitious behavior as do traditional village dwellers of Central Mexico (Chapter 6).

Another type of magical behavior fueled by NIMBs is certain forms of social communication, such as suggestion. As argued in Chapter 9, this form of communication descended from early magical practices that aimed to bond individuals together and encourage cooperation. Using the fundamental mechanism of magical beliefs—participation—various lobbyists and institutions secure obedience and compliance in the population. Political rhetoric, commercial advertising, certain forms of psychotherapies, and controversial religious leaders all successfully target people's PERSIM objects by exploiting, consciously or unconsciously, hidden magical beliefs.

Reactions of disgust, fear of contagion, and other manifestations of sympathetic magic in feelings and reasoning represent another category of magical behavior. As Nemeroff and Rozin (1994; 2000) persuasively argue, these reactions are widespread, are easy to elicit in an experimental setting, and perform a useful heuristic function. Like other mechanisms based on participation (see Chapter 9), in Western cultures today, these reactions operate implicitly. They are stripped of their original magical context and renamed in a way that makes them acceptable in the science-dominated cultural atmosphere.

Another kind of behavior that draws on NIMBs is curiosity toward magical events. TV programs such as "The X-Files" and "The Twilight Zone" are examples. Many people, independent of their religiosity or magical beliefs, happily read or watch programs about divine miracles, ghosts, UFOs, and other magical things.

A special kind of exploratory behavior powered by NIMBs is psi research. Indeed, such phenomena as precognition, extrasensory perception, and direct interaction between the mind and physical devices are essentially instances of mind-over-matter and mind-over-mind magic. Yet parapsychology researchers claim that these phenomena exist as effects in ordinary reality and can be proven by the methods of science. Despite the fact that methods employed by most psi researchers are rigorous and on par with methods used in physical sciences, the results are disputable and have not met with wide recognition in the scientific community to date. Putting the question of this research reliability aside, motivation for such research can, at least partially, come from NIMBs. Otherwise, one could hardly explain why such labor- and time-consuming studies, which are poorly funded, are nevertheless being conducted.

Paradoxically, subconscious NIMBs can also explain the growing interest of modern scientists in studying magic and religion. Being nonreligious themselves, many scholars nevertheless experience a strong attraction toward religious, magical, and other spiritual matters. Studying the history of magic and religion, providing rational justifications and proof of the existence of God, and explaining magical and religious thought on the basis of results of cognitive research in psychology and other empirical scientific disciplines may be viewed as a substitute for the metaphysical vacuum that appears in a human being when there is no explicit belief in the supernatural, yet there exists a subconscious intuition that supernatural things are nevertheless there.

Altogether, the studies reviewed in this book show that magical thinking and magical beliefs are a necessary part of human life; not only do they persist throughout the lifespan, but they also develop with age. An argument has even been made in favor of the reconstitution of the original (and long-lost) unity between magic and religion. According to Pyysiäinen (2004, p. 107), the "optimal combination of magic and religion are culturally more successful than magic or religion alone." In its competition with the growing monster of modernity—science—religion may find a useful ally in the mode of thought it has for centuries viewed as its rival and as such has worked to exterminate, magic.

There is a bridge between a person and the universe that is imperceptible to the rational mind. For millennia, religion explored this bridge, and in the last centuries this bridge became an object of close attention from theories, such as existentialism, phenomenology, psychoanalysis, psychology, parapsychology, and even physics. At the level of an individual's intuition, NIMBs are another manifestation of this invisible bridge.

Epilogue: Plunging Into a Utopia

One way to appreciate the role that magical thinking plays in our everyday lives is to conduct an imaginary experiment. So, let us imagine a little utopia—a world without magical thinking and magical beliefs.

THE WORLD WITHOUT MAGIC

Where shall we start? Childhood. Imagine children's books without magical characters—no fairies, no monsters, no magical land of Oz. What else would be missing? There would be no Alice and no adventures in Wonderland. There would be no Peter Pan, nor any tales by Andersen, Grimm, or Goffman. We would never meet the Girl in the Red Hat, Sleeping Beauty, the Nutcracker, the Ugly Duckling, or the Bremen Musicians. And of course Tolkien's Middle Earth and Rowling's Harry Potter would never have appeared. What a dull childhood—and what a dull parenthood!

And what about art? If we were to believe that cave art served the magical purpose of negotiating with animal spirits, then cave art would never have existed. Modern painting and sculpture would be strictly realistic. Michelangelo Buonarotti could still leave us his statue of David in Florence, but no fresco for the Sistine Chapel's ceiling in the Vatican. Entire trends in art, such as surrealism and magical realism, would be impossible. We could still enjoy novels, albeit reduced, by Leo Tolstoy and Fyodor Dostoevsky, but there would be no *Faust* by Goethe, nor many of the novels by Aleo Carpentier, Gabriel Garcia Marquez, or Jorge Louis Borges. We would never get to enjoy the weird and fantastic art of Pieter Breugel and Hieronymus Bosch. Music and poetry, deprived of magical imagination, would become totally mundane: hard rock and heavy metal—yes. Mozart's "Magic Flute" and Tchaikovsky's "Swan Lake"—no.

Religion? There would be none. No Bible, no Koran. With religion absent, there would be no biblical stories to inspire artists, painters, and composers. Rembrandt's wonderful portraits might exist, but Botticelli's "Birth of Venus" and Raphael's "Sistine Madonna" would vanish. The world's museums would lose much of their stock. Our cities and landscapes would be robbed of churches and cathedrals.

There would be no ancient mythologies. Imagine Egypt without its temples and "The Book of the Dead." The world's history would be completely different—no crusades, no religious wars. Without gods, atheists would be rendered impotent, for whom would they be proud of not believing in? For people, there would be no outlet for grappling with existential problems such as the fear of death and the meaning of life.

Physical science would probably survive, but its progress could be seriously impeded due to the deficit of creative imagination. The German chemist Kekule, discoverer of the structure of benzene, would not have made his discovery without magical thinking, as he claimed that he had discovered the ring shape of the benzene molecule after having a daydream of a snake seizing its own tail (this is a common mythological symbol in many ancient cultures, known as the Ouroboros). Einstein would not have been able to imagine traveling on a light beam, and Maxwell's demon would never have sorted molecules out into the flocks of fast and slow.

For psychology, a world without magical thinking would be a devastating blow. Indeed, in this utopian world all our dreams would be strictly realistic. There would not be much to interpret for Freud, as the seven magical wolves would never be seen sitting on a tree, staring at a dreamer through the window,[1] and the distortions and displacements of dream content would be impossible, since they violate the order of ordinary reality. The Jungian "depth psychology" that heavily relies on myths and religions would not exist either.

Beyond the science of psychology, human psychology in its own right would be different. We would be unable to fulfill wishes in our dreams (talk to our dear ones who passed away) or to experience catharsis and the feeling of "resurrection" by plunging ourselves into the magical worlds of imagination through art or psychedelic compounds. Love would no longer have its "chemistry"—that irrational element based on participation—and love relations would reduce themselves to marriage contracts and prenuptial agreements. Moral rules would lack the backing of divine origin and turn from moral imperatives into a set of rationally planned and temporary social conventions. Such feelings as disgust and fear of contagion would disappear as they are based on magical laws of similarity and contagion. We would be unable to immerse ourselves in the fantastic worlds of imagination. With magical reality absent, "paranormal events" would be impossible—no ghosts, apparitions, seeing the future (precognition), or reading the stars. Such disciplines as astrology and parapsychology could never emerge. With animistic constructions (such as "running water" or "a welcoming landscape") being impossible, even our language would change, coming closer to the language of computer programming.

Perhaps in our magic-free utopia some problems that we have today would disappear. There would be no drug dealers, as nobody would be using psychedelic drugs to plunge themselves into the world of alternative reality. There would be no superstitions. Religious war and suicidal terrorists would be nonexistent. There would be no Holy Inquisition, no witch hunting, and no stake burning. Manipulation of human minds based on the magical law of participation would be impossible, and such phenomena as compliance and obedience to authority would be based strictly on rational persuasion, surveillance, and law enforcement. Newspapers, magazines, and TV advertising would be free of seductive messages from all sorts of charlatans and fake "specialists" with paranormal abilities.

With all its losses and gains, a magic-free world would be very different from the one we live in. It is up to the reader to choose whether he or she would like to live in such a world; I would rather not. Since the utopia we speak of is impossible, here I will briefly summarize what magical thinking *can* do for us in the "real world."

A WORLD WITH MAGIC

According to Bruno Bettelheim (1977), in children, magical beliefs are fuel for imaginary role-play and fantasizing that help children to cope with the chaos of their subconscious desires and to master difficult problems of life. I would add to this that thinking and playing with magical things helps young children to maintain a feeling of independence and power—something that they mostly lack in real life.

But how can adults benefit from magical thinking? First, magical thinking can make this world a more interesting and exciting place. Tired of the monotony of everyday life, many of us are tempted by the enchantment of magic. Those who disagree may try to find an alternative explanation for the phenomenal success of works of imagination like *The Lord of the Rings* and the Harry Potter series, and that nearly every bookshop accommodates a spacious section for occult readings. Second, magic can give us a helpful hand in circumstances that are beyond rational control. For example, Keinan (1994) has shown that people under stress become more tolerant toward magical beliefs. Some theorists argue that the illusion of control is a typical feature of the human mind and has an important adaptive function (Langer, 1975; Zusne & Jones, 1982). Although an illusion, it pushes a person toward greater achievements and helps us cope with the troubling diversity and unpredictable nature of everyday life. Thus, when we set off for a flight, we can never be 100% certain that we are going to make it. In this kind of situation, some of us resort to magical behavior, like crossing fingers or knocking on wood. In more serious situations, such as the case of an incurable illness, a person is even more likely to turn to magical thinking. For those who believe in God, prayer can stand for magic, but for those who do not, a belief in magic and in the supernatural is sometimes the only way to establish and maintain hope. The alternative is hopelessness and despair. That is why there have always been (and, perhaps, always will be) people who claim they have special supernatural healing powers. In fact, contemporary psychotherapy uses techniques that are similar to (or based on) those pioneered by magic and religion, such as traditional shamans' techniques of autosuggestion and the creation of an imaginary reality for healing and other purposes (Mindel, 1993).

Third, magical thinking makes the nonanimate world more understandable and humane (Subbotsky, 2000b). When we are in a rush and our car will not start, we may speak to it. This animistic function of magical thinking is heavily exploited by advertising: in a TV clip, a speeding car can turn into a running jaguar, and a piece of chocolate can take a human shape. Last but not least, magical thinking constitutes a foundation for the way our individual and social minds work (Nemeroff & Rozin, 2000). Our emotional and communicative reactions are literally based on the laws of sympathetic magic. The phenomena of emotional contagion, hypnotic suggestion, magical healing, and placebo effects are just a small sample of those reactions. Magical thinking is important for establishing and maintaining human relations. In love and in parenting, we frequently perform little rituals (hugging, making presents, doing small things together) that, from the strictly rational view, are unnecessary.

Just as rational thinking helps us to cope with problems in the physical world, magical thinking and magical beliefs come to our aid when we deal with problems in our personal, social, and emotional lives. That is why, despite the popular view, magical thinking and magical beliefs (religion included) go well with common logic and are a useful complement to scientific thinking and rational reasoning.

LOOKING INTO THE FUTURE

Does magical thinking have a future? Having survived for many thousands of years, it is unlikely to disappear. One can only speculate about what will have happened to magical thinking and noninstitutionalized magical beliefs (NIMBs) hundreds and thousands years from now, and this book is not an exercise in science fiction. However, there are a few global problems in connection with magical thinking and NIMBs that face people today, and in regard to these problems a cautious prognosis is possible.

The first problem is the tension between by-products of human activities and the natural environment. If this tension reaches a breaking point, a global ecological catastrophe is inevitable. Early humans did not oppose themselves to their environment; rather, through the mechanism of participation, they felt that a spiritual bond linked them to the animals, plants, and landscapes around them (Frazer, 1923; Ingold, 1992; Lévy-Brühl, 1984). It would therefore seem unthinkable that early peoples would knowingly and over the long term commit harm to their environment. Today, the future of the planet and its environment is a precious and personally significant object for every person on Earth, just like in the past, yet few people feel and act this way. If humanity is to survive, it will have to start treating the global natural environment in the same way as most people today treat their personal future lives. As the studies reported in this book have shown, personally significant imagined (PERSIM) objects are the objects that elicit in people protective superstitious behavior. This means that something similar to the ancient animistic attitude toward nature, both animate and inanimate, should replace the exploitative rational attitude that dominates today. I hold that the unrestricted exploitation of natural resources and contamination of the environment with the waste products of human activity can only be stopped if rational and scientific thinking toward the global environment is taken under control by ethical and animistic thinking. Forests, lakes, planes, and oceans can be inanimate objects if taken in separation, but taken together, they are a system that has nurtured us as a species, and this system will destroy us if we ignore or disrespect its needs.

Another issue concerns the division between magical and ordinary realities. Evidence is accumulating that some human beings have an ability to exercise mind-over-matter (the direct interaction between the mind and machines, extrasensory perception) and mind-over-mind (telepathy) causality (Bem & Honorton, 1994; Eysenck & Sargent, 1993; Jahn & Dunne, 2007; Stanford & Rust, 1977). In the majority of people, this ability is present to such a small extent that it can effectively be ignored, but there are exceptional individuals, and even in ordinary people this ability can be amplified. If (and when) such amplification will be achieved, this ability will open a whole range of exciting new opportunities, such as mind-controlled technical devices and transmission of information between individuals without a physical medium. This may also change the structure of the individual's mind. At present, magical and ordinary realities in the mind of an individual are separated and isolated one from another (Chapter 1). In the world where psi will be controlled, the line between the two realities will soften, and the realities will intertwine. This can have important consequences for the everyday life of people, for our view of the universe and man's role in it, and for the traditional division between social and physical sciences. The existing isolation and alienation of the human individual from his or her physical environment will be overcome, and the link between people and nature that once used to exist will be restored.

Finally, it is not unlikely that disciplines studying the human mind and brain will solve the mystery of the afterlife. It is impossible to predict what impact on our beliefs such a discovery might have, except that it will be a major one. All that can be said with certainty is that the modern science-dominated view of the human mind and the universe is a historical creation and will be replaced, probably more than once, by different visions of the world. Magical thinking and magical beliefs may in fact play a more important role in this new world. Altogether, the global problems we face may demand the use of magical thinking and magical beliefs. This kind of thinking has a future, and as such is an exciting and important topic for multidisciplinary research.

Notes

CHAPTER 1

1. According to archeological data, for early modern humans there was not a division between people who have minds and natural things that do not. "For them [modern hunter-gatherers] there are not two worlds of persons (society) and things (nature), but just one world – one environment – saturated with personal powers and embracing both human beings, the animals and plants on which they depend, and the landscape in which they live and move" (Ingold, 1992, p. 42)
2. Of course, this depends on what one means by "consciousness." Currently, most philosophers agree that, being a product of brain processes, consciousness is nevertheless not a physical or material entity (see Hardcastle, 1993; McGinn, 1989; Mills, 1998).
3. Unless, of course, we define consciousness as a physical force, similar to electric or magnetic fields.

CHAPTER 3

1. Here and elsewhere in this book, I use the term "belief in the universal power of physical causality" as applied only to manual physical objects that are a part of children's everyday practical experience. In judgments about remote objects (like stars) and complex phenomena (like dreams), verbal magical beliefs persist in children and adolescents (Bolton, Dearsley, Madronal-Luque, & Baron-Cohen, 2002; Laurendeau & Pinard, 1962; Piaget, 1927).

176

2. In this book, effects that involve an element of the supernatural will be called "truly magical," in contrast to tricks that imitate magical effects. Independently of whether "truly magical effects" can or cannot happen in real life, they certainly can happen in dreams or imagination and therefore merit a strict definition.

CHAPTER 4

1. As in most studies of the effects of TV and movies on children's behavior, in constructing methodology for this study, we suspended the issues of whether the effect of exposure to a movie clip on children's creative performance is universal and stable or whether this effect is context dependent and short lived. These issues are important ones, yet they can only arise if the effect of exposure to a particular movie clip on a particular type of children's behavior is established in the first place. The aim of this study was to find out if the effect of watching a magical movie on children's creative performance exists; examining this effect on context dependence and stability could make a topic for a special study.
2. Further studies have shown that exposing 6- and 9-year-old children to the movie with magical content significantly increased their ability to discriminate between complex visual displays, whereas showing a similar movie without magical content did not (Subbotsky, 2010). In a delayed recognition memory test, adolescents and postgraduates recognised a significantly larger number of components from commercial TV adverts based on magical effects than from equally attractive and interesting non-magical adverts (Matthews, 2010).

CHAPTER 5

1. Some phenomena of magical thinking and behavior shown in Figure 5.1 (such as participation-based mechanisms of communication and suicidal terrorism) will be discussed in Chapters 6, 8, and 9 of this book.
2. This is an idea that was posed by the French philosopher Blaise Pascal that even though the existence of God cannot be determined through empirical knowledge or logically proven, a person should "wager" that God exists, because by doing so, one potentially has a lot to gain and very little to lose.

CHAPTER 6

1. This magical transmutation of one thing into another will be discussed in detail in Chapter 9 as the magical law of participation.
2. The participants' magical beliefs can also be evident from the following episode. One day, after the experimenter had tested a few female participants, a group of men approached and accused the experimenter of the intention to bewitch their children. The men then threatened to hang the experimenter. At that moment, the community leader arrived and explained to the group that the experimenter was a teacher from the city who was conducting the study that had been approved by him. The men apologized and even offered the experimenter some small gifts; however, for a moment, the experimenter did feel a serious concern for her life.

CHAPTER 7

1. Not to be confused with a magic trick that looks like a true magical effect.
2. Although the method employed in this study was similar to that in studying children's and adults' magical beliefs (Chapters 2 and 5), the motivation behind the action (putting a valuable object at risk) in this study was different from the one in the aforementioned study. Whereas in the study of magical beliefs participants' decisions of putting their valuable objects at risk were motivated by the desire to show their disbelief in magic, in this study it was motivated by the curiosity to see if the unusual effect would happen again. This may account for the fact that the 6- and 9-year-olds and adults in this study showed different patterns of behavior from those shown in the study of magical beliefs.

CHAPTER 8

1. Boyer and Walker (2000) make a similar distinction between "the realm of imagination" and "the world of fantasy." In this study, I refer to two kinds of imagined worlds—physical and fictional—to capture the fact that the fictional domain is based on the same mechanisms of imagination as the imagined physical domain, the only difference being that the physical constraints of the perceived world apply only to the imagined physical domain.
2. The term "real objects" is often used to contrast tangible physical objects with imagined objects. However, as many of imagined objects are, in some respects, real although not actually perceived, in this book I prefer to contrast imagined and perceived objects rather than imagined and real objects.

CHAPTER 9

1. Participation-based manipulation should not be confused with "pseudo-rational" forms of manipulation, in which a skillful debater or a political leader can befuddle and manipulate people with rational arguments by "bending" the truth or simply preying on people's trust and insufficient information. This kind of manipulation, known as Machiavellianism, is based on deception and secrecy. As soon as the recipients of this kind of manipulation attempt become aware of it, the manipulation becomes ineffective and is usually aborted (Kara-Murza, 2007). In contrast, participation-based manipulation is immune to rational arguments; the recipients follow the suggested message while being fully aware that what they are doing is untrue and/or contrary to their interests.
2. While the absence of the difference between the effects of magical and ordinary suggestions does not necessarily imply that they are based on the same psychological mechanism, it certainly increases the probability that these mechanisms are the same.
3. This type of suggestion was classified as ordinary because in this condition, unlike the magical suggestion condition, the suggestion explicitly did not refer to the supernatural forces. Indeed, changing simple numbers on computer screens is something that most participants do (or see being done) on a daily basis, and there are no superstitions in Western societies that link working with a computer with participants' future lives.
4. Although it does not follow with necessity that if participants have mixed motivations to allow or not allow the good spell then these motivations would balance the responses about equally, this might be the case. And, as was established in the previous study (Chapter 8),

this is the case. Certainly, this is an empirical fact, yet, once established, it can be used as a basis for prediction in subsequent research. Similarly, Miller's experiments showed that in adults the limit of short term memory capacity was around seven elements, regardless of whether the elements were digits, letters, words, or other units (Miller, 1956). There is no necessity for Miller's "magical number" to be 7, and not 5 or 9, yet it is 7, and this does not make this empirical fact unsuitable for making predictions.

5. In this study, as in the study reviewed in Chapter 8, participants' verbal responses ("yes" or "no") to the key questions are called behavioral. The reason is that, by acknowledging that they would allow or not allow a manipulation, participants had to reveal the actions they would choose if the imaginary situation presented in the interview were real. Generally speaking, it is quite often that in humans behavioral responses take the form of verbal actions (such as offending someone verbally or displaying verbal aggression). In this study, participants' behavioral answers were contrasted with their theoretical views about whether their allowing or not allowing a manipulation would have any real effect. For instance, a lot of participants said they would not allow the change of the numeric pattern on the computer screen, yet subsequently stated that even if they had then nothing would change in their future.

6. In psychoanalysis, "transference" is the fixation of the patient's libido on the therapist (simply put, the patient has to develop a sort of love attraction toward the therapist). Only if the transference occurs is the patient able to accept the therapist's interpretation of the cause of the patient's problem (for example, neurosis).

7. Indeed, persuading rational people that prayer can affect their lives, that buying a certain brand of jeans can make them rich, or that voting for a certain candidate can erase a paramount state budget deficit without raising taxes can only be successful if it appeals to people's magical thinking and not to their rational thinking.

CHAPTER 10

1. Cognitive PDAMI can be understood in terms of the "Multiple Drafts Model" by Dennet and Kinsbourne (1992). This model states that information processing in the brain is a pluralistic process of creating multiple models (or drafts) that unfold in parallel one to another and are "finalized" retrospectively. Applied to participants' reconstruction of the temporal order of events, this model would predict that such an order may be altered in the participants' memories, especially if the temporal intervals between the events are close to limits of the brain's power of temporal resolution, which is around 50msec for many tasks.

2. In this and other studies, the proportion of participants who accepted the offer of magical intervention depended on the magnitude of benefit that magical intervention promised. When the benefit was big (in the earlier hypothetical experiment [Subbotsky, 2005] and in Experiment 2 of this study), the number of participants willing to accept the offer was at chance level. When the benefit was small (in Experiments 1 and 3 of this study), the number of participants who accepted the offer was significantly above chance.

CHAPTER 11

1. Ordinary reality should not be confused with the everyday life of an individual. As it will be argued further in this chapter, the everyday life involves a mixture of ordinary and magical realities, rational and irrational thinking, and behavior.

2. Arguably, this dominant position of the ordinary reality in the structure of the individual mind is a relatively recent product of cultural and historical development. In earlier historical epochs, in Western civilizations (Greece and Rome) and in non-Western cultures (Egypt), magical realities (such as dreams, myths, and hallucinations) were given a higher role, comparable with that given to ordinary reality (see Al-Issa, 1995; Jaynes, 1976).

3. Perhaps it is an inability to immerse themselves into magical realities for this purpose in a normal way (through art, music, or imagination) that makes some people so vulnerable to hallucinogenic drugs.

4. For more on the role of theory-theory, reality monitoring, conceptual change, theory of mind, and other recent theoretical approaches in the development of phenomenalistic reality of the mind in children, see Subbotsky, 2000c.

EPILOGUE

1. The dream of a hysterical man described in the "Wolf man" case history (Freud, 1991).

Bibliography

Aaronson, B. S., & Osmond, H. (Eds.) (1971). *Psychedelics: The uses and implications of hallucinogenic drugs.* London: Hogart Press.

Aggernaes, A. (1994). Reality testing in schizophrenia. *Nordic Journal of Psychiatry, 48,* 47–54.

Aguirre, G., & D'Esposito, M. (1997). Environmental knowledge is sub-served by separable dorsal/ventral neural areas. *Journal of Neuroscience, 17,* 2512–2518.

Al-Issa, I. (1995). The illusion of reality or the reality of illusion: Hallucinations and culture. *British Journal of Psychiatry, 166,* 368–373.

Arieti, S. (1976). *Creativity: The magic synthesis.* New York: Basic Books.

Aristotle. (1976). *Works, in four volumes* (Vol. 1). Moscow: Mysl.

Asch, S. (1951). Effects of group pressure upon the modification and distortion of judgments. In H. Guetzkow (Ed.), *Groups, leadership, and men.* Pittsburgh, PA: Carnegie Press.

Atran, S. (2003). Genesis of suicidal terrorism. *Science, 2999,* 1534–1539.

Atran, S., Axelrod, R., & Davis, R. (2007). Sacred barriers to conflict resolution. *Science, 317,* 1039–1040.

Attneave, F., & Pierce, C. R. (1978). Accuracy of extrapolating a pointer into perceived and imagined space. *American Journal of Psychology, 91,* 371–387.

Babin, L. A., & Garder, S. T. (1996). Viewers' recognition of brands placed within a film. *International Journal of Advertising, 15,* 140–151.

Baillargeon, R. (1987). Object permanence in 3 1/2- and 4 1/2-month-old infants. *Developmental Psychology, 23,* 655–664.

Baron-Cohen, S., Leslie, A. M., & Frith, U. (1985). Does the autistic child have a "theory of mind"? *Cognition, 1,* 37–46.

Barrett, J. L. (2001). How ordinary cognition informs petitionary prayer. *Journal of Cognition and Culture, 1*(3), 259–269.

Barrett, J. L., & Keil, F. (1996). Conceptualizing a non-natural entity: Anthropomorphism in God concepts. *Cognitive Psychology, 31,* 219–247.

Barrett, J. L., Richert, R. A, & Driesenga, A. (2001). God's beliefs versus mother's: The development of nonhuman agents concepts. *Child Development, 72*(1), 50–65.

Barrett, M. D., & Light, P. H. (1976). Symbolism and intellectual realism in children's drawings. *British Journal of Educational Psychology, 46,* 198–202.

Belli, R. F., Schuman, H., & Jackson, B. (1997). Autobiographical misremembering: John Dean is not alone. *Applied Cognitive Psychology, 11,* 187–209.

Bem, D. J., & Honorton, C. (1994). Does psi exist? Replicable evidence for an Anomalous process of information transfer. *Psychological Bulletin, 115,* 4–18.

Bering, J. (2006a). The cognitive psychology of belief in the supernatural. *American Scientist, 94,* 142–149.

Bering, J. (2006b). The folk psychology of souls. *Behavioral and Brain Sciences, 29,* 453–498.

Berlyne, D. E. (1960). *Conflict, arousal and curiosity.* New York: McGraw-Hill.

Bettelheim, B. (1977). *The uses of enchantment: The meaning and importance of fairy tales.* New York: Vintage Books.

Bleuler, E. (1951). Autistic thinking. In D. Rapaport (Ed.), *Organization and pathology of thought* (pp. 199–437). New York: Columbia University Press. (Originally published in 1912.)

Bloom, P. (2004). *Descartes' baby: How the science of child development explains what makes us human.* New York: Basic Books.

Bloom, P., & Weisberg, D.S. (2007). Childhood origins of adult resistance to science. *Science, 316,* 996-997.

Bolton, D., Dearsley, P., Madronal-Luque, R., & Baron-Cohen, S. (2002). Magical thinking in childhood and adolescence: Development and relation to obsessive compulsion. *British Journal of Developmental Psychology, 20,* 479–494.

Borel, A. (1934). La pensée magique dans l'art. *Revue Française de Psychanalyse, 7,* 66–83.

Bower, T. G. R. (1971). The object in the world of an infant. *Scientific American, 225*(4), 30–38.

Bower, T. G. R. (1974). *Development in infancy.* San François: Freeman.

Bower, T. G. R. (1989). *The rational infant: Learning in infancy.* New York: Freeman.

Boyer, P. (1994). *The naturalness of religious ideas: A cognitive theory of religion.* · Berkley; Los Angeles; London: University of California Press.

Boyer, P. (2008) Religion: Bound to believe? *Nature, 455,* 1038–1039.

Boyer, P., & Bergstrom, B. (2008). Evolutionary perspectives on religion. *Annual Review of Anthropology, 37,* 111–130.

Boyer, P., & Walker, S.(2000). Intuitive ontology and cultural input in the acquisition of religious concepts. In K. S. Rosengren, C. N. Johnson, & P. L. Harris (Eds.), *Imagining the impossible: Magical, scientific and religious thinking in children* (pp. 130–156). Cambridge, UK: Cambridge University Press.

Brehm, S. S., & Kassin, S. M. (1996). *Social psychology* (3rd ed.). Boston: Houghton Mifflin.

Bremner, G. J., & Moor, S. (1984). Prior visual inspection and object naming: Two factors that enhance hidden feature inclusion in young children's drawings. *British Journal of Developmental Psychology, 2,* 371–376.

Browne, C. A., & Woolley, J. D. (2004). Preschoolers' magical explanations for violations of physical, social, and mental laws. *Journal of Cognition and Development, 5*(2), 239–260.

Bruck, M., & Ceci, S. J. (1999). The suggestibility of children's memory. *Annual Review of Psychology, 50,* 419–439.

Bulgakov, M. (1967). *The Master and Margarita.* Translated from Russian by Michael Glenny. London: Collins and Harviell Press.

Bullock, M. (1985). Animism in childhood thinking: A new look at an old question. *Developmental Psychology, 21,* 217–225.

Bullock, M., & Gelman, R. (1979). Preschool children's assumptions about cause and effect: Temporal ordering. *Child Development, 50*(1), 89–96.

Burns, J. E. (1991). Contemporary models of consciousness: II. *Journal of Mind and Behavior, 12,* 407–420.

Butler, R. A. (1954). Curiosity in monkeys. *Scientific American, 190,* 70–75.

Cahill-Solis, T. L., & Witryol, S. L. (1994). Children's exploratory play preferences for four levels of novelty in toy construction. *Genetic, Social, and General Psychology Monographs, 120*(4), 393–408.

Cannon, W. (1957). Voodoo death. *Psychosomatic Medicine, 19,* 182–190.

Cantor, J. H., & Cantor, G. N. (1964). Observing behavior in children as a function of stimulus novelty. *Child Development, 35,* 119–128.

Carey, S. (1985). *Conceptual change in childhood.* Cambridge, MA: MIT Press.

Carey, S. (1999). Sources of conceptual change. In E. K. Scholnick, K. Nelson, S. A. Gelman, & P. H. Miller (Eds.), *Conceptual development: Piaget's legacy* (pp. 293–326). Mahwah, NJ; London: Lawrence Erlbaum.

Carey, S., & Spelke, E. (1994). Domain-specific knowledge and conceptual change. In L. A. Hirschfeld & S. A. Gelman (Eds.), *Mapping the mind: Domain specificity in cognition and culture* (pp. 169–200). Cambridge, UK: Cambridge University Press.

Cartwright, R. D. (1974). The influence of a conscious wish on dreams: A methodological study of dream meaning and function. *Journal of Abnormal Psychology, 83,* 387–393.

Castiglioni, A. (1946). *Adventures of the mind.* New York: Alfred A. Knopf.

Ceci, S. J., & Bruck, M. (1993). Suggestibility of the child witness: A historical review and synthesis. *Psychological Bulletin, 113*(3), 403–439.

Ceci, S. J., & Huffman, M. L. C. (1997). How suggestible are preschool children? Cognitive and social factors. *Journal of the American Academy of Child and Adolescent Psychiatry, 36,* 948–958.

Ceci, S. J., Huffman, M. L. C., Smith, E., & Loftus, E. W. (1994). Repeatedly thinking about a non-event: Source misattribution among preschoolers. *Consciousness and Cognition, 3,* 388–407.

Champagne, A. B., Gunstone, R. F., & Klopfer, L. E. (1985). Instructional consequences of students' knowledge about physical phenomena. In L. H. T. West & A. L. Pines (Eds.), *Cognitive structure and conceptual change* (pp. 61–90). Orlando, FL: Academic Press.

Chandler, M. J., & Lalonde, C. E. (1994). Surprising, magical, and miraculous turns of events: Children's reactions to violations of their early theories of mind and matter. *British Journal of Developmental Psychology, 12,* 83–96.

Chi, M. T. N. (1992). Conceptual change within and across ontological categories: Implications for learning and discovery in science. In R. Giere (Ed.), *Minnesota studies in the philosophy of science: Vol. XV. Cognitive models of science* (pp. 129–186). Minneapolis, MN: University of Minnesota Press.

Chinn, C. A., & Brewer, W. F. (1993). The role of anomalous data in knowledge acquisition: A theoretical framework and implications for science instruction. *Review of Educational Research, 63,* 1–49.

Chinn, C. A., & Brewer, W. F. (2000). Knowledge change in response to data in science, religion, and magic. In K. S. Rosengren, C. N. Johnson, & P. L. Harris (Eds.), *Imagining the impossible: Magical, scientific and religious thinking in children* (pp. 334–371). Cambridge, UK: Cambridge University Press.

Christensen, S. M., & Turner, D. R. (1993). Introduction. In S. M. Christensen & D. R. Turner (Eds.), *Folk psychology and the philosophy of mind.* Hillsdale, NJ: Erlbaum.

Christiano, B. A., & Russ, S. W. (1996). Play as a predictor of coping and distress in children during an invasive dental procedure. *Journal of Clinical Child Psychology, 25,* 130–138.

Cialdini, R. B. (2007). *Influence: The psychology of persuasion.* New York: Harper Collins.

Clark, C. D. (1995). *Flights of fancy, leaps of faith: Children's myths in contemporary America.* Chicago: University of Chicago Press.

Clore, G. L., Schwarz, N., & Conway, M. (1994). Affective causes and consequences of social information processing. In R. S. Wyer & T. K. Srull (Eds.), *Handbook of social cognition* (2nd ed., pp. 323–341). Hillsdale, NJ: Erlbaum.

Cohen, F. W. (1981). Art therapy: Psychotic expression and symbolism. *Arts in Psychotherapy, 8,* 15–23.

Cole, M. (1996). *Cultural psychology: A once and future discipline.* Cambridge, MA: Harvard University Press.

Comerford, B., & Witryol, S. L. (1993). Information metrics for novelty level preference of first-and fifth-grade children. *Journal of Genetic Psychology, 154*(2), 155–165.

Comstock, G., & Scharrer, E. (2006). Media and pop culture. In W. Damon & R. M. Lerner (Series Eds.) and K. A. Reninger & I. Sigel (Volume Eds.), *Handbook of child psychology* (Vol. 4, 6th ed.). New York: Wiley.

Coriat, I. H. (1923). Suggestion as a form of medical magic. *Journal of Abnormal and Social Psychology, 18,* 258–268.

Craig, J., & Baron-Cohen, S. (1999). Creativity and imagination in autism and Asperger's syndrome. *Journal of Autism and Developmental Disorders, 29,* 319–326.

Damasio, A. (1994). *Descartes' error: Emotion, reason, and the human brain.* New York: Putnam Publishing.

Danilov-Danilian, V., Losev, K., & Reif, I. (2005). *The main challenge of civilization: The Russian view.* Moscow: Infra-M Publishers.

Dawkins, R. (2006). *The God delusion.* London: Transworld Publishers.

Delacour, J. (1995). An introduction to the biology of consciousness. *Neuropsychologia, 33,* 1061–1074.

DeLoache, J. S., Miller, K. F., & Rosengren, K. S. (1997). The credible shrinking room: Very young children's performance with symbolic and non-symbolic relations. *Psychological Science, 8,* 308–311.

Dennett, D. C. (1991). *Consciousness explained.* Boston: Little, Brown & Co.

Dennett, D. C., & Kinsbourne, M. (1992). Time and the observer: The where and when of consciousness. *Behavioral and Brain Sciences, 15,* 183–201.

Descartes, R. (1988). Meditations on first philosophy. In *Descartes, Select philosophical writings.* Translated by John Cottingham, Robert Stoothoff, and Dougald Murdoch. Cambridge, UK: Cambridge University Press. (Originally published 1641.)

Dias, M., & Harris, P. L. (1988). The effect of make-believe play on deductive reasoning. *British Journal of Developmental Psychology, 6,* 207–221.

Donald, M. (1995). The neurobiology of human consciousness: An evolutionary approach. *Neuropsychologia, 33,* 1087–1102.

Dowling, J. E. (1998). *Creating mind. How the brain works.* New York: W.W. Norton.

Dunne, B. J. (1991). Co-operator experiments with an REG device. Princeton Engineering Anomalous Research, School of Engineering and Applied Science, Princeton University, Technical Note PEAR 91005.

Dunne, B. J., Nelson, R. D., & Jahn, R. G. (1988). Operator-related anomalies in a random mechanical cascade. *Journal of Scientific Exploration, 2,* 155–179.

Eckblad, M., & Chapman, L. J. (1983). Magical ideation as an indicator of schizotypy. *Journal of Consulting and Clinical Psychology*, 51, 215–225.

Einstein, D. A, & Menzies, R.G (2004). Role of magical thinking in obsessive-compulsive symptoms in an undergraduate sample. *Journal of Consulting and Clinical Psychology, 51,* 215–225.

Eisenberger, R., Haskins, F., & Gambleten, P. (1999). Promised reward and creativity. Effects of prior experience. *Journal of Experimental social Psychology*, 35, 308–325.

Eriksen, H. R., Nordby, H., Olff, M., & Ursin, H. (2000). Effects of psychological defense on processing of neutral stimuli indicated by event-related potentials (ERPs). *Scandinavian Journal of Psychology, 41(4),* 263–267.

Estes, D., Wellman, H. M., & Woolley, J. (1989). Children's understanding of mental phenomena. In H. Reese (Ed.), *Advances in child development and behavior* (pp. 41–86). New York: Academic Press.

Evans, D. W., Milanak, M. E., Medeiros, B., & Ross, J. L. (2002). Magical beliefs and rituals in young children. *Child Psychiatry and Human Development, 33,* 43–58.

Eysenck, H. J., & Sargent, C. (1993). *Explaining the unexplained. Mysteries of the paranormal.* London; New York: Broadcast Agent Publishers.

Farah, M. J. (1994). Neuropsychological inference with an inactive brain: A critique of the 'locality' assumption. *Behavioral and Brain Sciences, 17,* 43–104.

Feldhusen, J. F., & Treffinger, D. J. (1975). Teachers' attitudes and practices in teaching creativity and problem solving to economically disadvantaged and minority children. *Psychological Reports, 37,* 1161–1162.

Feynman, R. (1974). Cargo cult science. *Engineering and Science, 7,* 10–13.

Filipowitch, A. (2006). From positive affect to creativity: The surprising role of surprise. *Creativity Research Journal, 18,* 141–152.

Flanagan, O. (1995). Consciousness and the natural method. *Neuropsychologia, 33,* 1103–1115.

Flavell, J. A., Green, F. L., & Flavell, E. R. (1986). Development of knowledge about the appearance-reality distinction. *Monographs of the Society for Research in Child Development, 51,* Serial No. 212.

Flavell, J. H. (1993). The development of children's understanding of false belief and the appearance-reality distinction. *International Journal of Psychology, 28,* 595–604.

Flavell, J. H., Green, F. L., Wahl, K. E., & Flavell, E. R. (1987). The effects of question clarification and memory aids on young children's performance on appearance-reality tasks. *Cognitive Development, 2,* 127–144.

Fodor, J. A. (1988). Precis of the modularity of mind. In A. Collins & E. E. Smith (Eds.), *Readings in cognitive science: A perspective from psychology and artificial Intelligence* (pp. 73–78). San Mateo, CA: Morgan Kauffmann Publishers.

Forgas, J. P. (1995). Mood and judgment: The affect infusion model (AIM). *Psychological Bulletin, 117,* 39–36.

Forgas, J. P. (2002). Feeling and doing: Affective influences on interpersonal behavior. *Psychological Inquiry, 13*, 1–28.

Frawley, W. (1997). *Vygotsky and cognitive science: Language and the unification of the social and computational mind.* Cambridge, MA: Harvard University Press.

Frazer, J. G. (1923). *The golden bough: A study in magic and religion.* London: Macmillan & Co. Ltd.

Freeman, N. H., & Janikoun, R. (1972). Intellectual realism in children's drawings of a familiar object with distinctive features. *Child Development, 43*, 1116–1121.

Freska, E., & Kulcsar, Z. (1989). Social bonding in the modulation of the physiology of ritual trance. *Ethos, 17*, 70–87.

Freud, S. (1935). *A general introduction to psychoanalysis.* New York: Liveright.

Freud, S. (1976). *Introductory lectures on psychoanalysis.* New York: Penguin Books. (Originally published 1916.)

Freud, S. (1991). *Case histories II.* New York: Penguin Books.

Freud, S. (1995). Creative writers and daydreaming. In E. Spector Person, P. Fonagy, and S. A. Figueira (Eds.), *On Freud's 'Creative writers and daydreaming'. Contemporary Freud: Turning points and critical issues* (pp. 3–13). New Haven, CT: Yale University Press. (Originally published 1908.)

Freyd, J. J., & Finke, R. A. (1984). Facilitation of length discrimination using real and imagined context frames. *American Journal of Psychology, 97*, 323–341.

Fromm, E. (1941). *Escape from freedom.* New York: Farrar & Rinehart.

Fromm, E. (1961). *The fear of freedom.* London: Routledge & Kegan Paul.

Gasper, K. (2004). Do you see what I see? Affect and visual information processing. *Cognition and Emotion, 18*, 405–421.

Gellner, E. (1989). *Plough, sword, and book: The structure of human history.* Chicago: University of Chicago Press.

Gelman, R., & Baillargeon, R. (1983). A review of some Piagetian concepts. In J. H. Flavell & E. M. Markman (Eds.), *Handbook of child psychology* (Vol. III, pp. 166–230). New York: Wiley.

George, L., & Neufeld, R. W. (1987). Magical ideation and schizophrenia. *Journal of Consulting and Clinical Psychology, 55*, 778–779.

German, T. P., & Leslie, A. (2000). Attending to and learning about mental states. In P. Mitchell & K. J. Riggs (Eds.), *Children's reasoning and the mind* (pp. 229–248). Hove, UK: Psychology Press.

Goldman, R. (1964). *Religious thinking from childhood to adolescence.* London: Routledge & Kegan Paul.

Gopnik, A., & Astington, J. W. (1988). Children's understanding of representational change and its relation to the understanding of false-belief and the appearance-reality distinction. *Child Development, 59*, 26–37.

Gopnik, A., & Wellman, H. M. (1992). Why the child's theory of mind really is a theory. *Mind and Language, 7*, 145–171.

Gopnik, A., & Wellman, H. M. (1994). The theory theory. In L. A. Hirschfeld & S. A. Gelman (Eds.), *Mapping the mind: Domain specificity in cognition and culture* (pp. 257–293). Cambridge, UK: Cambridge University Press.

Gregory, R. L. (1980). *The intelligent eye.* London: Weidenfeld and Nicolson.

Grobstein, P. (1990). Strategies for analysing complex organization in nervous system: I. Lesion experiments. In E. L. Schwartz (Ed.), *Computational neuroscience* (pp. 19–37). Cambridge, MA: A Bradford Book.

Guilford, J. P. (1950). Creativity. *American Psychologist, 5*, 444–454.

Gupta, P. B., & Lord, K. R. (1998). Product placement in movies: The effect of prominence and mode on audience recall. *Journal of Current Issues and Research in Advertising, 20*(1), 47–59.

Hardcastle, V. G. (1993). The naturalists versus the sceptics: The debate over a scientific understanding of consciousness. *Journal of Mind and Behavior, 14,* 27–50.

Harlow, H. F. (1953). Mice, monkeys, men, and motives. *Psychological Review, 60,* 23–32.

Harris, P. L. (2000). *The work of the imagination.* Malden, MA: Blackwell.

Harris, P. L., Brown, E., Marriot, C., Whittal, S., & Harmer, S. (1991). Monsters, ghosts and witches: Testing the limits of the fantasy–reality distinction in young children. *British Journal of Developmental Psychology, 9*, 105–123.

Harris, P. L., & Kavanaugh, R. (1993). Young children's understanding of pretence. *Monographs of the Society for Research in Child Development, 58*(1), Serial No. 231.

Heidegger, M. (1959). *The introduction to metaphysics.* New Haven, CT: Yale University Press.

Henderson, B., & Moore, S. G. (1980). Children's responses to objects differing in novelty in relation to level of curiosity and adult behavior. *Child Development, 51*(2), 457–465.

Henkel, L. A., & Franklin, N. (1998). Reality monitoring of physically similar and conceptually related objects. *Memory and Cognition, 26,* 659–673.

Hergovich, A. (2003). Field dependence, suggestibility and belief in paranormal phenomena. *Personality and Individual Differences, 34,* 195–209.

Howse, B. (1993). *Cradle to college.* Green Forest, AR: New Leaf Press.

Huang, I. (1930). Children's explanations of strange phenomena. *Psychologische Forschung, 14,* 63–183.

Humphreys, W. C. (1968). *Anomalies and scientific theories.* San Francisco: Freeman, Cooper & Co.

Husserl, E. (1970). *Cartesian meditations: An introduction to phenomenology.* The Hague: M. Nijhoff.

Huston, A. C., & Wright, J. C. (1998). Mass media and children's development. In W. Damon (General Ed.) and I. E. Sigel, & K. A. Reninger (Volume Eds.), *Handbook of child psychology: Vol.4. Child psychology in practice* (pp. 999–1058). New York: Wiley.

Huston-Stein, A., Fox, S., Greer, D., Watkins, B. A., & Whitaker, J. (1981). The effects of TV action and violence on children's social behaviour. *Journal of Genetic Psychology, 138,* 183–191.

Ingold, T. (1992). Comment on "Beyond the original affluent society" by N. Bird-David. *Current Anthropology, 33,* 34–47.

Jackendoff, R. (1987). *Consciousness and the computational mind.* Cambridge, MA: MIT Press.

Jahn, R. G., & Dunne, B. J. (2007). Change the rules! Princeton Engineering Anomalies Research, School of Engineering and Applied Science, Princeton University, Technical Note PEAR 2007.01.

Jahoda, G. (1969). *The psychology of superstition.* London: Allen Lane.

James, W. (1980). *The principles of psychology* (Vol. II). London: Macmillan and Co. Ltd. (Originally published 1901.)

Jaynes, J. (1976). *The origin of consciousness in the breakdown of the bicameral mind.* Boston: Houghton Mifflin.

Jersild, A. T. (1943). Studies of children's fears. In R. G. Barker, J. S. Kounin, & H. F. Wright (Eds.), *Child behavior and development* (pp. 329–344). New York: McGraw-Hill.

Jersild, A. T., & Holmes, F. B. (1935). Methods of overcoming children's fears. *Journal of Psychology, 1,* 75–104.

Johnson, C., & Harris, P. L. (1994). Magic: Special but not excluded. *British Journal of Developmental Psychology, 12,* 35–52.

Johnson, C. N., & Wellman, H. M. (1980). Children's developing understanding of mental verbs: Remember, know and guess. *Child Development, 51*(4), 1095–1102.

Johnson, M. K. (1988). Reality monitoring: An experimental-phenomenological approach. *Journal of Experimental Psychology: General, 117,* 390–394.

Johnson, M. K., Foley, M. A., Suengas, A. G., & Raye, C. L. (1988). Phenomenal characteristics of memories for perceived and imagined autobiographical events. *Journal of Experimental Psychology: General, 117*(4), 371–376.

Kant, I. (1929). *Critique of pure reason.* Translated by N.K. Smith. London: MacMillan. (Original work published 1781.)

Kara-Murza, S. G. (2007). *The power of manipulation.* Moscow: Academical Project.

Karmiloff-Smith, A. (1989). Constraints on representational change: Evidence from children's drawing. *Cognition, 34,* 57–83.

Karrh, J. A. (1998). Brand placement: A review. *Journal of Current Issues and Research in Advertising, 20*(2), 31–49.

Kaufman, A. M. (1990). The role of fantasy in the treatment of a severely disturbed child. *Psychoanalytic Study of the Child, 45,* 235–256.

Keil, F. C. (1989). *Concepts, kinds, and cognitive development.* Cambridge, MA: MIT Press.

Keinan, G. (1994). Effects of stress and tolerance of ambiguity on magical thinking. *Journal of Personality and Social Psychology, 67,* 48–55.

Kelly, M. H., & Keil, F. C. (1985). The more things change . . .: Metamorphoses and conceptual structure. *Cognitive Science, 9,* 403–416.

Killeen, P. R. (1977). Superstition: A matter of bias, not detectability. *Science, 199,* 88–90.

Kisch, I., & Braffman, W. (2001). Imaginative suggestibility and hypnotizability. *Current Directions in Psychological Science, 10,* 57–61.

Knight, N., Sousa, P., Barrett, J. L., & Atran, S. (2004). Children's attributions of beliefs to humans and God: Cross-cultural evidence. *Cognitive Science, 28,* 117–126.

Krellenstein, M. F. (1995). Unsolvable problems, visual imagery and explanatory satisfaction. *Journal of Mind and Behavior, 16*(3), 235–253.

Kuhn, D. (1989). Children and adults as intuitive scientists. *Psychological Review, 96,* 674–689.

Kuhn, G., Amlani, A., & Rensink, R. A. (2008). Towards a science of magic. *Trends in Cognitive Science, 9,* 349–354.

Kuhn, T. S. (1970). *The structure of scientific revolutions* (2nd ed.). Chicago: University of Chicago Press.

Kun, A. (1978). Evidence for preschoolers' understanding of causal direction in extended causal sequences. *Child Development, 49*(1), 218–222.

Lacatos, I. (1970). Falsification and the methodology of scientific research programmes. In I. Lakatos & A. Musgrave (Eds.), *Criticism and the growth of knowledge* (pp. 91–196). London: Cambridge University Press.

Langer, E. J. (1975). The illusion of control. *Journal of Personality and Social Psychology, 32,* 311–328.

Larkin, J. H. (1983). The role of problem representation in physics. In D. Gentner & A. Stevens (Eds.), *Mental models* (pp. 75–98). New York: Academic Press.

Laurendeau, M., & Pinard, A. (1962). *Causal thinking in the child.* Montreal, Canada: International University Press.

LeDoux, J. (1996). *The emotional brain: Mysterious underpinnings of emotional life.* New York: Simon and Shuster.

Leevers, H. J., & Harris, P. L. (1998). Drawing impossible entities: A measure of the imagination in children with autism, children with learning disabilities, and normal 4-year-olds. *Journal of Child Psychology and Psychiatry, 39*, 399–410.

Lehman, A. C., & Mayers, J. E. (1985). *Magic, witchcraft, and religion.* Palo Alto, CA: Mayfield.

Leslie, A. M. (1982). The perception of causality in infants. *Perception, 11*(2), 173–186.

Leslie, A. M. (1984). Infant perception of manual pick-up event. *British Journal of Developmental Psychology, 2,* 29–32.

Leslie, A. M. (1986). Getting development off the ground: Modularity and infant's perception of causality. In P. L. C. van Geert (Ed.), *Theory building in developmental psychology* (pp. 405–437). Amsterdam: North Holland Publishers.

Levin, I., Siegler, R. S., Druyan, S., & Gardosh, R. (1990). Everyday and curriculum–based physics concepts: When does short-term training bring change where years of schooling failed to do so? *British Journal of Developmental Psychology, 8,* 269–279.

Lévy-Brühl, L. (1966). *Primitive mentality.* Boston: Beacon Press. (Original work published 1923.)

Lévy-Brühl, L. (1985). *How natives think.* Princeton, N.J.: Princeton University Press. (Original work published 1926.)

Lewis, C., & Mitchell, P. (1994). *Children's early understanding of mind: Origins and development.* Hove, UK: Lawrence Erlbaum.

Long, D., Elkind, D., & Spilka, B. (1967). The child's conception of prayer. *Journal for the Scientific Study of Religion, 6*, 101–109.

Losev, A. F. (1978). *Estetika Vosrozhdenija [Aesthetics of the renaissance].* Moscow: Mysl.

Luhrman, T. M. (1989). *Persuasions of the witch's craft: Ritual magic and witchcraft in present-day England.* Oxford, UK: Blackwell.

Lundahl, C. R. (1993). The near-death experience: A theoretical summarization. *Journal of Near-Death Studies, 12*(2), 105–118.

Luria, A. R. (1931). Psychological expedition to Central Asia. *Science, 74,* 383–384.

Luria, A. R. (1971). Toward the problem of the historical nature of psychological processes. *International Journal of Psychology, 6*, 259–272.

Luria, A. R. (1976). *Cognitive development: Its cultural and social foundations.* Cambridge, MA: Harvard University Press.

Luria, A. R. (1980). *Higher cortical functions in man.* New York: Basic Books.

Malinowski, B. (1935). *Coral gardens and their magic.* London: George Allen and Anwin.

Matthews, J. (2010). Magical thinking and commercial advertising: Adolescents' and adults' memories for magical and non-magical adverts. A dissertation in partial fulfilment of the requirements for the degree of BSc (Hon) in Psychology. Lancaster University, Psychology Department, UK.

Matuga, J. M. (2004). Situated creative activity: The drawings and private speech of young children. *Creativity Research Journal, 16,* 267–281.

May, E. C. (2006) *Anomalous cognition: Two protocols for data collection and analysis.* Unpublished manuscript. Available from http://www.lfr.org/LFR/csl/library/ACtrials&Analysis.pdf

May, E. C., Faith, L. V., Blackman, M., Bourgeois, B., Kerr, N., & Woods, L. (1999). A target pool and database for anomalous cognition experiments. Parapsychological

Association Meeting, Stanford, CA. Available from http://www.lfr.org/LFR/csl/academic/whitepapers.html

McCloskey, M. (1983). Naïve theories of motion. In D. Gentner & A. Stevens (Eds.), *Mental models* (pp. 299–324). Hillsdale, NJ: Erlbaum.

McGinn, C. (1989). Can we solve the body-mind problem? *Mind, 391,* 349–366.

Mead, M. (1932). An investigation of the thought of primitive children, with special reference to animism. *Journal of the Royal Anthropological Institute, 62,* 173–190.

Mendel, G. (1965). Children's preferences for differing degrees of novelty. *Child Development, 36,* 453–465.

Michotte, A. (1962). *Causalite, permanence et realite phenomenales.* Paris: Editions.

Milgram, S. (1992). *The individual in a social world: Essays and experiments* (2nd ed.). New York: McGraw-Hill.

Miller, G. A. (1956). The magical number seven, plus or minus two: Some limits on our capacity for processing information. *Psychological Review,* 63, 81-97.

Mills, F. B. (1998). The easy and hard problems of consciousness: A Cartesian perspective. *Journal of Mind and Behavior, 19,* 119–140.

Mindel, A. (1993). *The shaman's body: A new shamanism for transferring healthy relationships and community.* San Francisco: Harper.

Mitchell, P., Robinson, E. J., Isaacs, J. E., & Nye, R. M. (1996). Contamination in reasoning about false belief: An instance of realist bias in adults but not children. *Cognition, 59,* 1–26.

Mithen, S. J. (2005*). The prehistory of the mind: A search for the history of art, religion and science.* London: Phoenix.

Moody, R. (1976). *Life after life: The investigation of a phenomenon—survival of body death.* New York: Bantam Books.

Moor, C., Pure, K., & Furrow, P. (1990). Children's understanding of the modal expression of certainty and uncertainty and its relation to the development of a representational theory of mind. *Child Development, 61,* 7222–7730.

Morrison, P., & Gardner, H. (1978). Dragons and dinosaurs: The child's capacity to differentiate fantasy from reality. *Child Development, 49,* 642–648.

Mouchiroud, C., & Lubart, T. (2001). Children's original thinking: An empirical examination of alternative measures derived from divergent thinking tasks. *Journal of Genetic Psychology, 162,* 382–401.

Needham, J. (1925). Science, religion and reality. London: The Sheldon Press.

Nelson, R., Bradish, G., Jahn, R. G., & Dunne, B. J. (1994). A linear pendulum experiment: Effects of operator intention on damping rate. *Journal of Scientific Exploration, 8,* 471–489.

Nemeroff, C. (1995). Magical thinking about illness virulence: Conceptions of germs from "safe" versus "dangerous" others. *Health Psychology, 14,* 147–151.

Nemeroff, C., & Rozin, P. (1992). Sympathetic magical beliefs and kosher dietary practice: The interaction of rules and feelings. *Ethos, 20*(1), 96–115.

Nemeroff, C., & Rozin, P. (1994). The contagion concept in adult thinking in the United States: Transmission of germs and an interpersonal influence. *Ethos, 22*(2), 158–186.

Nemeroff, C., & Rozin, P. (2000). The making of the magical mind: The nature and function of sympathetic magical thinking. In K. S. Rosengren, C. N. Johnson, & P. L. Harris (Eds.), *Imagining the impossible: Magical, scientific and religious thinking in children* (pp. 1–34). Cambridge, UK: Cambridge University Press.

Pavlov, I. P. (1927). *Conditioned reflexes.* London: Oxford University Press.

Penfield, W. (1975). *The mystery of the mind.* Princeton, NJ: Princeton University Press.

Perleth, C., & Sierwald, W. (1993). Selected results of the Munich longitudinal study of giftedness: The multidimensional/typo- logical giftedness model. *Roeper Review, 15,* 149–155.

Perner, J. (1991). *Understanding the representational mind.* Cambridge, MA: MIT Press.

Perner, J., Leekam, S. R., & Wimmer, H. (1987). Three-year-olds' difficulty with false belief: The case for a conceptual deficit. *British Journal of Developmental Psychology, 5,* 125–137.

Petty, R. E., & Cacioppo, J. T. (1986). *Communication and persuasion: Central and peripheral routes to attitude change.* New York: Springer-Verlag.

Phelps, K. E., & Woolley, J. D. (1994). The form and function of young children's magical beliefs. *Developmental Psychology, 30,* 385–394.

Piaget, J. (1927). *La causalite physique chez l'enfant.* Paris: Alcan.

Piaget, J. (1937). *La formation du symbol chez l'enfant.* Neuchatel-Paris: Delachaux et Niestle.

Piaget, J. (1954). *The construction of reality in the child.* New York: Basic Books. (Originally published 1937.)

Piaget, J. (1962). *Play, dreams, and imitation in childhood.* Translated by C. Gattegno and F. M. Hodgson. New York: Norton. (Original work published in 1937.)

Piaget, J. (1971). *The child's conception of the world.* London: Routledge & Kegan Paul. (Original work published in 1929.)

Piaget, J. (1976). *The grasp of consciousness: Action and concept in the young child.* Cambridge, MA: Harvard University Press. (Originally published 1974.)

Plato. (1968). *Works, in three volumes* (Vol. 1). Moscow: Mysl.

Pliner, P., Pelchat, M., & Grabski, M. (1993). Reduction of neophobia in humans by exposure to novel food. *Appetite, 20*(2), 111–123.

Plotkin, H. (1998). *Evolution in mind: An introduction to evolutionary psychology.* Cambridge, MA: Harvard University Press.

Plucker, J. A. (1999). Is the proof in the pudding? Reanalyses of Torrance's (1958 to present) longitudinal data. *Creativity Research Journal, 12,* 103–114.

Prawat, R. S., Anderson, A. H., & Hapkiewicz, W. (1983). Is the scariest monster also the least real? An examination of children's reality classification. *Journal of Genetic Psychology, 146*(2), 7–12.

Prentice, N. M., Manosevitz, M., & Hubbs, L. (1978). Imaginary figures of early childhood: Santa Claus, Easter Bunny, and the Tooth Fairy. *American Journal of Orthopsychiatry, 48,* 618–628.

Principe, G. F., & Smith, E. (2008). Seeing things unseen: Fantasy beliefs and false reports. *Journal of Cognition and Development, 9,* 89–111.

Procter, P. (Ed.). (1995). *Cambridge international dictionary of English.* Cambridge, UK: Cambridge University Press.

Punamäki, R. L., Kanninen, K., Qouta, S., & El-Sarraj, E. (2002). The role of psychological defences in moderating between trauma and post-traumatic symptoms among Palestinian men. *International Journal of Psychology, 37*(5), 286–296.

Pyysiäinen, I. (2004). *Magic, miracles and religion: A scientist's perspective.* Walnut Creek, CA: AltaMira Press.

Redfield, R. (1968). *The folk culture of Yucatan.* Chicago: University of Chicago Press.

Reisman, F. K., Pellegrini, A. D., Floyd, B., Paguio, L., & Torrance, E. P. (1980). *Performance on Torrance's thinking creatively in action and movement as a predictor of cognitive development.* Unpublished research report, Department of Early Childhood and Elementary Education, University of Georgia. Cited in Torrance, E. P. (1981). *Thinking creatively in action and movement.* Bensenville, IL: Scholastic Testing Service, Inc.

Rice, C. K., Koinis, D., Sullivan, K., & Tager-Flusberg, H. (1997). When 3-year-olds pass the appearance-reality test. *Developmental Psychology, 1,* 54–61.

Richards, R. (1993). Everyday creativity, eminent creativity, and psychopathology. *Psychological Inquiry, 4,* 212–217.

Richardson, G., & Kelly, T. P. (2004). A study in the relationship between interrogative suggestibility, compliance and social desirability in institutionalized adolescents. *Personality and Individual Differences, 36*(2), 485–494.

Richert, R. A. (2003). *The effect of fantasy context on preschoolers' analogical problem solving.* Poster presented at the 2003 meeting of the Jean Piaget Society, Chicago, IL.

Rittenhouse, C. D., Stickgold, R., & Hobson, J. A. (1994). Constraint on the transformation of characters, objects, and settings in dream reports. *Consciousness and Cognition, 3,* 100–113.

Roffwarg, H. P., Herman, J. H., Bowe-Anders, C., & Tauber, E. S. (1978). The effect of sustained alterations of waking visual input on dream content. In A. M. Arkin, J. S. Antrobus, & S. J. Ellman (Eds.), *The mind in sleep* (pp. 295–349). Hillsdale, NJ: Erlbaum.

Rosengren, K. S., & Hickling, A. K. (1994). Seeing is believing: Children's explanations of commonplace, magical, and extraordinary transformations. *Child Development, 65,* 1605–1626.

Rosengren, K. S., & Hickling, A. K. (2000). Metamorphosis and magic: The development of children's thinking about possible events and plausible mechanisms. In K. S. Rosengren, C. N. Johnson, & P. L. Harris (Eds.), *Imagining the impossible: Magical, scientific, and religious thinking in children* (pp. 75–98). Cambridge, UK: Cambridge University Press.

Rosengren, K. S., Kalish, C. W., Hickling, A. K., & Gelman, S. A. (1994). Exploring the relation between preschool children's magical beliefs and causal thinking. *British Journal of Developmental Psychology, 12,* 69–82.

Rozin, P., Markwith, M., & McCauley, C. R. (1994). The nature of aversion to indirect contact with another person: AIDS aversion as a composite of aversion to strangers, infection, moral taint and misfortune. *Journal of Abnormal Psychology, 103,* 495–504.

Rozin, P., Markwith, M., & Nemeroff, C. (1992). Magical contagion beliefs and fear of AIDS. *Journal of Applied Social Psychology, 22,* 1081–1092.

Rozin, P., Markwith, M., & Ross, B. (1990). The sympathetic magical law of similarity, nominal realism, and neglect of negatives in response to negative labels. *Psychological Science, 1,* 383–384.

Rozin, P., Millman, L., & Nemeroff, C. (1986). Operation of laws of sympathetic magic in disgust and other domains. *Journal of Personality and Social Psychology, 50,* 703–712.

Runco, M. A., Nemiro, J., & Walberg, H. J. (1998). Personal explicit theories of creativity. *Journal of Creative Behavior, 32,* 1–17.

Russ, S. W. (1998). Play, creativity, and adaptive functioning: Implications for play interventions. *Journal of Clinical Child Psychology, 27,* 469–480.

Russ, S. W., & Kaugars, A. S. (2001). Emotion in children's play and creative problem solving. *Creativity Research Journal, 13,* 211–219.

Russ, S. W., Robins, A. L., & Christiano, B. A. (1999) Pretend play: Longitudinal prediction of creativity and affect in fantasy in children. *Creativity Research Journal, 12*, 129–139.

Samarapungavan, A. (1992). Children judgements in theory choice tasks: Scientific rationality in childhood. *Cognition, 45,* 1–32.

Sasaki, T. (2006). *Magical thinking as a function of educational background and religious belief.* A dissertation in partial fulfilment of the requirements for the degree of BSc (Hon) in Psychology. Lancaster University, Psychology Department, UK.

Scott, F. J., & Baron-Cohen, S. (1996). Imagining real and unreal things: Evidence of a dissociation in autism. *Journal of Cognitive Neuroscience, 8,* 371–382.

Scott, F. J., Baron-Cohen, S., & Leslie, A. (1999). If pigs could fly: A test of counterfactual reasoning and pretence in children with autism. *British Journal of Developmental Psychology, 17,* 349–362.

Sejourne, L. (1976). *Burning water: Thought and religion in ancient Mexico.* Berkeley, CA: Shambala.

Selby, H. A. (1974). *Zapotec deviance: The convergence of folk and modern sociology.* Austin, TX: University of Texas Press.

Sextus Empiricus. (1976). *Works, book 1.* Moscow: Mysl.

Shafran, R., Thordarson, M. A., & Rachman, S. (1996). Thought-action fusion in obsessive compulsive disorder. *Journal of Anxiety Disorders, 10,* 379–391.

Sharon, T., & Woolley, J. D. (2004). Do monsters dream? Young children's understanding of the fantasy/reality distinction. *British Journal of Developmental Psychology, 22,* 293–310.

Sherif, M. (1966). *The psychology of social norms.* New York: Harper and Row.

Shtulman, A., & Carey, S. (2007). Improbable or impossible? How children reason about the possibility of extraordinary events. *Child Development, 78*(3), 1015–1032.

Shultz, T. R., Fisher, G. W., Pratt, C. C., & Rulf, S. (1986). Selection of causal rules. *Child Development, 49,* 143–152.

Shweder, R. A. (1977). Likeness and likelihood in everyday thought: Magical thinking in judgments about personality. *Current Anthropology, 18,* 637–658.

Singer, M., Goldstein, H., Langone, H., Miller, J. S., Temerlin, M. K., & West, L. J. (1986). *Report of the APA task force on deceptive and indirect techniques of persuasion and control.* www.rickross.com/reference/apologist/apologist23.html

Singer, D., & Singer, J. (Eds.). (2001). *Handbook of children and the media.* Thousand Oaks, CA: Sage.

Singer, D. L., & Singer, J. (1990) *The house of make-believe.* Cambridge, MA: Harvard University Press.

Skinner, B. F. (1948). 'Superstition' in the pigeon. *Journal of Experimental Psychology, 38,* 168–172.

Skolnick, D., & Bloom, P. (2006). What does Batman think about SpongeBob? Children's understanding of the fantasy/fantasy distinction. *Cognition, 101,* 9–18.

Smith, G. J. W. (2005). How should creativity be defined? *Creativity Research Journal, 17,* 293–295.

Smith, C., Carey, S., & Wiser, M. (1985). On differentiation: A case study of the development of the concepts of size, weight, and density. *Cognition, 21,* 177–237.

Sobel, D. M. (2006). How fantasy benefits young children's understanding of pretense. *Developmental Science, 9,* 63–75.

Sperber, D. (1997). Intuitive and reflective beliefs. *Mind and Language, 12*(1), 67–83.

Stafford, P. (2003). *Psychedelics.* Oakland, CA: Ronin Publishing.

Staley, A. A., & O'Donnell, J. P. (1984). A developmental analysis of mothers' reports of normal children fears. *Journal of Genetic Psychology, 144,* 165–178.

Stanford, R. G., & Rust, P. (1977). Psi-mediated helping behavior: Experimental paradigm and initial results. In J. D. Morris, W. G. Roll, & R. L. Morris (Eds.), *Research in parapsychology* (pp. 109–110). Metuchen, NJ: Scarecrow.

Sternberg, R. J. (1985). Implicit theories of intelligence, creativity, and wisdom. *Journal of Personality and Social Psychology, 49,* 607–627.

Strandberg, T., & Terry, J. D. (2004). *Are you rapture ready? Signs, prophecies, warnings, and suspicions that the endtime is now.* New York: Penguin Books.

Stuss, D., & Benson, D. F. (1986). *The frontal lobes.* New York: Raven Press.

Subbotsky, E. V. (1985). Preschool children's perception of unusual phenomena. *Soviet Psychology, 23,* 91–114.

Subbotsky, E. V. (1991a). Existence as a psychological problem: Object permanence in adults and preschool children. *International Journal of Behavioral Development, 14*(1), 67–82.

Subbotsky, E. V. (1991b). A life span approach to object permanence. *Human Development, 34,* 125–137.

Subbotsky, E. V. (1993*). Foundations of the mind: Children's understanding of reality.* Cambridge, Massachusetts: Harvard University Press.

Subbotsky, E. V. (1994). Early rationality and magical thinking in preschoolers: Space and time. *British Journal of Developmental Psychology, 12,* 97–108.

Subbotsky, E. V. (1996). Explaining impossible phenomena: Object permanence beliefs and memory failures in adults. *Memory, 4,* 199–223.

Subbotsky, E. V. (1997a). Explanations of unusual events: Phenomenalistic causal judgments in children and adults. *British Journal of Developmental Psychology, 15,* 13–36.

Subbotsky, E. (1997b). Understanding the distinction between sensations and physical properties of objects by children and adults. *International Journal of Behavioral Development, 20,* 321–347.

Subbotsky, E. V. (2000a). Causal reasoning and behavior in children and adults in a technologically advanced society: Are we still prepared to believe in magic and animism? In P. Mitchell & K. J. Riggs (Eds.), *Children's reasoning and the mind* (pp. 227–347). Hove, UK: Psychology Press.

Subbotsky, E. (2000b). Phenomenalistic perception and rational understanding in the mind of an individual: A fight for dominance. In K. S. Rosengren, C. N. Johnson, & P. L. Harris (Eds.), *Imagining the impossible: Magical, scientific and religious thinking in children* (pp. 35–74). Cambridge, UK: Cambridge University Press.

Subbotsky, E. (2000c). Phenomenalistic reality: The developmental perspective. *Developmental Review, 20,* 438–474.

Subbotsky, E. V. (2001). Causal explanations of events by children and adults: Can alternative causal modes coexist in one mind? *British Journal of Developmental Psychology, 19,* 23–46.

Subbotsky, E. (2004). Magical thinking in judgments of causation: Can anomalous phenomena affect ontological causal beliefs in children and adults? *British Journal of Developmental Psychology, 22,* 123–152.

Subbotsky, E. (2005). The permanence of mental objects: Testing magical thinking on perceived and imaginary realities. *Developmental Psychology, 41,* 301–318.

Subbotsky, E. (2007) Children's and adults' reactions to magical and ordinary suggestion: Are suggestibility and magical thinking psychologically close relatives? *British Journal of Psychology, 98,* 547–574.

Subbotsky, E. (2009a). Can magical intervention affect subjective experiences? Adults' reactions to magical suggestion. *British Journal of Psychology*, 100, 517–537.

Subbotsky, E. (2009b). Curiosity and exploratory behavior towards possible and impossible events in children and adults. *British Journal of Psychology* (accepted for publication)

Subbotsky, E. (2010). Discrimination between fantastic and ordinary visual displays by children and adults (Unpublished manuscript).

Subbotsky, E., Chesnokova, O., & Greenfield, S. (2002). *Object permanence beliefs and memory failures in children and adults.* Paper presented at the conference on memory, University of Tsukuba, Japan, March 8–10, 2002. Available from www.lancs.ac.uk/staff/subbotsk

Subbotsky, E., & Hysted, C. (2008). *Magical thinking and creativity in preschool children.* Paper presented at XXth Biennial Meeting of the International Society for the Study of Behavioral Development, July 13–17, 2008, Wurzburg, Germany.

Subbotsky, E., Hysted, C., & Jones, N. (2009). Watching Harry Potter: *Magical thinking and creativity in children.* Unpublished manuscript. Available from www.lancs.ac.uk/staff/subbotsk/

Subbotsky, E., & Quinteros, G. (2002). Do cultural factors affect causal beliefs? Rational and magical thinking in Britain and Mexico. *British Journal of Psychology, 93*, 519–543.

Subbotsky, E., & Ryan, A. (2009). *Motivation, belief and geomagnetic activity in a remote viewing task.* Paper presented at the Society for Psychical Research Annual Conference, Nottingham, UK, September 4–6, 2009.

Subbotsky, E. V., & Trommsdorff, G. (1992). Object permanence in adults: A cross-cultural perspective. *Psychologische Beiträge, 34*, 62–79.

Swinburne , R. (1979). *The existence of god?* New York: Oxford University Press.

Swinburne, R. (1996). *Is there a god?* Oxford; New York: Oxford University Press.

Tambiah, S. J. (1990). *Magic, science, religion, and the scope of rationality.* Cambridge, UK: Cambridge University Press.

Taylor, M., & Carlson, S. (1997). The relation between individual differences in fantasy and theory of mind. *Child Development, 68*, 436–455.

Taylor, M., & Carlson, S. (2000). The influence of religious beliefs on parental attitudes about children's fantasy behavior. In K. S. Rosengren, C. N. Johnson, & P. L. Harris (Eds.), *Imagining the impossible: Magical, scientific and religious thinking in children* (pp. 247–268). Cambridge, UK: Cambridge University Press.

Taylor, M., & Flavell, J. H. (1984). Seeing and believing: Children's understanding of the distinction between appearance and reality. *Child Development, 55*, 1710–1720.

Taylor, M., & Hort, B. (1990). Can children be trained in making the distinction between appearance and reality? *Cognitive Development, 5*, 89–99.

Taylor, B., & Howell, R. (1973). The ability of three-, four-, and five-year-old children to distinguish ordinary from magical reality. *Journal of Genetic Psychology, 122*, 315–318.

Thalbourne, M. A. (1994). Belief in the paranormal and its relationship to schizophrenia-relevant measures: A confirmatory study. *British Journal of Clinical Psychology, 33*, 78–80.

Thalbourne, M. A., & Delin, P. S. (1994). A common thread underlying belief in the paranormal, creative personality, mystical experience and psychopathology. *Journal of Parapsychology, 58*(1), 3–38.

Thalbourne, M., & French, C. C. (1995). Paranormal beliefs, manic-depressiveness and magical ideation: A replication. *Personality and Individual Differences, 18*(2), 291–292.

Thomas, K. (1971). *Attitudes and behavior*. Baltimore, MD: Penguin Books.

Tissot, R., & Burnard, Y. (1980). Aspects of cognitive activity in schizophrenia. *Psychological Medicine, 10,* 657–663.

Torrance, E. P. (1962). *Guiding creative talent*. Englewood Cliffs, NJ: Prentice-Hall.

Torrance, E. P. (1981). *Thinking creatively in action and movement*. Bensenville, IL: Scholastic Testing Service, Inc.

Tulviste, P. (1991). *The cultural-historical development of verbal thinking*. Commack, NY: Nova Science Publishers.

Vikan, A., & Clausen, S.E. (1993). Freud, Piaget, or neither? Beliefs in controlling others by wishful thinking and magical behavior in young children. *Journal of Genetic Psychology, 154*(3), 297–314.

Vinden, P. (1996). Junin Quechua children's understanding of mind. *Child Development, 67,* 1707–1716.

Vygotsky, L. S. (1982). Memory and its development in childhood. In L. S. Vygotsky (Ed.), *Works, in six volumes, Volume 2*. Moscow: Pedagogica.

Vygotsky, L. S. (1999). Tool and sign in the development of the child. In *The collected works of L.S. Vygotsky. Volume 6: Scientific legacy*. New York: Kluwer/Plenum. (Original work written in 1930.)

Vyse, S. A. (1997). *Believing in magic: The psychology of superstition*. New York; Oxford, UK: Oxford University Press.

Walker, S. (1992). Developmental changes in the representation of word-meaning: Cross-cultural findings. *British Journal of Developmental Psychology, 10,* 285–299.

Wegner, D. M. (1994). Pink elephant tramples white bear: The evasion of suppression. *Psycoloquy, 5,* 40.

Wegner, D. M., & Erskine, J. A. K. (2003). Voluntary involuntariness: Thought suppression and the regulation of the experience of will. *Consciousness and Cognition, 12*(4), 684–694.

Wegner, D. M., Schneider, D. J., Carter, S. R., III, & White, T. L. (1987). Paradoxical effects of thought suppression. *Journal of Personality and Social Psychology, 53*(1), 5–13.

Wellman, H. M., & Bartsch, K. (1988). Young children's reasoning about beliefs. *Cognition, 30,* 239–277.

Wellman, H. M., Cross, D., & Watson, J. (2001). Meta-analysis of theory-of-mind development: The truth about false belief. *Child Development, 3,* 655–684.

Wellman, H. M., & Estes, D. (1986). Early understanding of mental entities: A re-examination of childhood realism. *Child Development, 57,* 910–923.

Wertsch, J. (1991). *Voices of the mind*. Cambridge, MA: Harvard University Press.

Westen, D. (2007). *The political brain: The role of emotion in deciding the fate of the nation*. New York: Public Affairs.

Wimmer, H., & Perner, J. (1983). Beliefs about beliefs: Representation and constraining function of wrong beliefs in young children's understanding of deception. *Cognition, 13,* 103–128.

Wiseman, R., & Watt, C. (2004). Measuring superstitious belief: Why lucky charms matter. *Personality and Individual Differences,* 37, 1533–1541.

Wiser, M., & Carey, S. (1983). When heat and temperature were one. In: D. Gentner & A. Stevens (Eds.), *Mental models* (pp. 75–98). New York: Academic Press.

Wolpert, L. (2006). *Six impossible things before breakfast: The evolutionary origins of beliefs*. London: Faber & Faber.

Woolley, J. D. (1997). Thinking about fantasy: Are children fundamentally different thinkers and believers from adults? *Child Development, 98,* 991–1011.

Woolley, J. D. (2000). The development of beliefs about direct mental-physical causality in imagination, magic, and religion. In K. S. Rosengren, C. N. Johnson, & P. L. Harris (Eds.), *Imagining the impossible: Magical, scientific and religious thinking in children* (pp. 99–129). Cambridge, UK: Cambridge University Press.

Woolley, J., Boerger, E. A., & Markman, A. B. (2004). A visit from the Candy Witch: Factors influencing children's belief in a novel fantastic entity. *Developmental Science, 7*, 456–468.

Woolley, J. D., Browne, C. A., & Boerger, E. A. (2006). Constraints on children's judgments of magical causality. *Journal of Cognition and Development, 7*(2), 253–277.

Woolley, J. D., & Cox, V. (2007). Development of beliefs about storybook reality. *Developmental Science, 10*, 681–693.

Woolley, J. D., & Phelps, K. E. (1994). Young children's practical reasoning about imagination. *British Journal of Developmental Psychology, 12*(1), 53–67.

Woolley, J. D., Phelps, K. E., Davis, D. L., & Mandell, D. J. (1999). Where theories of mind meet magic: The development of children's beliefs about wishing. *Child Development, 70*, 571–587.

Woolley, J. D., & Wellman, H. M. (1993). Origin and truth: Young children's understanding of imaginary mental representations. *Child Development, 64*(1), 1–17.

Zaitchek, D. (1990). When representation conflict with reality: The preschoolers problem with false beliefs and "false" photographs. *Cognition, 35*, 41–68.

Zusne, L. (1985). Magical thinking and parapsychology. In P. Kurtz (Ed.), *A sceptical handbook of parapsychology* (pp. 688–700). New York: Prometheus Books.

Zusne, L., & Jones, W. H. (1982). *Anomalistic psychology: A study of extraordinary phenomena of behavior and experience*. Hillsdale, NJ: Erlbaum.

Index

Little Red Riding Hood, 35

Magic, 3
   as anomalous experience, 24–27
   beliefs in, 4
   cultural support for, 43–44
   future of, 173–75
   personal destiny and, 91–95
   religion and, 4–5, 117
   science and, 8–12, 116–17
   uses and misuses of, 60–62
   world with, 172–73
   world without, 170–72
Magical behavior, 7, 18, 20, 154
Magical beliefs, 7
   in Britain, 58, 60
   history of political power and, 111–13
   institutionalized, 12
   noninstitutionalized, 12
   in Mexico, 57–60
   in Russia, 112–13
   testing entrenchment of, 27–33
Magical causality, 5, 6, 94, 98, 144
Magical causation, 5, 79, 83
Magical condition (MC), 66–67, 73
Magical contagion, 96
Magical Ideation scale, 4–5, 50
Magical reality, 5
   functions of, 136–40
   ordinary reality and, 144–45, 150–54
   as realm of religion, 145
   structure of mind and, 134–36
Magical suggestion, 97–98
   logical persuasion and, 100
   ordinary suggestion and
      experiment, 103–5
   hypothesis, 102–3
Magical thinking, 7
   adulthood and, 165–69
   autistic thinking and, 7–8
   children and, 163–65
   fantasy orientation, 8
   hypotheses and predictions, 14–17
   imagination, 79–95
   mass media and, 167
   mind. See Mind and magical thinking
   role on human mind functioning, 14
   scientific thinking and, 11
   studies of, 13–14

Magical versus counterintuitive physical
      effect, 65–78
   action trial, 66
   causes of, 76
   counterintuitive physical condition
      (CPC), 66, 67
   definition, 65
   demonstration trial, 66
   experiments with, 65–78
   magical condition (MC), 66–67
   "violation of expectation" paradigm, 65
Mann, Thomas, 117
Mass media and magical thinking, 167
MC. See Magical condition (MC)
Meaning-creating function of magical
      thinking, 138
Mental objects, permanence of, 80–81
Metamorphoses (Ovid), 80
Mind and magical thinking, 132
   differentiation between ordinary and
      magical realities, 150–54
   existentialization
      developmental research and, 154–62
      as work of mind, 147–50
   human mind, view of, 132–34
   functions of magical reality, 136–40
   magical reality and religion, 144–47
   structure of mind, 134
      individual, 146
      magical reality, 134–36
      ordinary reality, 134–36
Mind-over-matter magic, 5–6, 28
Mind-over-mind magic experiment, 84–91,
      121
   comparison of perceived and imagined
      objects, 89–91
   fantastic objects, permanence of, 87–89
   imagined physical objects trial, 84–87
   issues in, 84

NIMBs. See Noninstitutionalized magical
      beliefs (NIMBs)
Noninstitutionalized magical beliefs
      (NIMBs), 12, 33, 46, 54, 63, 114,
      165, 174
Nonmagical effects, difference between
      magical and, 9
Nonpermanence magic, 5, 6, 28
Nonverbal tests, 83